Karen Hugg

LEAF YOUR TROUBLES BEHIND

How to Destress and Grow Happiness through Plants

Prometheus Books

Guilford, Connecticut

Prometheus Books

An imprint of Globe Pequot, the trade division of
The Rowman & Littlefield Publishing Group, Inc.
4501 Forbes Blvd., Ste. 200
Lanham, MD 20706
www.rowman.com

Distributed by NATIONAL BOOK NETWORK

British Library Cataloguing in Publication Information Available

Library of Congress Cataloging-in-Publication Data

Names: Hugg, Karen, author.
Title: Leaf your troubles behind : how to destress and grow happiness
  through plants / Karen Hugg.
Description: Lanham, MD : Prometheus, [2022] | Summary: "With personal
  stories, fun activities, scientific research, and the original approach
  of #GreenLeisure, Leaf Your Troubles Behind shows how plants and nature
  can help you de-stress and live a fuller, more joyful life"— Provided
  by publisher.
Identifiers: LCCN 2021048901 (print) | LCCN 2021048902 (ebook) | ISBN
  9781633888173 (paperback) | ISBN 9781633888173 (epub)
Subjects: LCSH: Environmental psychology. | Nature—Psychological aspects.
  | Plants—Psychological aspects.
Classification: LCC BF353.5.N37 H84 2022 (print) | LCC BF353.5.N37
  (ebook) | DDC 155.9/1—dc23/eng/20211014
LC record available at https://lccn.loc.gov/2021048901
LC ebook record available at https://lccn.loc.gov/2021048902

♾™ The paper used in this publication meets the minimum requirements of
American National Standard for Information Sciences—Permanence of Paper
for Printed Library Materials, ANSI/NISO Z39.48-1992.

For my sister, Anne,
who despite illness still enjoys the trees

Contents

Introduction

If you look the right way, you can see that the whole world is a garden.—Frances Hodgson Burnett, author

CALIFORNIA DREAMING IN A CLOUD TOWN BACKYARD

Happiness. It's what we all want, right? Well, when I think of the word *happiness*, I think of plants. It's the delight I feel when a closed blossom on a cherry tree suddenly opens. When a delicate white bean sprout emerges from black soil. A massive tangle of tree roots decaying in a forest. Even the common, annoying, ubiquitous, never-dying dandelion. Sometimes when I see their tiny yellow heads peppering the lawn, I think, *I need to get out there and pull those damn things.* Then a bee lands on a sunshiny flower and I think, *It's feeding the little bee! How could you even consider yanking it?* These silly, wondrous moments make my heart—forgive the pun—bloom. I pause when I see these teeny green miracles, feeling a wild surge of excitement in my chest, in awe of how they did what they did so fast, wondering where the energy came from and why I, a longtime gardener and apparently still a rookie of the natural world, once again missed the signs.

I mean, I am a certified ornamental horticulturalist (which, let's face it, is a fancy term for garden designer), so I should be used to all of this nature stuff by now. But I never am. Every fall when I see those purple pearls on a beautyberry, I shake my head in disbelief at their perfectly round iridescence. Every summer when my rugosa rose creates a complexly intertwined blossom that steams with fragrance, I smell it for the billionth time. And every spring when I pass a zelkova tree in a mall parking lot, I smile at its new corrugated leaves unfurling on a forlorn winter skeleton, impressed that it bounced back despite being surrounded by heavy concrete.

This is why I go on. How I cope. How, in years past, I've survived the stresses of a fast-paced tech job and my husband's stage-four cancer treatment (which, thankfully, he survived). How we got through raising three traumatized, loudly active adopted children, one who is cognitively delayed, into happy-enough teenagers. And today, as I deal with the aftereffects of the pandemic and my sister's cancer diagnosis, plants offer me silent, steady hope for renewal.

If you're anything like me, you've been—or are—a stressed-out human living in a noisy home with lots of busy chaos and distractions. Every time you turn on the news, you see more corruption, violence, and discrimination. If you have kids, you may bounce from concentrating on work for your job to helping a child with homework to changing a diaper. The toilet and sink are dirty—again. And a year or so ago during the pandemic, you bundled up like a giant burrito just to brave the germy grocery store to feed your family. That's when you're not *already* grieving the loss of a family member or friend or coworker or job. Then, in the evening, when all is said and done, forget about seeing friends or taking in a movie, because you're supposed to be disciplined enough to exercise and not eat pasta and not drink away your feelings, right? Yeah, right.

So how do we cope with all of this? Well, one way is by getting outside. Yes, that place without glowing screens or vacuums or diapers. And by "outside," I mean a park or woods or, if you're lucky, your own backyard. Every day, I spend at least some time amid greenery, which can mean a variety of things. Strolling up the street amid the tall firs and cedars with my husband. Trimming the dry leaves from my houseplants. Even kneeling before weeds and yanking them from the ground. What it doesn't mean is growing the perfect peony or arranging a beautiful vase of exotic leaves. Forget that idea and the social media platform it rode in on.

On days when I have the most time, coping with stress means putting on my gloves and hiking to the back of my yard. It takes only a minute, but when I get there, it feels like I've arrived in California, somewhere coastal and pristine, like Santa Barbara without the outrageous prices. It's a whole other world there, full of bright light and sandy soil and hot-weather shrubs. Happy bees buzz around ceanothus and lavender. The rockrose leaves waft spicy scents. I can even see my house in the short distance—you know, that stressful place with the vacuums and screens and diapers? What I've discovered is that, by placing myself in this sunny garden, I gain a strange, calming sense of relief. A relaxed feeling like—dare I say it—everything will be okay? I don't know why I feel this way. I just do.

Wait—yes, I know why. It's because I'm in an aimless state among greenery, almost as if I'm on a break from work or regular life. Down in my own California dream, I don't have much of an agenda. My goal is to tidy up the plants, but mostly I'm walking a little, observing, kneeling, digging, trimming, and clearing. It's leisurely. I have no big goals. Above me, the fir trees sway in the breeze. Birds tweet and swoop. Lilacs cast a sweet scent. The varying textures of leaves create a serene playscape. I don't have to turn on any devices or laptops. I don't have to read or speak as if I'm an intelligent human being. I don't have to scold or praise or form opinions or feel outraged. In fact, I don't have to have any thoughts or feelings at all. Instead, I just help small lives survive. My mind is quiet. Time is not important. I'm on vacation among those teeny—or giant, as it were—green miracles called plants.

CREATING A VACATION DESTINATION FOR OTHERS

About twenty years ago, I decided to make a career out of "vacationing" with those green miracles. I fell in love with this one brilliant shrub (which I'll tell you about a little later) and never looked back. Since then, I discovered a recurring trend I couldn't shake.

First, let me tell you, during my years as a professional gardener, I did a lot of yucky stuff. I mean, do you know what it's like when hemlock needles wedge in your undies? Not fun. Anyway, while working on clients' yards, I'd prune branches in the rain while sawdust sprinkled my face. I'd crawl through mud to grab that last bit of morning glory vine. I'd clear brambles of blackberry whose thorny canes whapped my face. I even raked away leaves with my hands to be suddenly scared by a dead rat. (Thank God I had gloves on.) But the one thing that made up for my unfun troubles was the response I got from my clients like Dana.

Dana lived in a spacious cottage in a charming neighborhood of Seattle. She knew nothing about plants, and she didn't really care to find out (enter me, the gardener), but she knew she loved having a garden. In fact, before I started my work, she always gave me a quick tour of the beds to chat about how the plants were doing. We'd amble around the yard as she'd update me about how wonderful the "bush with the flat blue flowers" (hydrangea) was growing, and how the "purple leaf things" (coral bells) were her favorite, and how stumped she was about why the "pointy swords" (iris) were brown and, by the way, was brown bad? (answers: water and yes).

Every quarter, I maintained her yard and occasionally designed new perennial beds. The biggest area was a small courtyard in her backyard, not much more than a patio, containing a small Japanese maple and a shade border. Each time I finished up my work there, Dana came outside to check in. At nearly every meeting when she saw my progress, she'd squeal and jump up and down and clap her hands, a huge smile on her face. She loved the sight of her tidy garden. Her unguarded joy gave me joy.

Not all of my clients jumped up and down about their gardens, although they too were often overjoyed after their garden had been tidied or installed. Lots of beaming smiles. Like Dana, most of my clients were not gardeners, not in the slightest. They were busy folks with more money than time. They were frequently stressed, working long hours in offices or whatnot, raising kids, struggling with a constant stream of tasks, relationships, and random thoughts. Uniformly, they all yearned for peace. So I saw my gardener job as designing and maintaining a sanctuary. In fact, a kind of sacred sanctuary. An outdoor space of interesting foliage, colorful flowers, and sweet scents. A place where they could relax and escape the overwhelming responsibilities of their lives. A place where they could breathe a sigh of relief, or "releaf" as it were.

And that's what they did. During follow-up maintenance or future project visits, clients often mentioned how their stress drastically lessened or even disappeared after spending time in the garden. Whether they were sitting, weeding, watering, puttering about, or even taking a phone call, they felt renewed and more peaceful. The garden actually evolved into their sanctuary, their special refuge where they healed from the stress of the day.

Again and again, I heard the phrases, "I can get away from the stress here," and "I feel so much better after we spend time out here."

One time, I asked a client, "Do you feel like you feel when you're on vacation?"

"Definitely," she said. "It's my happy place."

Happy place, indeed.

Your "Releaf" from Stress

As the years went on, I sometimes wondered whether the mental health benefits of being among plants was limited to people who had a garden. I asked myself whether apartment dwellers could heal from their stress with either a small or no outdoor area. Was it possible to create a soothing green space indoors with houseplants? For those who were either physically unable or uninclined to grow plants, could they benefit by mimicking a green space, such as with photos and decor? Then, in recent years, I started reading the growing scientific research about the healing effects of nature, which gave me the answer to all of those questions: *yes*.

In a society growing quickly with technological advancements and whose citizens are squeezed by the responsibilities of careers, childrearing, elder caretaking, political polarization, and social media chatter, people struggle to stay happy. The pandemic has devastated families who lost loved ones. A weak economy has created severe financial distress. So many people, especially parents, lie in bed at night wondering if they can make ends meet before getting sucked into the whirlwind of the day, navigating commitments in a mostly indoor world of work, school, and home, where screens, not nature, dominate their lives.

Folks need a break from that whirlwind, a window of time when they can be idle to restore their energy and inspire inner harmony. And studies show that spending time with plants accelerates that soul-healing time. Nowadays, many people, especially millennials, appreciate nature and the importance of protecting our environment. People are ready, more than ever, to explore nature's happy-making effects. But oftentimes they don't know how. Or they may have tried to grow a few plants and weren't successful. Hence, that exploration gets shelved to an indefinite future to-do list.

Are you overwhelmed by the busyness of everyday life, or worried about illness, or do you find it hard to focus on the deep work of a job or hobby? Does social media pull you into its void of rumors, opinions, and shallow infotainment snippets? Do you feel like there's no time to relax?

If so, I think I can help you.

It entails, metaphorically, at least, stepping carefully down a new path, maneuvering over fallen logs, ducking under broken branches, and avoiding the prickly canes. But the risk will be worth it.

Though this book may not solve all of your problems, it can at least help you find some respite from the stress of the day. The early chapters focus on how to disengage from electronic screens and find more time in our busy lives. Then I share my concept of "green leisure," the method I've developed for dialing into nature's healing benefits. It involves seven basic destressing strategies rooted in scientific research. You'll hear stories from my life and from those of my clients and various friends. You'll learn about the amazing studies on the psychological benefits of plants and nature coming out of not just Japan and east Asia, but America, Europe, Australia, and India. I include some exploratory and quirky exercises I hope you have fun doing. Lastly, I wrap up with a section about how to make the best use of an indoor or outdoor space for a "green leisure lounge" before offering resources to further explore.

After reading, I hope you'll feel like you know how to reconnect with plants and nature to reduce stress and increase happiness in a way that's right for you. You may even become an expert at "leafing" your troubles behind!

Part One

DIGGING IN THE SOUL'S DIRT

To destress and grow happiness through plants, where do we begin? First, it's helpful to do a little soulful excavation in our lives. Unearth where we're at right now. What are our sources of stress and what changes could make our life better? Also, to what extent, if any, do we participate in the green world? And did we in the past but, for whatever reason, don't now? Regardless, solid research gives us some basic strategies for becoming happier and nature can fast-track those. We just need to dig around to discover what's right for us.

This section addresses our modern dilemma, green leisure, and one's green personality. We'll examine our indoor, tech-oriented, busy lives while covering how to disengage from technology, work less, and find more time. We discuss the concept of green leisure, my system for dialing into nature's healing benefits that's rooted in happiness research. Lastly, we assess what your green personality might be, your preferences as they relate to nature and what plant-oriented activities are right for you.

Chapter One

A Modern Dilemma
of Our Own Making

One of the things I missed most while living in space was being able to go outside and experience nature. After being confined to a small space for months, I actually started to crave nature—the color green, the smell of fresh dirt, and the feel of warm sun on my face. That flower experiment became more important to me than I could have ever imagined.—Scott Kelly, astronaut

LIVING LIFE IN A SMALL WHITE SCREEN

During the late 1990s, I discovered an important revelation about stress. At the time, I was intimately familiar with stress because of my job. I worked in tech as a content editor at an online retailer whose sales, reputation, and organization were exploding by the minute. Every day our stock price shot up, giving executives the justification to pressure employees into sixty-hour workweeks while human resources couldn't build teams fast enough to keep up with the work that needed covering. We had a charismatic, type-A CEO who often brainstormed ideas he wanted implemented in two days. In turn, everyone dropped what they were doing and scrambled in a different direction to jump on the project, sacrificing what scant free evening time they had. Some employees even slept under their desks.

Feeling grateful that a young nobody English major like me had the opportunity to use my skills, I managed a mountain of work. I rendered website pages with complex technology that interacted with databases and hopefully didn't break pipelines. I assigned and edited content that existed only in a network of communicating packets. I wrote reviews, planned a schedule, and managed product information. Every day, the mail guy delivered a tower of boxes and envelopes to my desk. Every hour, dozens of emails jammed my inbox. The tasks flew in from all directions, at light speed and in an endless stream. All I did was react and execute. React and execute. React and execute.

And so I spent years tweaking with thousands of worries while staring at a small white screen. For around ten of my fifteen waking hours, my life was limited to the images and text inside that glowing fifteen-by-fifteen-inch panel. I sat in a scentless office under white fluorescent lights in a climate-controlled room with white walls. Sometimes I wore headphones playing white noise. Rarely did I go outside.

During the weekends, I had about thirty waking hours to decompress before jumping on the merry-go-round again, and, of course, half of that time was spent grocery shopping, taking care of family, walking the dog, running personal errands, and fixing home-related problems. My one highlight was sharing dinner or playing music with my husband. By the time I'd finally sorted through my feelings of anxiety and frustration and jettisoned some of my zig-zagging thoughts, it was already Sunday evening. So I struggled on, gaining thirty pounds of weight while losing hundreds of hours in happiness.

Sound familiar? You may not work in tech, but chances are good you spend most of your day staring at a screen for several hours. Chances are even better that you too feel anxiety and frustration and experience zig-zagging thoughts. If you're a parent, the stress is even greater.

How do I know? Well, in 2018 a Wrike poll found that 94 percent of Americans reported feeling stressed at their workplace, with nearly a third describing it as high to unsustainably high.[1] Around the same time, a Gallup poll found 51 percent of workers were "mentally checked out" while at work.[2] Generally, women are more stressed than men, according to the American Psychological Association, and younger people are more stressed than older folks.[3] In the end, stress is not only bad for our minds and bodies, it's bad from a corporate perspective, too. Stanford researcher Leah Weiss found that chronic stress makes productive workplaces deteriorate. Employee engagement and morale nosedives. Ultimately, chronic stress leads to fatigue, anxiety, and confusion about "the setting of priorities."[4]

I've been confused about my priorities, that's for sure, which explains why I didn't quit. We all need jobs, right? We have to put up with the bullcrap in order to get the paycheck. Admittedly, I got a decent paycheck at that job. So decent that my husband and I were able to buy a house. That house led me to my important revelation about stress.

Can One Plant Heal a Soul?

As you might expect, the house came with a backyard. It was a pathetically brief plot of land, part neighbor's garage, part rotting raised beds, all neglected with a scattering of shrubs and a sickly lawn. But I loved it; it was mine. And because it was mine, I wanted to care for it. But I didn't know a cactus from a lamppost, so I started reading gardening magazines and books. I signed up for too many plant catalogs. At night, exhausted and in need of a refuge from corporate mania, I'd climb into bed with my stack of literature and peruse. I saw lovely photos of cheery plants: pointy hosta leaves, orange dahlias, gnarly redwoods. I read about their needs, their gifts. The ritual was a soothing salve for my angsty soul. I'd drift to sleep with images of green sanctuaries in my mind, a place where no annoying colleagues or glitching software or soul-sucking rat race existed.

Then the turning point came. One night after my husband and I ripped out the rotted beds in the backyard and installed a fresh square of lawn, I got in the bathtub and soaked my sore muscles. With the idea of freshening up the yard with new plants, I scanned and dog-eared pages in a nursery catalog. Halfway in, my eyes landed on a butterfly bush. It was a perfectly rounded shrub covered in tubular violet flowers. The photo beamed with spots of dark purple and bright green. My eyes feasted on the beauty. It was called *Buddleia davidii* 'Black Knight.' Above the plant's description, a headline read: "Bring Butterflies to Your Garden!"

I blinked. I wanted to bring butterflies to my garden. Could that really happen? And how? How could a plant manipulate a butterfly? I had no idea. It seemed crazy. Didn't butterflies just magically appear and fly around randomly, born to look pretty and remind people it was summer? Butterflies weren't related to me or plants. They just did what they wanted to do whenever they felt like it.

Of course, now I know how wrong I was, but back then I didn't. Reeling with the possibility that I might somehow make butterflies magically appear by simply planting a shrub, and in fact disbelieving that I could, I got up the next day and headed to a local nursery where I bought the alluringly named Black Knight. Convinced the advertising was overblown, I didn't expect anything to happen, but the shrub with its grayish leaves and long indigo blooms stunned me. Its shape was so strange and cool. I couldn't wait to see it grow into what the picture looked like.

You can guess that the plant didn't exactly grow into a perfectly pruned, perfectly fertilized, perfectly rounded shrub. Instead, it was tall and gangly, and its flowers hung at weird angles like hoses. But the flowers—wow—they did sport that deep dark color. The purple moodily glowed against the crisp blue sky. When I looked closely at them, I noticed the blooms were actually a compendium of tiny flowers jammed in all directions along the stem. How did it do that? How did it know to create itself that way?

I never did figure out the long answer, but I did experience a different revelation: that butterfly bush, that one silly plant whose more common species relative, *Buddleia davidii*, is considered a weed in some states, completely neutralized my stress. Instantly—every day. In the morning before work, I gazed at its deep velvety flowers through the window while drinking tea, and in the evening, I checked on how it had changed. I liked to rub its fuzzy gray leaves, marveling at how prettily they contrasted against the glossy leaves of a nearby laurel. I enjoyed pulling out the hose and doing the simple act of watering before being surprised by fresh new growth a few days later. Most of all, I loved that, on a warm day in summer, a yellow and black swallowtail butterfly landed on that tubular flower, as promised.

When my attention focused on that plant, I didn't think about my job. I didn't think about anything office related at all: the convoluted meetings, the hundreds of emails, the mountain of work. No interpersonal politics, no complex technology, no messy responsibilities. It all melted away like magic. I felt as if I'd been taken out of a harsh, busy cage where I was swatted every day and gently laid in a peaceful, warm nest where I was not only *not* swatted but actually hugged.

Needless to say, I grew addicted to the feeling. Soon, I was outside in the sunlight (or, in Seattle's case, "cloudlight") almost every day. I planted more plants, playing and experimenting. I got exercise as I hauled pots around, dug holes, and took thousands of steps. Whatever my day had been like at the office, it mattered little, because as soon as I was immersed in my garden, I felt relaxed. I cared for innocent living things. I felt grateful for my teeny backyard. Even in winter when I wasn't outside much, I daydreamed and read about plants, then designed and installed plans as the weather warmed. I met and had fun with other people who liked plants, too. In essence, I was practicing the essential strategies of destressing via the natural world. And little by little, my soul healed.

NATURE CALLED BUT WE WEREN'T HOME

Perhaps you're working at a stressful office job as well. Maybe you have to work late on a project a coworker tossed in your lap, but you have to leave on time because your child needs a ride home from soccer practice. Or you should be answering your boss's email, but the cat vomited on the rug again. Your sister might need your ear to vent about her marriage, but you and your own spouse may be barely speaking. Maybe you're starving but forgot to hit the grocery store on the way home and have nothing but old ketchup in the fridge. Or perhaps money is a constant worry, or you or a loved one is suffering from a serious illness. What about laundry and dishes? There's always laundry and dishes. You may feel like *not* drinking an extra glass of wine or *not* watching another TV show is a win.

Getting a decent night's sleep is a flat-out triumph. Losing weight or volunteering or organizing the junk in the basement seems a million miles away.

Well, you're not alone.

The Happiness Research Institute in Denmark, founded by the ever handsome and seemingly placid Meik Wiking, says that although happiness is subjective, the institute has found some interesting, objective facts about it.[5] One of those is the surprisingly low rank of the United States when it comes to happiness. As of 2019, it was eighteenth, quite low considering our country's vast wealth.[6] It's not surprising that the institute cites stress as an enemy of well-being. And, of course, the 2020 pandemic didn't help, with parents, especially moms, carrying the brunt of the stress due to a weak economy and at-home schooling.

Meanwhile, we're spending more time than ever indoors. According to researcher Neil Klepeis, Americans spend 87 percent of their time indoors. The average American spends two hours and six minutes a day on social media. Twelve-year-olds spend about nineteen hours on electronic media a week.[7] That's a lot of life spent inside and stressed out!

In fact, journalist Richard Louv coined a term for the experience. It's not stuck-in-an-office-with-a-small-screen syndrome, though I suppose it could be. He calls it nature deficit disorder.[8] In his 2005 book, *Last Child in the Woods*, he found that behavioral problems and depression in children were often linked to their lack of time outdoors. Though his research applied to children, he later found the symptoms applied to adults as well. We've become stressed out from a fast-paced, indoor-based, technological world. We don't interact with nature like we used to, which has led to poor behavior and physical softness. We lack the sunlight we used to get working on farms and have developed vitamin D deficiencies. No wonder so many of us are depressed.

But the good news is plants can help.

In the last ten years, scientists have been proving that time spent in nature heals us. Both mentally *and* physically. We've learned about *shinrin-yoku* (or forest bathing) research from Japan;

how surgical recovery accelerates in hospital rooms with natural views; how taking in the scents, sights, and textures of plants lowers our heart rates and blood pressure. Green spaces make neighbors friendlier, and offices with plants increase worker productivity and improve attitudes.

In some ways, the idea isn't surprising, right? It makes sense. After all, nature was our first home on this planet. Plants give us life and air and food and beauty. We survived and evolved thanks to plants. In his 1984 book, E. O. Wilson popularized the concept of biophilia, the idea that humans possess an innate desire to connect with natural living systems.[9] Plants, forests, gardens, prairies, and landscapes are part of those. In short, we're biologically wired to crave nature (see Scott Kelly's thoughts in the chapter's opening quote).

What I unknowingly was doing with that butterfly bush is what researchers Stephen and Rachel Kaplan called attention restoration theory (ART).[10] In their studies, they found evidence that nature has the capacity to renew our attention after long bouts of exerting mental energy. You probably have already experienced ART. After a stressful busy week at work, you take a hike or camping trip in the woods on the weekend and afterward feel renewed. That's what vacations are for. But the Kaplans scientifically proved this feeling as it relates to plants. They also identified which natural interactions heal us best, along with the duration of the healing effects. In some ways, the healing effects have lasted for nearly my entire adult life, and I'll share what I've learned with you.

DOES NATURE *REALLY* HELP US RECOVER FROM STRESS?

Most of us work hard. I mean, really, really hard. Whether we're burning the midnight oil on a complex work project, doing homework, caring for active children, or completing a difficult puzzle, that mental effort sucks away our energy and leaves us feeling wiped out. As we say, our brains "feel fried." We have to take a break.

Environmental psychology researchers Stephen and Rachel Kaplan thought that break was key, so they started studying natural environments and whether they restored our ability to focus. For the last thirty years, the Kaplans have found nature is highly effective at healing our minds after intense stress. Whether we go on a camping trip or even watch nature scenery on a screen, we can recover via nature. They termed the phenomenon attention restoration theory (ART).

There are four components of effective attention restoration.

1. *Being away.* We have to remove ourselves from the usual work that's draining us. That can be physical (as in leaving the home, office, workplace, or classroom) or psychological. The point is to be psychologically detached or distracted from the source of stress.
2. *Soft fascination.* We need to be mildly fascinated by our surroundings. Interested but not highly stimulated or stressed by whatever we're looking at.
3. *Extent.* We need to be in a comfortable, familiar environment that's not jarring or surprising but one that encourages us to engage our minds without being disturbed or worried.
4. *Compatibility.* We need an environment we jibe with. One that's safe, congruent with what we know, enjoyable, easy to navigate, and not a place we feel obligated to visit.

They found that the natural environment provides these components more than any other. In fact, in an overview of the research on ART, Italian researcher Rita Berto found that engaging in nature produces positive mood changes, mediates negative effects of stress, has a restorative influence on disposition, and reduces anger and fear. People think better, are friendlier, more physically fit, and sociable. Those who spend time in nature experience reduced physiological symptoms of stress.[11] So, yes, nature really can heal us!

But Do You Have to Garden?

So am I saying everyone should buy a house and tend a garden and all will be well? No. There's no need for such drastic solutions. And nowadays, many people can't afford to buy a home. Others aren't interested in the headaches of maintaining one. A lot of people live in apartments by choice, and some folks are physically challenged, which puts gardening in a yard out of the question. Also, with prickly shrubs, uneven ground, and poisonous plants, nature can be a bit treacherous. And let's face it, some of us don't want to get our hands dirty with mucky soil and creepy insects. All of that is valid. The good news is you don't need a garden. You just need the willingness to change your life a bit.

And how do we do that? Well, it's different for different people, but it's helpful to first assess our stress. If we can pinpoint from where our stress emanates, we can start taking small steps toward a happier, more relaxed life. Then we can explore the various strategies of destressing and how nature plays a part. And afterward, we might even figure out how to create a personal plant refuge, or what I call a green leisure lounge, like my client's "happy place" from the introduction. So I encourage you to do the following activities to start leafing your troubles behind. The first one is the easiest of all.

ACTIVITIES

Picturing a Happy Plant Place

RATING: **Clean hands, no tools, indoors or outdoors, no cost**

Here's an activity to remind you of what a happier, more relaxed life might feel like, a taste of what we're aiming for. You can do it anytime, anywhere: at home or at the office, school, library, or even while waiting for a table in a restaurant. I like to do this at home, right after lunch but before resuming work, to transition from active stuff to a calm feeling of restored relaxation.

1. Close your eyes and imagine you're in an outside "happy place" that's green with plants. It can be a beach, a wooded grove, a valley of wildflowers, a bench in a secret garden. Even your grandma's front porch. Wherever you are, it's the perfect day.
2. Take three deep breaths. Feel the sun's warmth on your face. Hear the wind rustling the leaves. The birds singing. Smell the fresh air, the moist soil, the sweet flowers. Take three deep breaths. Your

hands rest against a smooth chair, or soft grass, or a velvety blanket. Notice the sun beaming through the trees, brightening the flowers, reflecting off the waves. Your heart beats in a steady quiet rhythm.
3. Breathe out the events of the day. Breathe out the tension. Let it drain from your face to your neck to your arms and torso and legs, straight out your toes. Inhale and exhale deeply, without thought. Let the stress go. You can think, "goodbye angst, hello peace." Your body is serenely heavy; your heart beats slowly.
4. Look at the beautiful natural surroundings. Breathe deeply again. Notice the sky, the leaves, the ground. If a random dark image enters the scene, silently say, "no, thank you." Stay there for several more breaths. In fact, stay as long as you like. This is the happy plant place of your mind.
5. When you're ready, open your eyes. How do you feel? If you feel relaxed, more whole, better in any way, congrats! You've done the first step in destressing through nature. And remember, you can visit your happy plant place whenever you want.

An Escape-to-Nature Notebook

RATING: Clean hands, no tools, indoors, low cost ($10–$50)

Creating this notebook is optional but worth it. I love mine. It's a journal, an artistic outlet, and cheery reminder of possibilities. It provides a centralized location for all of your destressing work and fun, nature-related endeavors. Plus, it functions as a chronicle of your progress. You can use it well after you finish this book.

Make or buy a binder or scrapbook to hold all of your journal writings, diagrams, sketches, photos, pressed plant material, two-dimensional crafts, and calendar related to this journey. I include a list of supplies below but if you can't afford them, download a mini-workbook from my website, www.karenhugg.com. It has the pages you'll need along with bonus information, photos, and additional activities.

What you'll need:

- binder or scrapbook
- pockets or pocket folders

- lined paper
- blank paper or sketch paper
- stiff background paper
- writing tool
- photos of favorite plants from magazines or books (if you don't have favorites, refer to the activities in chapter 3)
- calendar, either purchased or drawn, that fits in the pocket or three-ring binder

1. Write or draw "Escape to Nature" on the cover. If you're inclined, decorate it. You can write words or draw plant pictures or create a collage of photos, whatever you like.
2. Insert your folder pockets. If you have pressed plants, put those in there.
3. If you have favorite plants, like a collection of houseplants, take photos of them or use magazine photos to build a visual inventory on the stiff paper and write out the common and Latin names of the plant.
4. Insert your calendar into the folder pocket or three-ring holder.
5. Keep at the ready for future activities!

The Stress Bramble

RATING: **Clean hands, no tools, indoors, low cost ($0–$10)**

Here's the first activity to put in your notebook: a "mind map" of the most tense, angsty aspects of your life. You'll draw a diagram of the sources of stress in your life by freely associating thoughts and feelings.

What you'll need:

- Escape-to-Nature notebook or blank paper
- writing tool

1. In the center of the paper or notebook, write the word "stress" within a leaf shape (or circle).

2. Draw a stem, and in another leaf, write the first source of stress that pops into your head. Then draw another stem from the word "stress" and another source of stress inside another leaf. You might have listed "home" and "work." If one of those words makes you think of a person or something related, create another small stem and leaf and write it down. As sources of stress and images come to you, write them in mini-lists or clustered. It's up to you. Keep free associating thoughts and feelings. Work rapidly without much thinking. Let your stream of consciousness guide you. Keep clustering until you've poured all of the ways that life stresses you out on the paper. Include everything until you have a giant bramble of stress.

3. Circle or highlight the worst offenders. Notice where there are clusters. Wherever you notice a large cluster, you'll discover a "hot zone" of stress.

Keep it handy. We'll examine this bramble in the next chapter.

Chapter Two

―――――――― ✧ ――――――――

Slowing the Stress
and Getting into
Green Leisure

Sorry, I have plants this weekend.—Zahrada na niti, interior designer

Now that you're more familiar with how relaxed you could feel as well as the kinds of stressors you struggle with, the next thing you'll need to do is prioritize yourself and not feel guilty about it. Can you? I bet you prioritize the people and pets you love all the time. But now it's time to put yourself first. As they say, whatever age you are now, that's the youngest you'll ever be from this point on, so let's make this time in your life a healthy, happy one.

SAYING "NO" TO OTHERS IN ORDER TO SAY "YES" TO YOURSELF

I know putting yourself first is easier said than done. I get that. It wasn't like my stress never returned after I discovered my butterfly bush. It did. Stress is like a reoccurring storm. A few years after I fell in love with gardening and left the tech world, my husband was diagnosed with cancer. After he recovered (knock on wood), we were so thrilled that we adopted three children from Poland. But my youngest daughter was cognitively delayed and needed occupational therapy and special education classes. My husband and

I both still worked, he as a software architect, me as a professional gardener. We took in four stray pets, one of which was an intelligent shepherd mix who'd been abused as a puppy and often behaved in random hyper ways. Don't get me wrong, I'm grateful for my and my husband's jobs, grateful for our kids and pets, but I mistakenly allowed my life to get jammed with overwhelming responsibilities.

We had a packed calendar: work commitments that went into evening most nights, then music lessons, band recitals, business meetings, travel visits, family gatherings, school events, homework projects, vet appointments, doctor and dentist appointments, occupational therapy groups, tutoring, and more. Sound familiar? Oh, and did I mention that I tried to write creative fiction in my spare time? Life was crazy.

In retrospect, I'm not particularly proud that it was crazy. That's because I mostly blame myself. You see, I brought it on. And in a very direct way. I said "yes" too often. I couldn't control my husband's illness, that's for sure, but after he recovered, we adopted not one, but *three* children (mostly because we had no idea what we were in for), and we took in not one or two, but *four* pets! Also, I took on a lot workwise. I always said "yes" to gardening jobs (because y'know, three kids and four pets eat a lot). I often said "yes" to the kids' activities. I said "yes" to volunteer work. I said "yes" to extended family commitments. I said "yes" to others for years when I should have been saying "no."

Perhaps you're in a similar boat. Researchers have found that Americans want to be viewed as productive, and so sometimes we take on more work to prove to ourselves (and our bosses) that we are productive. And, of course, bills *are* a reality, and they need to be paid. But psychologists say we often measure our self-esteem by how busy we are.

By contrast, Europeans, especially in countries like France and Denmark, feel less hardship in saying "no" to things. They don't need to be constantly busy to prove their worth to themselves or their bosses. In fact, the opposite is true. Happiness and recreational time are highly valued. Years ago, I worked in a French office outside of Paris, and I can testify that *not one* employee ever felt guilty about taking days off for a long weekend or vacation. Once, when I mentioned working on Saturday to a colleague, he looked at me with a mix of horror and confusion, as if I'd just thrown up on my desk. "You mean, here?" he said. "At this office?" The French understand that leisure time is vital to recovering from stress.

So can you, right now, decide to say "no" to commitments that you know, deep down, will strain your time? Are you ready to say "yes" to yourself and dedicate some time to your happiness? If it feels difficult because you feel like you *should* be doing all of these things, I understand. I felt like a taut rubber band whose attention was pulled in opposing directions for years. But guess what? If you're not happy, no one else around you will be. If you don't devote the time to your well-being, later in life you'll regret how miserable you were during those years. Speaking as a middle-aged Gen Xer, trust me on that one. Don't let the storms of stress overtake your life. Even if you're working two jobs to make ends meet, you can still relax via plants in less time than you think. For instance, one day I took my daughters blackberry picking at our local beach. I was convinced it would take all morning, but it barely took an hour. The silence, fresh air, and sight of soft green shrubs renewed our spirits. Not to mention the three bags of free organic berries we gained! So remember to make a little time for yourself. You deserve it.

Shutting Off an Addictive Screen

Once you say "yes" to yourself, you've begun the process of destressing. You've already found a few bits of time you can devote to yourself. However, you probably know the lure of a screen is strong. It can eat away at unscheduled free time. In fact, I still wrestle with it.

For instance, in the evenings on most nights, my husband and I watch a favorite television show. For a while, we finished at about 9:30, when he'd practice piano before bed. At the time, I was redesigning an area of my garden that required research into plants native to the Northwest that could handle sunlight. Every night I intended to research those plants. But feeling mentally exhausted, I mindlessly scrolled through Twitter. Suddenly, thirty minutes had flown by.

Over several weeks, while my husband was progressing to Bach's Partita and Chopin's Ocean Etude, I'd accomplished laughing at a few funny posts. (And hey, I'm into laughter.) At first, I shrugged it off, saying it was only a half hour, but later I felt guilty and disappointed with myself. I could have shut off my screen and used my time better. So I suggested to my husband that we meet later in the evening, after he'd practiced and before our nightly TV hour. The switch worked out great! I actually discovered the rare natives I needed for my garden and watched TV later, when my mind was spent.

My point is, time is hiding in plain sight. And if you shut off your screen, you will experience life in a fuller, more meaningful way. What's more, you'll disconnect from the shallow, addictive, sensory-less experience a screen offers. I know that's hard; I struggle, too. Technology is ingrained deeply in our lives; it's been hyped

as the coolest thing ever, and it can be enormously useful. It's difficult to escape. But remember this: computers are appliances. Your
laptop is an *appliance*. Your phone is an *appliance*. Your TV is an
appliance, a technological device used for a chore. So treat them as
such. Use them when you need them and shut them off. To honor
our lives, we need to be the one controlling technology, not allowing
it to control us.

So far, as a country, we haven't been able to do that. In 2018,
the Nielsen research group found that Americans spent eleven of
their waking hours interacting with some kind of media on a screen.
Television makes up almost five of those hours, and the combination of computer, tablet, and smartphone usage is not far behind at
more than three hours. The rest involves game consoles, DVD play-
ers, etcetera.[1] We settle in front of screens because screens offer re-
warding distractions with little effort. They're easy but also empty.

THE LURE OF "SHOW-OFF" MEDIA

In particular, social media is excellent at luring us in. Science shows
us that we visit Twitter, Facebook, and Instagram because we crave
approval from our communities. Though we do use them to catch
up with folks, what really keeps us sucked in are the small hits of
dopamine we get via "likes." Who has "liked" you today? How many
people have "liked" you? It's impressively insidious and ultimately
harmful to our mental health. When we don't get "liked" very much,
we may feel disappointed. We can feel inferior to our peers. And
if we too often expose ourselves to others' wonderful news and
dreamy photos, we can feel downright depressed. As Meik Wiking
says, "social media is a constant bombardment of great news that
happens for everybody else."[2]

Over the years, I've struggled with social media. I'd log on to
Facebook or Instagram and see perfect photos of people or vacations or parties or babies whose dreaminess or hipness or accomplished style I felt I couldn't achieve. Inevitably, I'd toss myself
facedown on the couch, complaining into my pillow, caught in a

"less-than" spiral in which I'd think, "God, my hair's so flat and my old T-shirts look so faded and lame. My kid's not an uber genius. I've eaten too much bread that's migrated to my butt, and I never go anywhere cool. No glam parties for you, loser." Then later, I'd realize I'd probably announced some award or vacation or food pic in the past that made someone else feel lousy. Then I felt guilty. That push-pull feeling drove me nuts for a long time.

In the end, I didn't want to feel like a loser because of other people's good news, and I didn't want to make anyone else feel like a loser. Yet I wanted to inform the people who truly supported me about news they might be interested in or photos they might feel better after seeing. So I renamed social media "show-off media" in my head. I decided not to engage with the apps for more than five minutes at breakfast, lunchtime, and in the evening. I promised myself I wouldn't post unless my message was aimed at helping others. These small rules curbed my usage by two-thirds and gave me a wholesome, free feeling in my soul.

I encourage you to examine how your screen time, and in particular social media, serves you. Does it *really* align with what you value? Or do you feel more shallow, envious, depressed, even frustrated, afterward? I mean, are we really meant to continually attend cocktail parties with thousands of people all the time? Do we really need to see someone else's perfect vacation photos or, conversely, swollen, injured foot? Probably not. As computer science professor Cal Newport recommends in his excellent book *Digital Minimalism*, to be happy, you have to "focus your online time on a small number of carefully selected and optimized activities that strongly support things you value, and then happily miss out on everything else."[3]

Put another way, what do you want to give your attention to? What do you want to spend your brief time on this beautiful planet looking at and thinking about? We have only so many days and hours left here on Earth, which makes our time the most precious thing of all. And I understand that many of you need to use screens at work. I myself still do. I'm staring at a screen as I write this. But we can control what we give our attention to *after* work. Think of your attention as a gift. Are you going to "gift" a news site your attention? A social media app? A phone game? Any of those is valid as long as you know *why* you're doing it. If you use technology with intention, then you won't have a guilt hangover later. But for our purposes, let's aim to divert our attention away from screens so we can become more aware of our tangible surroundings. Especially those that help us the most, like the lovely landscapes of plants.

ARE YOU EVEN SLEEPING?

Forget about leisure a minute. Let me ask you, are you sleeping? Research shows sleep is the first activity to go when we're busy. Lack of sleep creates a bunch of harmful effects.[4] Here are six big ones:

1. *Foul mood.* You're always grumpy, and if you're like me, always "hangry."
2. *Weakened immunity.* This is a no-brainer. Wanna catch a cold in winter? Don't sleep.
3. *High blood pressure.* When your blood pressure rises so does your risk of heart attack.
4. *Weight gain.* I mean, when you're "hangry," you're *definitely* ordering the fries!
5. *Diabetes risk.* Your blood sugar release gets all out of whack when you don't sleep.
6. *Alzheimer's risk.* Dangerous toxins that stick in the brain are washed away by sleep.

Years ago, after tennis star Roger Federer had won more than ten Grand Slam championships, a journalist asked his secret to phenomenal success. Long hours of practice? A secret technique? Special racket? Without hesitation, he said, "I love my sleep." No wonder he's still competing in his early forties! Here are seven tips that give me world-champion sleep:

1. *Shut off screens.* Obvious, right? But I work on a laptop, glance at a phone, and check email on a tablet into the evening, sometimes in bed. Also, ebook readers count! They generate blue light, disturbing sleep patterns. Instead read a light-hearted book.
2. *Limit or eliminate caffeine.* I've found that even a cup of caffeinated tea in the morning disturbs my sleep at night. So I subbed decaf and it helped a bunch.

3. *Drink little or no alcohol.* If I drink one glass of wine at dinner, I sleep *way* better. When the light goes out, my mind shuts down until morning.
4. *Darken the room.* A while ago, I realized the green signal from our electric toothbrush cast light into our bedroom. I unplugged it and slept more soundly.
5. *A second pillow for a snoring spouse.* If he snores, you're not sleeping. Or she, or they. See if you can elevate your partner's head. You love 'em but you also need to get some rest.
6. *Keep the room cool.* If I'm hot, I not only wake up during the night, I have nightmares. What's up with that?
7. *Don't sleep too long.* If I sleep late or nap after lunch, I can't fall into solid sleep at night. So I sleep about seven and a half hours. That way I'm tired enough to fall asleep when my head hits the pillow.

The Seven Strategies of Destressing

In my almost two decades as a professional gardener and in my own personal research, I've found there are essentially seven strategies for destressing. Some of these activities my clients have mentioned more than once after I finished working in their garden and some I found reoccurring in the psychological literature. What's encouraging is that the latest scientific research proves nature provides an instant direct line to these strategies. They are: learning something new, fully experiencing our experiences, spending time being idle in play, supporting other living beings, uniting for a common cause, recognizing what we're grateful for, and of course, exercise. Let's look more closely at each.

Learning for fun is about discovery and exploration. When we learn, we find out what fascinates us, what we're most attracted to, what gets us excited, what interesting possibilities our future might hold. It's a key part of destressing, because when we learn, our brains reorganize themselves and build neural connections that enhance our well-being. For instance, when you read about a new topic, person, or place, your brain lights up with surprise, interest, and delight. Plus, sometimes you discover the next great passion of your life.

Experiencing the present is about intentionally existing in each moment. When we're aware of what we're doing or what's happening to us, we're living fully in the moment with all of our senses. We don't think about the future or the past, only the present. We breathe deeply and observe our thoughts. We set aside our own egos and simply perceive being alive with intention. I know: that's easier said than done, right? But fully experiencing a moment helps us redirect our thoughts away from what's troubling us and feel it as a more profound event that reminds us we're alive.

Idleness in play is about setting aside goals and relaxing. It's not about being lazy; it's about taking a break from our hectic schedules and engaging in low-stakes play. When we play, we indulge in an activity that seemingly has no purpose and only inconsequential goals. It stimulates our brains but doesn't tax them. We play a game because we don't know what to expect, but we won't die afterward, we won't even lose our job or spouse or car. Idle play is about curiosity and camaraderie, which researchers recently have found leads to super-charged levels of creativity and joy. Doing something for the sake of fun is exhilarating.

Supporting others is about finding meaning by caring for a living thing other than ourselves. It gives us a higher purpose in life, which experts believe is key to feeling a sense of placement on this planet. When we care about a person or family or pet or social issue, we feel a stronger sense of belonging to a community. Similarly, when we care for a plant, we reflect our valuation of the vast network of nature. When we carry an elderly neighbor's groceries into their house or volunteer for a cause we believe in, we get a jolt of happy warmth in our heart.

Similarly, *uniting with others* is about relationships. And relationships make us feel not so alone as we struggle through life. Unfortunately, as our lives have become busier and more technology oriented, we're losing our in-person connections to each other. And of course, the 2020 pandemic put that phenomenon on steroids. Still, overall, we're not gathering in person as much as we did decades ago, and we're not communicating as much. We're all suffering loneliness because of it. Hopefully, we can restore those bonds.

Recognizing what we have is about feeling grateful. Gratitude may be the most significant factor in reducing stress. Studies show that when we spotlight the people, objects, and experiences we already have in our minds, we feel happier and more at ease. Studies also show that keeping a gratitude journal or list of people, events, and memories we're grateful for makes us happier. To stay in touch with what we're thankful for every day rather than yearning for what we don't powerfully reminds us of how good our lives actually are.

Exercise seems an obvious way to jettison stress. We all know how, after working out at a gym or playing a game of tennis, we feel energized. We're high from the endorphin rush, which stays with us for hours after the activity's done. Plus, not only do our minds supercharge into a different, healthier space, but our muscles, tendons, and heart strengthen. Our cells regenerate and expel the waste. Our physical endurance and mobility improve. Exercise is a fast, healthy way to improve our mood.

IN THE NATURE HEALING ZONE

These seven strategies explain a lot about the experience I had with the butterfly bush. When I was reading those plant catalogs, I was *learning* about horticulture, which was novel and interesting. When I planted, deadheaded, and pruned the shrub, I was *idly playing*, engaging in a low-stakes activity whose outcome I was unsure of. When I was outside puttering in the garden, I could see the butterfly bush's gorgeous blossoms, smell the grass and soil, touch fuzzy leaves, and fully *experience* those moments with my senses. Of course, while planting the plant and working in the garden, I was *exercising* and getting my blood circulating. By *supporting* another living being, I felt responsible, which in turn made me feel *united* with the natural world and provided a small sense of purpose. That those dark purple flowers brought me so much joy triggered my grateful *recognition* of the garden and in turn brought on an overall state of happiness that felt like a beam of sunshine.

In short, I was unconsciously employing the seven strategies of destressing, which may have been why I went on to not only tend that little garden but to head full throttle into a horticulture career. Gardening and tending plants was the one activity I felt relaxed and whole while doing. I lost track of time and felt in "the zone." In fact, when people have asked me about my switch from high tech to horticulture, I always joke that I love gardening because "plants don't talk back or schedule meetings."

What happened from a slightly more scientific point of view was my innate urge to be in nature (*biophilia*) manifested through gardening, where I destressed and recharged my soul (*attention restoration theory*) and reconnected to nature (*nature-deficit disorder*). I was practicing, in essence, a kind of healing through a plant-focused diversion.

Others may view it through a different kind of lens. Meditation and yoga practitioners might see it as a kind of plant practice. Doctors and psychologists might see it as horticulture therapy. Self-help and business experts might see it as a beneficial, plant-oriented habit. But I see it more as an activity that's directed and intentional but not high stakes or particularly goal oriented. It's goofing off for a pleasurable psychological outcome; it's playing with plants for its own sake; it's a nature-based hobby that makes us happy. Ultimately, it's engaging in nature-related activities with the small aim of clearing our cluttered minds. What it truly is, is "green leisure."

TEN TINY IDEAS TO "RELEAF" YOUR STRESS

1. Keep a plant (real or fake) on your office desk.
2. Stop and smell the flowers at the grocery store.
3. Set your phone's home screen to a plant photo.
4. Stretch on tiptoes and reach for a tree branch.
5. Hang three landscape postcards on your bulletin board.
6. Listen to the wind rustle trees for an entire minute.
7. Create a tiny diorama of leaves, twigs, and moss.
8. Sit at the coffee shop table closest to leaves.
9. Watch a bee swoop from flower to flower.
10. Touch the bark on the first tree you see when you leave the house.

WHAT KIND OF GREEN LEISURE IS BEST?

That the seven strategies above actually spell the word "leisure" is no accident. Think of it as taking a mini-vacation with the natural world—what I'd accidentally created for my clients during all of those years as a professional gardener. And if it is indeed taking a nature-related mini-vacation, then what kind of green leisure is best for us? What kinds of activities? For how many days a week? And for how long? I have opinions on that, which I share as we go along, but the most important considerations are *your* interests and *your* time—what's right for you.

The good news is that there are a lot of activities to choose from. Some require a greater time commitment, like a few hours a week. Others require a few minutes a day (See "Ten Tiny Ideas to 'Releaf' Your Stress" for ideas). Some offer quicker results than others. They can be free, inexpensive, or require some money. Most are just plain fun. And if you already have one you love, help others by sharing how you do it on social media with the handle #greenleisure.

So let's explore what makes *your* spirit soar, the nature-related activities in which you feel most alive. You probably already know what kinds of recreational leisure you like, but you may not be totally sure of what kinds of nature-related hobbies you like. Usually, though not always, our opinions and feelings about nature can be traced back to our childhoods. So in the next chapter, let's explore how our green personality formed, what it looks like today, and how to incorporate green leisure into a personal plan.

ACTIVITIES

The Less-Stress Challenge

RATING: Clean hands, no tools, indoors, no cost

Remember how we located the hot spots of stress by creating a Stress Bramble in chapter 1? Now let's focus on those stress sources, the people, events, and situations that plague our minds, and see if we can cool those down.

What you'll need:

- Escape-to-Nature notebook
- writing tool

1. Examine the stress hot spots on your Stress Bramble. Make a separate list of all stress sources and the people involved. Is there a person who continually leans on you for help when he or she could probably care for themselves a bit better? Or perhaps a friend who forwards emails or calls you with dark, aggressive political opinions? Does something happen on the regular that you wish you could ditch? Are you a person of color who worries about the increase in hate crimes? Is it simply damn global warming? (I am so ridiculously worried about global warming.) Zero in on those areas and make a detailed list.
2. Strategize about how to neutralize those stress hot spots. For instance, I used to stress about my kids bickering all the time. I'd be helping my son with homework while my daughters were fighting. I constantly played referee. Finally, I decided I'd reward the girls with extra screen time every time they worked out their own problems and didn't interrupt me. (I know, I know, that's more screen stuff, but hey, I was busy.) Guess who solved their problems? Then, because I finished helping my son with his homework more quickly, I gained a half hour of my own time. Is there something

similar for you? Brainstorm some solutions. What are you doing that you shouldn't have to do? Who can help you? What can you say "no" to? I think we often know but don't want to cause discomfort for others. Well, time to cause discomfort!

3. If you find that you're able to gain a few minutes here and there, write down the time of day and amount of time. For instance, if you decided not to eat out on Fridays so you can pay down your student loans, then you've not only neutralized that stress a bit, you've gained twenty to forty minutes by not traveling to a restaurant.

Sifting Your Time Soil

RATING: Clean hands, no tools, indoors, low cost ($0–$10)

The next step is to assess your time. It's a valuable tool in making change happen. When we take a clear look at how we spend our hours, we get in touch with what's working for us and what isn't, thus allowing us to find the detritus to discard. We're sifting the soil of our time so we can toss the rocks that get in the way of all the good growing time.

What you'll need:

- Escape-to-Nature notebook
- writing tool
- five colored markers

1. On the first page, list the following five categories in five rows: Must Do, For Later, Hand Off, Let Go, Me Time. These are, what's important and ongoing, like a job (Must Do). Then, what's important but not ongoing, like cleaning out the garage (For Later). Next, what's important and ongoing but could be delegated, like chores or automated bill paying (Hand Off). What's not important or ongoing, like posting personal stuff to social media (Let Go). Lastly, the time you already set aside for yourself (Me Time). Assign each category a different color: red, blue, green, black, whatever. Leave a space beside each.

2. Starting on the next page, keep a time log of how you spend your waking hours for *three* days. It's good to choose a couple weekdays and a weekend day. Try to round to a half hour or fifteen-minute increments.
3. After three days, highlight each activity with a chosen category color.
4. Add up the amount of time in each category and put those totals in their corresponding rows.
5. Examine how you spend your time. Was most of your time spent at your job? Taking care of kids? Dealing with someone who's ill? Check for correlations between the activities on your Less-Stress Challenge and here. Do they align? Or do they *not* align, which is the problem?
6. Focus on the activities listed under "Hand Off" and "Let Go." How can you modify those to give yourself more time? During those three days, did you do something that you didn't plan on? Did you take care of a task that a family member could have? Did you do a mindless activity that afterward made you feel regretful? To what activities did you say "yes" when you could have said "no"?
7. See if you can sift through your time soil and find a half hour, an hour, a couple hours here and there. Identify those days and times by putting a box around each.
8. Look at your "Me Time." Was there enough of it? Too little on certain days? We focus more on this in the next chapter, but for now, circle them. These are the sacred slots you'll keep for your enjoyment, your fun, your relaxation, and some nature-related activities of your choice.
9. Write out the time windows you've gained in capital letters at the bottom of the page.

Congratulations, you're already making your "plants" for the weekend.

Chapter Three

========== ✍ ==========

Growing Your
Green Personality

Memory is a way of telling you what's important to you.—
Salman Rushdie, author

Unearthing Our Attitude toward Plants

Now that we've examined our stress and our schedules, let's explore
our attitude toward nature. What are your feelings about plants?
Do you have any? Are they nice but mostly form the background of
life? That's how I used to view landscapes. Kinda like wallpaper. I
saw them but didn't *see* them. There was green stuff on the horizon.
If that's where you're at, that's okay, though I bet we can uncover
some kind of viewpoint. Discovering it takes a bit of soulful excavation. As in diving into our past. Oftentimes our attitude toward
plants is in the depths of our memories. And most often, our key
memories of nature are made during childhood.

So let me ask you a few questions.

Do you remember your first memory of a plant? If so, how old
were you? Where was it?

Was it the early 2000s, the 1990s? The 1980s? For me, it was
the hot funky 1970s.

My first plant memory goes back to Chicago, where I grew up.
Northwest side. Go Cubs! Back then, people didn't think about

plants that much. Yards were for lawn chairs and kiddie pools. Trees were for shade. We lived in a two-unit apartment building with a square of grass and one tree for a backyard. Outside of a couple occasional tomato plants, neither of my parents gardened. We rarely used the yard, mostly for barbecues and to hang laundry. But in front of our house, my life was different.

On the parking strip, that wide patch of grass between the sidewalk and street, two catalpa trees grew. They were huge, towering far above our house and massive in diameter. Every August, they dropped their long seed pods, and every October, their papery leaves fluttered to the ground. They always captured my imagination. I played around them continually, pretending they had sentience and personalities. Needless to say, after reading about Ents in the *Lord of the Rings*, I found a kinship in those trees. They were mighty and powerful and, like Ents, kind and gentle. Of course, like Ents, they were expressive, too. Days after my father died, a lightning strike split one of the trees in two, which I interpreted as a message that the trees were distraught because we'd lost my dad.

Later, as a young adult, I saw Seattle for the first time on a trip to visit my aunt. I was stunned by the huge evergreen trees that grew everywhere: in parks, on golf courses, along highways, even in people's backyards. They towered over houses and commercial buildings, making those structures seem like toys. Furthermore, out in the country just beyond the suburbs, I found masses of coniferous forests. Evergreen tree after tree after tree. I couldn't believe so many trees grew in one place. Velvety hills covered in dark green spires folded into the snow-laced mountains. The whole area was like a giant wonderland. The Fangorn Forest come to life.

In an instant, I knew I was home. It was as if I'd arrived where I was supposed to be, though I didn't know why. It took a mere two months for me to go back to Chicago, pack up the few things I owned, and move to Seattle. To my mother's dismay, I never moved back to the Midwest, but when she visited the Pacific Northwest, she understood why I'd stayed.

Oddly, it took me almost twenty years before I finally realized why I'd really moved here. Before, when people had asked me, I'd said I needed a job and my aunt lived in Tacoma and I had nothing going on in Chicago. But that wasn't the deeper reason. The reason I'd moved to the Pacific Northwest was because I'd fallen in love. With giant trees. And by giant trees I mean *those giant catalpa trees* from my childhood. Two natural beauties of Chicago, of which at least one still stands today. My Ent-like trees had imprinted their majesty on my soul. Now, twenty-five years later, I'm blessed to live in a house on land where several giant conifers grow.

WHAT IF YOU'RE NOT *THAT* INTO NATURE?

Not everyone has a dreamy experience of books and trees. And to be honest, I don't have a lot of dreamy experiences because my dad dying young created a pretty sad childhood for me. But thankfully that time is past. I'd rather focus on you. What kinds of experiences with plants did *you* have as a child? Perhaps you grew up gardening with your grandma and it was awesome. Or perhaps you lived in a high rise and only saw trees when you visited a park. Or perhaps your park didn't even have trees, just dirt and broken glass. You might have even had an experience with plants that made nature repulsive to you.

For instance, take my husband's experience. He grew up on a small farm in Bellingham, Washington. His family home was surrounded by trees of all kinds. Nature was literally his backyard for miles. As a boy, he was able to play in open fields, climb trees, explore a creek, build forts inside thickets, and ride his bike on dirt trails. But once he grew up, he couldn't wait to leave town. During his college years, he chose to attend the University of Washington in Seattle. Since then, he's always lived in the city and has zero interest in returning to rural life. He doesn't dream of managing his own small farm or growing vegetables or raising animals. Nor is he interested in gardening, backpacking, or camping. He has a vastly different kind of green personality than me. Why?

Well, the answer is in his childhood. When my husband was a boy, his family had an enormous kitchen garden. Vegetables, fruit trees, berry bushes. It needed continual tending. Every other day and every weekend, he had to pull weeds, which of course he found boring and repetitive. He didn't get chore money for his work, and he didn't get enough time to play. (He even had to often eat mushy squash for dinner, which he disliked.) So his memories associate plants with work and icky food, not fun or positive times. His interest in the natural world was crushed by well-intended parents who wanted to teach him the value of work but didn't provide the higher meaning the natural world offers. For him, plants are chores, not filled with imaginative dreams, wonder, or solace. So as an adult, he has a green leisure activity that doesn't involve tending plants but that works for him. I'll share it with you later in this chapter.

AMERICANS ARE AVOIDING THE SCENERY

This disconnection from nature happens for many people. In fact, according to a 2019 American Public Media survey, one in six American adults reported never spending any time in nature. About 30 percent of those surveyed said their job or work-related issues left them little time to spend in nature. In particular, millennials, who said they felt happier after spending time in or with nature, avoided doing so because of long working hours and the associated costs.[1] Similarly, the Outdoor Foundation learned that Americans went on one billion fewer outings in 2018 than they did in 2008. Children went on fewer outings as well: 15 percent fewer than in 2012. One small gift from the pandemic was 7.1 million more people participated in outdoor recreation but ultimately that increase didn't reverse long-term trends.[2] While we're getting a lot done in the indoor working world, we're missing out on the pleasures of outdoor life.

FIFTEEN IDEAS FOR FIFTEEN MINUTES OF GREEN

We can connect with the soothing green world of plants in lots of brief ways. Here are fifteen. Can you think of more? If so, let me know via my website (www.karenhugg.com)!

1. Hop off the subway or bus a stop early and walk down a street with trees.
2. Find a green space on the map of your town. Park there and eat lunch.
3. Color with your kids in a botanic coloring book using green crayons or markers.
4. Visit a museum courtyard garden on free admission days.
5. Walk your dog and search for birds in trees you pass.
6. Relax in the bathtub while gazing at a plant on a stand or sill.
7. Dance barefoot with your sweetheart at sunset in a leafy park.
8. Lie on the floor and stare at the upward perspective of your largest houseplant.
9. Drive down that wooded lane you often see but haven't explored.
10. Sip a cocktail decorated with mint leaves with your roommate.
11. Chat with a neighbor about his or her beloved roses.
12. Peruse a glossy gardening magazine in bed.
13. Decorate your home with fallen leaves, branches, vines, and pine cones.
14. Jog to that one beautiful house with a lush garden.
15. Enjoy a meal at an outdoor restaurant with pretty flower boxes.

What's strange is how starkly this trend contradicts the geography of our country. Land-wise, America is the third largest country in the world, behind Russia and Canada. Unlike many countries, we have more than a dozen mountain ranges, several massive lakes, countless rivers, including thirty-eight that are more than five hundred miles long, wetlands in every state, precious saguaro-rich desert, vast coastal areas, and diverse forests. Plus, we have more than 22,000 city parks. It's astonishing how we have so many natural areas in which to play, yet most of us don't bother taking advantage of them. For some reason, we're avoiding the scenery.

Actually, I guess it's not a mystery. In fact, I understand the impulse to stay inside. Half of the year, it's too cold to go outside. Inside is more comfortable. It's familiar. Temperature controlled. Clean. In contrast, the outside world can be unfamiliar, even exotic or dangerous depending on where you are. It can be so cold your nose hair freezes or so hot you melt into a puddle. Plus, nature is hard and rough, not cushy, or if it is cushy, it's soak-through-your-pants wet, like moss in the Pacific Northwest. Even to my middle-aged self, the idea of sleeping in a tent on a yoga mat that passes for a mattress doesn't seem enticing, forget cool or hip. Never mind the potential of large furry animals stomping your ribs or biting your neck. Relieving your bladder on a 45-degree morning doesn't sound exactly fun, either. I get it.

All of those attitudes are totally legit. Then again, maybe they're a bigger deal in our minds than they are in reality. The point is, you are who you are in part from your early childhood experiences and in part from your adult tastes. The most important thing is to discover what kind of relationship to the green world your soul craves and honor it. Engaging with nature can happen in as little as fifteen minutes (see "Fifteen Ideas for Fifteen Minutes of Green" for ideas). And it can be as easy as sitting on your balcony beside a container of flowers every day or gazing at the tree outside your window. So let's see if we can excavate the clues to your green personality by examining your childhood experiences and your current preferences.

WHAT'S YOUR GREEN PERSONALITY?

How interested in plants are you right now? Are you a city person whose imagination is captured by nature? Or do you have memories of the outdoor world as a source of chores or a scary place? Do you like to tinker with plants in your home or yard? Ever grown a butterfly bush or a houseplant? Maybe you don't know where to start with plants. Maybe you're not even interested, but you appreciate nature. Maybe you like to hike with a close friend on vacation or hang out with your kids at the local park. Or maybe you're just too darn busy for anything. Regardless, if you picked up this book, I imagine you're at least interested in finding out.

In my professional gardening work, I've noticed people tend to fall into three profiles in terms of their engagement with the natural world. Sometimes they overlap but not always. They are explorers, nesters, and greeners.

Explorers are people who like to go out into the world to spend time in nature. They walk, hike, bike, paddle, fish, camp, and so on. They're not interested in growing plants at home but would rather go out into nature to enjoy it. This is my husband. He likes to walk twice a day along our forested street. On weekends, he rides his bike on a leafy trail. Those single, repeating activities suit him well.

Nesters are people who like to bring nature into their home. They might grow houseplants indoors and decorate with plant imagery. They also like to grow plants outside if they have outdoor space, whether it be in containers or a garden.

Greeners like to go to nature *and* bring nature to their homes. They enjoy both kinds of green experiences. This might be someone who mountain bikes on the weekends but also grows herbs at home on a balcony. Someone who likes to read about plants and visit botanic gardens. A person who keeps several houseplants, maintains a garden, *and* camps every summer. Also, they might decorate with natural materials or green objects while also picnicking in parks.

Do you fit any of these profiles? You might be an explorer who likes to kayak on tree-lined rivers but doesn't grow houseplants.

Maybe you're a nester who once a year goes camping. I'm a greener. I like to hike in the woods but I also like gardening at home. Whatever you think you might be, try the activities below. Find a quiet, comfortable space in which to do them. Don't forget to read the follow-up text for guidance on how to meld this new information into the activities from chapter 2.

ACTIVITIES

Green Personality Germination

RATING: Clean hands, no tools, indoors, no cost

It's time your green personality grew from the seed of your intention into a full-scale plan.

What you'll need:

- Escape-to-Nature notebook
- writing tool

1. Write about your first memory (or memories) related to plants or green spaces generally. Answer these questions: How old were you? Where were you? Who, if anyone, was with you? Were you engaged in an activity? What time of year was it? Was it a positive experience or a negative experience? Include all of the sights and sounds and smells you remember. Talk about why you felt the way you did. You don't even need full sentences, phrases will do. Spend about fifteen minutes writing. You can start with, "My first memory of nature was . . ."
2. If that doesn't jog your memory, make a list of favorite people from your past. It need not be many, even one or two is fine. Now ask yourself, did you ever enjoy a nature-related activity with that person? Describe what you did. Why did it make you joyful? What

are the feelings related to the experience? Describe it in detail as vividly as you can. Write for fifteen minutes. Note: When I did these exercises with my husband, he couldn't recall his first plant memory. He was at a loss. Ironic for a farm kid, right? But when I asked him about a favorite person from his early life, he instantly named his father's mother and recalled how wonderful she was. He talked about how his family drove to California to see her when he was a boy. He remembered the amazing smell of her grapefruit tree flowers. He talked about how big and common to California the grapefruits were, how his cousin would bat them around for fun, which seemed exotic to a northern kid. This story is revealing to me. You know why? To this day, my husband loves eating grapefruit more than anyone in our family. So if you're stumped at first, keep going. There are more questions below.

3. If there are no joyful memories of plants or people in your past, is there a sad one you can pinpoint? What did that feel like? Describe it. Include your feelings without holding back. Afterward, in a new paragraph, answer how you can reclaim that sad experience and move on from it today. What can you do differently in your life now? Or what do you do differently with your own children? Write in detail for fifteen minutes if you can.

4. If money, time, and societal conditions weren't a factor, what would an engaged life with plants look like for you? Would you grow houseplants? Would you decorate with more greenery? Would you visit parks or gardens more? Hike? Camp? Fish? What would you like to try or do more of? Paint a verbal picture in your Escape-to-Nature notebook of what that would look like. If you're artistically inclined, draw it.

5. From all of the journaling and imagining you've done thus far, circle the words describing positive feelings. Some examples are carefree, loved, peaceful, accepted, fun, relaxed, healed, happy, content, etcetera. You can count related words like quiet, beauty, colorful, stress-free, soft, recover, escape, and so on. Make a list of words denoting positive feelings.

6. Now circle the activities that appeal to you. Some examples are swinging from willow tree branches, planting petunias in a

basket, rowing a boat on a lake, snuggling in a hammock with a parent, or walking through a nature preserve. Make a list of appealing activities.

7. Try to create a green personality mission statement. You want to make your intentions clear. The template is "I want to [activity], so I can feel [emotion or state of mind]." For instance, if your memory is of rowing a boat and you felt relaxed while doing so, write something like: "I want to spend some time in a boat on a secluded lake so I can feel relaxed." If your memory is of planting petunias, write something like: "I want to have/grow flowering plants so I can feel peaceful." For now, don't worry about the details. You'll explore more in part II. And it's okay to have more than one mission statement. I have four. If you can, list a rough estimate of the amount of time you'll need for each one.

Congratulations, you've reached the first milestone of destressing through green leisure!

Follow Up

Now that you have a loose portrait of your green personality, you may feel a mix of emotions. Digging into our buried past can reveal both joy and pain. Rediscovering joy is exciting because it means we can reclaim an object, ritual, or activity that makes us happy. You may now feel a strong yearning to do an activity you haven't done in years. Conversely, remembering a sad or melancholy experience triggers grief, which can be painful, but it also provides insight into how we *don't* want to live our lives, and that's useful too. The point is, you've empowered yourself to live your life in a healthier way.

Carving out Your Calendar Time

RATING: Clean hands, no tools, indoors, no cost

We're getting to the fun part! By now, hopefully you've identified some time from your Less-Stress Challenge and soil-sifting exercises that you can use here. And hopefully you've discovered a few plant-related activities you'd like to either pick up again or try out. This activity is the straightforward task of melding the two together.

Note: If this exercise seems overwhelming or you're not into calendars and schedules, consider this less formal approach. When you notice yourself wasting time, time you consider to be "Let Go" time, stop doing it and replace it with a green moment. Say "Nope. Green moment," then shift your attention (#greenleisure). Instead of reading news about a celebrity you don't really care about, go outside for five minutes and check on your raspberry bushes. If you don't have an outdoor area, give your houseplant a wipe down. If you don't have a houseplant, you can relax for five deep breaths by staring out the window at a weed growing through a crack in the sidewalk. The point is to redirect your attention to something green.

Now let's pinpoint your green leisure time windows.

What you'll need:

• Escape-to-Nature notebook
• writing tool

Flip back to the Less-Stress Challenge and Sifting Your Time Soil exercises. What were the windows of time you reclaimed? Remember those written at the bottom in capital letters? Can those blocks of time be added to any "Me Time" to create a larger chunk of a half hour, hour, or two hours?

1. Block out those bits of reclaimed time and/or "Let Go" time and label them as "Me Time."
2. Examine the "Hand Off" pieces of your time. Who can you hand off chores to? Spouse? Children? A babysitter? Maybe a housecleaner? If so, do it! Let your family know that you're trying to find some time to relax. Don't forget to mention that if they help out, you'll be a happier, more laid-back person. Everyone wins. If you speak up for yourself, you just might get a gift certificate for a cleaning service or an offer of babysitting for your birthday!
3. Look at the "For Later" category. If you can turn a "For Later" task into "Must Do," then do it! Call the car dealership and schedule the oil change. Block out time to bake the cookies for teacher

appreciation week. Then that task will become "Must Do" on your calendar. Also, deleting a "For Later" task is fine too. I mean, who *really* wants to clean out the garage?

4. After all that, identify the number of "Me Time" hours you have. Did you gain anything from the "Hand Off" or "Let Go" categories? Fifteen minutes? An hour? Two hours? Three even? If you can create a large block on the weekend, bravo! The largest amount of time gives you the most flexibility. On your calendar, block out those times and write in big letters "Me Time."

5. In at least one of those "Me Time" blocks, plug in one of the activities from your green personality mission statements. Be realistic but try to reserve one to three times a week devoted to favorite activities. Of course, they can be fitted in terms of time. You can put "water houseplants" for Wednesday evenings from 5:00 to 5:30 and "rent kayak at lake" for Saturday mornings from 9:00 to 12:00. Again, if you're not into calendars, then mark the time on a sticky note and hang it where you can see it to remind yourself to take time for yourself. Ultimately, this can be a rough sketch.

Congratulations! You've got a plan for how you'll honor your green personality.

Part Two

NO-GOALS
GREEN LEISURE

Hopefully in the last section you were able to identify your sources of stress, create more windows of "Me Time," and figure out at least one green leisure mission statement. But if you didn't, it's not a big deal. I have more ideas about growing happiness.

In fact, when surveying the research on happiness, I found common strategies reoccurring among all studies and recommendations. I applied those strategies to the natural world and created what I hope is the easy, memorable system of "green leisure" to help you heal from the stress of the day and restore energy. Part II explores these seven destressing strategies:

- **L**earning and imagining in green
- **E**xperiencing plants through the senses
- **I**dly playing in the plant world
- **S**upporting a green life
- **U**niting with like "nature minds"
- **R**ecognizing what we've grown
- **E**xercising outside without trying

We'll learn how folks I know have applied these concepts in their everyday lives, what the science tells us about each strategy's effectiveness, and how to apply them in your own life.

Chapter Four

=====================— ✑ —=====================

Learning and
Imagining in Green

Exploration is what you do when you don't know what you're doing.—Neil deGrasse Tyson, astrophysicist

In 2016, I met with a client called Ruby who taught me a valuable lesson about learning and imagination. Ruby owned a beautiful home on a small lake in north Seattle. She wanted a design for her garden, so we met and walked her property. As we strolled through a messy backyard to an uneven path with weeds and a densely overgrown front yard, she slumped forward, pointing to the various problem areas. These were the sections of the garden where, as she said, she'd "failed." She described how a long fence border hadn't turned out the way she'd hoped and how much it bothered her. She sighed at a dark corner where she wasn't sure what to grow. Her face scrunched with dismay as she told me all about the mature tangled shrubs she'd inherited with the house. Her voice even cracked with exasperation when she described growing a few lavenders that had died. An uneven path was unfinished. A nearby ash hung too low over the roof. When she finished, she said she'd always wanted to have a nice garden she could relax in but now her yard had become one "giant source of stress."

I interviewed her about what activities she and her family usually did in the backyard and what they wanted to do but couldn't with the yard in its current state. Then I described the changes that might enhance each area. As I talked, I noticed her face change. It softened. She peppered me with questions. She unfolded her arms, nodded, and gave me more feedback. The more I described where and how we'd start, what my design changes would be, and some outstanding plants she could easily grow, she grew more excited. Her imagination had booted up and started churning, her voice lightening, her eyes bright.

I had seen this before-and-after experience in my clients' eyes before. Whenever I met with them to discuss a garden, they were dismayed by the garden's present state but often turned animated when we talked possibilities. As I wrapped up my meeting with Ruby, I gave her a bit of homework (as I did with most clients). I asked her to make a list of favorite plants and a list of least favorite plants, plus the same for color preferences, if any. I asked her to include any "dream features" like a firepit, a flagstone patio, or an arbor. Again, she told me she didn't know anything about plants or garden features. She insisted she had no preferences, so I gave her a list of a few key gardening websites and books and went on my way.

A week later, when I returned for a second meeting, Ruby had totally transformed. I rang her doorbell, and she opened the door, smiling, emerging with coat and boots on, ready to walk the property. A notebook and pen were tucked at her chest. She ambled around with a more erect posture and even cracked a joke about the rainy weather. She told me she'd checked out a couple books from the library and had read about a bunch of plants on the internet. She said she had "a blast" looking through all of the photos. She buzzed with excitement, her expression loose and open. Later, in the house, she led me eagerly to her kitchen island, where a stack of glossy gardening books, folded-back magazines, and her laptop waited. Almost like a collage, she laid out all of the information and photos she'd found. These were what inspired her the most, she said. They made up her "dream garden."

I smiled. It seemed she *did* have preferences.

Ruby had been utterly stressed out about her garden. She'd claimed to know nothing about plants and have no opinions whatsoever and suddenly she was brimming with so many ideas she couldn't keep them straight. She not only made list within list on that notepad, but she'd also done a very rough sketch of what she wanted for that dark corner. She mentioned various aspects of garden design like "winter structure" and "mixed borders" and asked detailed, informed questions. Could we include red flowers to attract hummingbirds? Could we have a water feature as a focal point like the one she'd seen in a magazine? Could we screen out the neighbor's garbage cans? Did a rain garden exposed to the north make sense? And on and on.

What Ruby essentially had done was learn and imagine her way out of stress. She'd directed her mind's attention away from the overwhelming angst she felt at having a messy "failed" garden to thoughts and images that energized her spirit. And because the thoughts and images were about plants, she dialed into her biophilic connection to nature, which hit two buttons on her happiness meter. She taught me that learning and imagining are easy, fun ways to destress.

How Learning Leads to Lower Stress

Learning is our first destressing strategy, the *L* in green leisure. It engages the imagination and supercharges the brain. When we learn, we discover, explore, and, maybe most importantly, dream of a more perfect future. When we dive into a subject that interests us, we not only physically grow our brains through neural connections, we grow psychologically through the excitement of possibility. Plus, we focus that precious attention we talked about in chapter 2 on what ignites our spirit. We escape our flawed, day-to-day life where suffering is prevalent for a more perfect, fulfilling one. We abandon the ache of stress and enter a peaceful sanctuary. It's escapism, yes, but the best kind.

If we can enter a peaceful sanctuary of plants in our minds, we may benefit not only from the effects of learning, but from nature's healing effects as well. Not only are you discovering information you didn't know before, you're exposing yourself to images of real or imagined plant-related scenarios, whose physiological benefits I'll explain in the next chapter. And though it is better for us when that learning happens in the real world, learning through our imagination still helps to relax our minds and bodies.

What's more, learning is a low-cost ritual that requires no specific skill or tools. Information on the internet is free. Books in libraries are free. If you can get to a library, you can learn about a topic. You don't even need a computer in your home. Also, learning doesn't demand that you physically move. This is of course important for those whose bodies are challenged. But overall, the exciting thing is that learning requires only your focus and time.

So what if, unlike Ruby, you don't have a garden and aren't interested in creating one? That's the beauty of learning. It doesn't require you to actually buy plants or use tools. You can simply use it as an exercise in discovery. Discovering isn't really about implementing the final design or end result; it's about the exploratory process. In learning about whatever aspect of the natural world we like, we practice attention restoration therapy (ART). We divert our attention from worry and struggle to a more neutral ideal world. In fact, I have a particular gardening project that I'll probably never create in the real world, I only use it to make myself happier. I'll share it later in this chapter.

Putting the Process over an Outcome

Scientific research shows us why the learning process, rather than the outcome, is so important. In 2021, UK and US researchers found that test subjects were happier when they were figuring out the task of how to win a video game car race rather than actually winning the race. It wasn't the reward; it was the actual process of learning. "We found that happiness depends on learning, but surprisingly, it doesn't depend on reward," Bastien Blain, the lead researcher, said.[1] That's a strong argument for learning something new to lower stress.

Similarly, studies have found that as you repeat a complex task or practice a hobby, your brain grows its number of neural connections. Areas like the cerebellum can actually thicken.[2] Learning keeps us sharp as we age. Or as Professor Lisa Berkman at Harvard University found, "Your mind is really like a muscle and using it is a key [to long-term mental health]." Her 2012 study found that people who lived in states where the laws required them to attend school for longer had better cognitive functioning later in life.[3]

Forget the outcome; let's learn for fun.

THE POWER OF IMAGINATION

Still, learning is the rational, organized attempt to increase our knowledge by inputting straight-up information. When we do it, we are attempting to gain knowledge. And what happens inside our minds? Well, we create pictures, right? We see the images of what we're learning about in our mind. We imagine; we visualize. And there's a lot of power in visualizing, too.

For instance, when we imagine a positive scenario like a vacation, relaxing on a beach with a cocktail under a sunny sky, we feel excited and happy. You may recall a study from 2018 when Dutch researchers found their subjects' levels of happiness were highest when *planning* a vacation rather than actually taking it.[4] People felt an anticipatory joy in the act of gathering information, seeing images of their destination, and imagining the possibilities. We get our brains buzzing in a hopeful, positive way.

Sometimes the process can be destructive. We can obsess on the negative, the "what-if" problems that might go wrong. When we imagine a negative scenario like a business meeting going poorly or the boss ridiculing our ideas, we feel worried. The anxiety quickens our breathing. Our heartbeat increases. When we go to those negative scenarios in our head, we can consider what might go wrong and change our plans in light of those possibilities. But the way to neutralize stress is to redirect our attention and focus on a positive scenario. If we visualize the business meeting going well, the boss liking our ideas and shaking our hand, we move away from feeling anxious to feeling more confident and hopeful.

This shows how powerful our imagination is, and what a powerful tool it is for destressing. I mean, we have the ability to dream up what we need. Wow! It's easy; it's free; it's effective. And it often leads to tangible, real-world results. Psychotherapists use visualization with clients to reduce stress in those who suffer from anxiety. Athletes use it to aid in performance. Olympic swimmer Michael Phelps famously used visualization to win twenty-three gold medals.[5] Every night before a swimming competition, he would lie down and relax his body. Then he would imagine his perfect performance, taking into account all that could go wrong so he wouldn't panic during the competition. Similarly, people in the corporate world use visualization to motivate themselves to achieve goals. Anyone can use visualization. Whether the outcome happens or not, dreaming about it garners hope and happiness, which is essentially what happened with my client Ruby.

The next time you have a rotten day, do a Michael Phelps but apply it to your daily life. Steal away for ten minutes. Tell the kids to entertain themselves for a little treat later. Lie down and close your eyes. Relax your entire body, arms, legs, and all else. Imagine yourself in your favorite natural scenario: On that beach sipping a cocktail, the palm trees fluttering in the wind. Or at a trail viewpoint, high up, gazing at a rolling forest valley. What about a steady, rushing waterfall surrounded by mossy rocks and evergreen trees? Your ideal stress-free image is limited only by your imagination.

THE BENEFITS OF DAYDREAMING

Whereas learning and visualization have clear outcomes, daydreaming, albeit pointless and meandering, can also be helpful in destressing. When we daydream, we allow our minds to wander, skipping randomly from, perhaps, an image to a thought to a memory. We don't direct our minds; we allow our attention to wander as it wants. We detach ourselves emotionally. There's no goal, no results we're after.

Daydreaming is an impressive, somewhat mysterious, process. Seemingly disparate thoughts connect and creativity supercharges. Great works of literature and music and progress in science and technology have resulted when people allowed their minds to wander. Albert Einstein famously came up with the theory of relativity after taking a break and allowing his thoughts to roam.

In my own life, I've found that some of my strongest ideas popped in my mind when I wasn't actively thinking about the project at hand. For instance, when I was hired to design a client's garden, I often scheduled at least two weeks between our initial meeting and when I presented the design. I needed that time for my ideas to ferment, to not only solve problems in the yard but to edit my design choices. Same thing when I write novels. Sometimes while driving, I make sure to drive in silence so my mind wanders from one thought to another. I give myself a directed push but allow myself to skip around in thought. (This is when a phone's "Notes" feature comes in handy.) I also do this in the shower or while working in my own garden. Regardless, I always solve a design puzzle or discover a strong novel idea when I allow my mind to organically follow its path.

Researchers have found daydreaming has strong benefits as well. University of California at Santa Barbara researchers found that students who daydreamed during a break in a task in which they listed uses for mundane objects created 41 percent more ideas than those who hadn't daydreamed.[6] That's a big chunk! Similarly, psychologist Kalina Christoff at the University of British Columbia discovered that mind-wandering actually activates high-level problem-solving areas of the brain, which helps us figure out complex puzzles or issues.[7] These two studies prove that the brain needs a break to play around. Lastly, Matthew Lorber of Lenox Hill Hospital in New York City found that those who daydreamed were more motivated to achieve their goals.[8] So if you can find some time to give your brain a break, you may be able to relax, get creative, and accomplish more.

THE POTAGER I'LL NEVER PRODUCE

What I love about the natural world is that there's so much to learn and so much to imagine. It's endless. For instance, I've been involved with gardening for almost twenty-five years now, but there's lots I don't know. I discover new stuff every day: new plant cultivars, new design approaches, new products. Even existing plants I wasn't familiar with. There's a ton of fascinating information and images out there. And most of it isn't political or complex or underhanded or intense. It's just the natural world, waiting to be discovered.

In my own garden, I continually plan changes and imagine how I can improve areas, how I can squeeze in the latest whizzy-pretty plant. This imagining gives me a wonderful excuse to go back to my gardening roots and peruse catalogs and read up on plants. And what a crazy useful resource the internet is. Thirty years ago, we had to go to the library, look up numbers on little cards, and scan dozens of shelves for books. Now, learning about anything happens in five seconds. I take advantage of that. I make my laptop work for me like an appliance and enjoy diving down those "rabbit holes" of discovery.

With that in mind, I have to confess that I do use Pinterest, even though I discourage people from using screens. I keep several boards with images of gardens and plants that I like. Unlike other social media, Pinterest is not focused on likes and highlighting your own life. Some people use it this way and that's fine for them. But I use it as an effective search engine that expertly personalizes to my tastes. When I open it, I see a feed of images that helps me learn, imagine, and dream every day. It doesn't limit my experience or make me feel ashamed; it expands and encourages possibilities.

One ongoing project I like to dream about is a formal potager—a formal French kitchen garden—for my backyard. But it's a potager I'll never build. I know that. I mean, I have the space and I have the sun to build it, but I don't want to. I have enough garden to maintain already! I don't want the extra real-life work, just the dreamy fun. And the image of a certain kind of potager makes me swoon. I can see it in my mind's eye now.

I know exactly how it looks. It resembles the formal potagers you see in Italy or France. It's geometric in shape with a birdbath at the center. Beds of chives, rosemary, sage grow in a circular bed surrounding the birdbath. Then squarish vegetable beds radiate out from the bird bath with tomatoes, peppers, beans, and so forth. Paths of lime grit lay placidly and ever-weeded in between. The weather is warm and sunny, *always*, unlike damp, misty Seattle, and the plants are healthy. Cicadas and bees buzz in the distance. The air is dry and still. I can smell the lemon balm.

Sometimes when I'm stressed, I retreat to my European potager. I collect images related to it; I wonder whether I could rent a house with one for a summer; I curl up on the couch and read about exotic herbs and heirloom tomatoes. There's no pressure. I expect nothing of myself. I use it to relax my mind, escape the day. I feel calm; I feel engaged in a positive way. Difficult, complex life doesn't exist when I'm in my imaginary potager. It's just a virtual vacation to dream country.

LEARNING AS INTENTIONAL ATTENTION

What is the garden you'll never grow? Or the plants you're curious about? Maybe you have houseplants and you want to care for them better. Or maybe deepen your growing skills with a small outdoor space with plants (more of that in chapters 11, 12, and 13). Whatever it is, keep in mind that when we explore with intention, we discover what nurtures us in the purest way. You're not unconsciously scrolling through random photos or micro-bits of info on social media. You're focusing on what *you* want to actively pursue, not mindlessly be fed. *You're* steering your life in the direction *you* want to go, no one else. Plus, you're bettering yourself as a person as you expand your knowledge, explore your imagination, and dream up ideas! Look at you, what tremendous power. Go!

ACTIVITIES

Sleuthing a Special Plant

RATING: Clean hands, no supplies, indoors or outdoors, low cost ($0–$10)

When you explored your early plant memories in chapter 3, did you discover a plant you were fond of? Was there a sweet apple you ate? Flowers you cut? A tree that you climbed and made you feel safe? Maybe nowadays, there's a rose you pass by every day that smells sweet. Or an unusual plant in your dentist's waiting room, but you don't know the name of the plant. Let's find out!

This week, learn more about that special plant. Photograph it. Investigate. Inquire. Search online. Consult a friend. Do you know that you can search via a photo using Google Images? If you download a plant identification app on your phone, you can take a photo and learn the name there. (See the appendix for app suggestions.) Or take a photo to your local nursery folks or master gardener program for help.

See if you can solve the mystery of this plant that draws you in. After you learn the name, look up where it natively lives. What conditions it likes. You could even give it a nickname. Then use the photo as your computer wallpaper. Or print it out and hang it up where you can see it. Grow it, if possible. Post it on social media. If you want to send it to me through my website, I'll post it on www.karenhugg.com.

The Garden I Might Grow Someday

RATING: **Clean hands, no supplies, indoors, low cost ($0–$20)**

If you don't have a plant collection, why not dream one up? Pretend I'm your garden designer and you're my client. In your Escape-to-Nature notebook, create a scrapbook of your ideal houseplant or outdoor garden collection. What would be in it? It doesn't matter if you grow it in real life. Just fill your imagination with a dreamy plantscape. If you like tangible objects, gather physical photos, quotes, postcards, and bits of botanical information about plants. These can come from catalogs, magazines, old books, outdated calendars, bookmarks, or anything else you come across. If you're artistically inclined, sketch your favorite plants and scenes and write bits of what you've learned around them. Keep this scrapbook or board wherever you will see it regularly. It's great to keep it by your bed or desk. You can page through it for some calm images to relax with before sleep and take notes about what you want to learn about in coming days.

If you find exploring online easier, create a collection using an online board site. Make a personalized feed of images and plant growing tips based on your interests. Don't limit yourself to plants, either. Explore the spaces that make you feel good. Perhaps it's a cabin in a deep forest, a flowering prairie, a castle with an enormous English garden. Maybe even your own kitchen window jammed with plants. Whatever it is, don't hold back your imagination. Learn about what grows there. Include anything and everything you've ever desired. This is about filling your mind with images, information, and exciting possibilities. If you want some inspiration, you can find my real garden and my dream potager at www.pinterest.com/karenhugg.

Nerdy Plant Family Newsletter Exchange

RATING: Clean hands, no supplies, indoors, low cost ($0–$20)

You know how you might get a newsletter in the mail from relatives or friends at Christmastime? Well, what if you wrote one, to no one in particular—or, even better, to a real-life friend or a plant-loving pen pal (see below)—about your garden, houseplants, or "only child" houseplant?

Share your plant or plants' names. Write about what the Latin names mean in English. Share your personal nicknames for your plants. Describe what they look like and what they like. Talk about their history, where you bought them, or their baby origins as a seed or cutting.

Share what they've accomplished this year (as if they were your kids). Brag about them a bit. Describe how they looked earlier this year and what they look like now. Are they putting on new leaves? About to bloom? Sagging? Browning lower leaves? Describe all that. Are there any losses? Share who died and who's sick, as if they are your dear relatives, and what you're doing to improve their lives. Water more? Less? Feed with fertilizer? Or cut a stem to rid the plant of pests? Don't be shy about asking for advice.

Finally, write about whether there will be any new additions to the family. Will the plants get any little brothers or sisters in the future? If so, what kinds of plants are you thinking about adding to your collection? Ask for ideas from your pen pal. If you don't have one, contact me at www.karenhugg.com. I'm collecting names for correspondence!

Chapter Five

※

Experiencing Plants through the Senses

It is very rare to find a human being today. They are always going somewhere, hardly ever being here. That is why I call them "human goings."—Ajahn Brahm, joyful monk

In 2007, my friend Melanie started an intriguing habit of destressing. Every morning, she walks through her local park right after waking up (which impresses me because I'm barely conscious right after I wake up). She does it rain or shine, from March through October or until the severe snow or cold hits. Sometimes she drives to the park and sometimes she walks. With a path around a soccer field, various trees, a pond encircled by thick trees and shrubs, and a small botanical garden, the park offers a peaceful green experience to start her day. Interestingly, Melanie makes a point to slowly stroll, breathing in the smell of trees, the rain, fragrant flowers, and all else. She touches the soft leaves of lamb's ear or dusty miller in the park's hanging baskets. She listens to the birds tweeting and pond gurgling. Every now and then, when in the botanical garden area, she'll notice spearmint or oregano and pluck a leaf to chew. For about a half hour, all five of her senses are engaged.

What does that do for her? Well, she feels calmer, more relaxed, more appreciative. She says it helps ground her and start her day. There are no commercial signs, no traffic, no argumentative voices in the garden. Once in a while, there's the buzz of a lawnmower or kids playing at the playground, but she views such activity as part of the park's relaxed, enclosed world. Walking through is a soothing salve for her soul. That she does it every day impresses me. I mean, she does it in a snowy big city! But it's a habit she's committed to, albeit a leisurely one. There are no goals. The only task is to pay attention. To be mindful. To slow down, pause to see and touch the plants, inhale the outdoor scents, and listen to the ambient sounds, whatever they are. She doesn't judge or worry but exists in the landscape. Melanie's walk-through is like a form of walking meditation. She experiences the park in the most authentic way possible: with utter nonjudgmental presence.

THE STRUGGLE FOR EVERY MOMENT AS A GIFT

What Melanie's doing is practicing the second strategy of destressing: experiencing—the *E* in green leisure. When we live utterly present in the moment, we're giving ourselves the gift of true raw experience. We're making the most of being alive, living not carelessly but rather care*fully*. It's like living inside a sharp, colorful painting rather than a dull, fuzzy backdrop. We breathe deeply. We soak in every color, smell, sound, surface, and taste. Savor every second. And as we savor the seconds, we honor our beautiful but brief life. By doing that, later when we're about to leave this giant verdant garden, we'll feel satisfaction in knowing we enjoyed every moment we were given.

I know that sounds dreamy, right? And maybe a bit unrealistic. I know we can't all become Buddhist monks who dress in robes and beg for donations. Well, we could, but that would make for some weird rock concerts and football games. What we can do is engage in small acts of mindfulness. We can make time to exist in the "here and now." We can focus on *intentionally* existing. Being more aware of what we're doing and our surroundings, calming ourselves with deep breathing, fully living through the senses, not thinking about the future or the past, only the present. Trying to observe rather than getting tangled in our triumphs and failures. Simply *experiencing* life.

Sometimes this requires a chunk of dedicated time. So I encourage you to ask for help. Years ago, when my kids were little, my husband took them to the playground every Saturday morning, leaving me a delicious hour or two to do as I liked. Usually, I tended plants or read books. I *never* cleaned. Like Melanie, the simple act of spending time amid greenery softened my mood. Even if I accomplished little by wandering around my garden, I'd find the sane mind I'd lost days earlier. I could breathe in the lemony scent of a magnolia flower or listen to the rain fall. In winter, I'd lie on the couch and watch the leaves rustle outside. Be bored on purpose. I'd breathe and relax.

By focusing my attention on the natural world, which offered no opinions and very little needs, I restored my soul. By the time the car pulled into the driveway, I indeed felt like a calm monk who'd been away on silent retreat. Of course, the feeling was fleeting but it lasted long enough for me to recover. Later, when my energetic kids streamed in the house, I'd wipe the ice cream off their faces, feeling like they were no longer a chore but a gift.

OUR FIVE SENSES MIGHT SAVE US

Growing scientific research from the last twenty years supports this ritual of experiencing nature as a destressing strategy. Unlike urban surroundings, a natural setting helps us recover faster and more fully. Here's a look at what nature does for our five senses.

Sight

Perhaps the most powerful means of experiencing the natural world is through our sense of sight. Though anyone who appreciates nature knows its value, as a society, we hadn't really studied nature's effect on our bodies until the 1980s. Two early pioneers were environmental psychology researchers Stephen and Rachel Kaplan.

They found that when people experienced mental fatigue from extended stimulation and thinking, their brains could be renewed by focusing attention on nature. As I mentioned in chapter 1, they originated the concept of attention restoration theory (ART).

As I also said, you've probably already employed ART in your life. When you camp or hike or fish in a natural setting, your brain restores itself simply by seeing what the Kaplans call the "soft fascination" of the greenery around you. You return to work feeling refreshed and relaxed and like, "Hey, my job doesn't suck that much." That's no accident. Our visual cortex actually is built to click in a harmonious way with nature, which I'll explain later. But what's even more exciting is that seeing nature through the eye translates to physical body healing as well.

Take Roger Ulrich's landmark study conducted in the 1980s. He found that gallbladder surgery patients whose beds faced windows with views of greenery recovered more quickly and with fewer medical issues than patients who faced a blank wall. Patients facing greenery needed fewer doses of pain relief medicine. They experienced fewer postsurgical complications.[1] Though Ulrich was able only to speculate on the reasons for this effect, he did know that it had something to do with patterns and the green color of plants.

Later, this theory was confirmed by researchers Branka Spehar and Richard Taylor. They studied stress levels as they related to images of nature. When people looked at images of nature, their stress lowered by 60 percent.[2] Wow! It turns out that's because of the way the human eye and brain work in concert with patterns of nature. Our eyes naturally follow the patterns in the same manner as some natural phenomena arrange themselves, which is basically (and I mean very basically) via mathematically spaced distances that self-divide into smaller and smaller pieces. They're called "fractals" and they exist in nature and even space.

For example, take a leaf. When looking closely at its surface, you see the network of veins called its vascular system, the tiny tubes used for sending food and water throughout the plant's body. You'll see how the main branching network divides into a similar but smaller branching network, then divides again, and again, and so forth. If you're visually challenged, you could try running a finger

along the veins of stiffer leaves like oaks or maples. That brief journey of repetitive patterns is the same journey your visual process takes when seeing an image. The correlation makes logical sense to our human brains, and therefore produces alpha brain waves, which relax our physiological system.

Fractal patterns exist not only in leaves, but in tree branch structure, ocean waves, spiral seashells, snowflakes, hurricanes, galaxy formations, river deltas, and flowers. In fact, Japanese researcher Yoshifumi Miyazaki found that the mere process of staring at flowers relaxes the human body by an impressive degree (see "An Easy, Sensory-Rich Bouquet"). So feel free to take a few minutes to gaze at a tree's scaffolding or a bouquet of flowers. It's scientifically proven to heal you.

AN EASY, SENSORY-RICH BOUQUET

The simplest way to experience plants with our five senses is to do what people have done for ages: create a bouquet. Bouquets, whether with flowers or leaves or both, are direct stress reducers. The science tells us so. Take, for instance, this fascinating study from Japan.

Yoshifumi Miyazaki and his team wanted to know if any changes occurred in the body when subjects looked at flowers. He had 127 people gaze at pink roses while the team measured the subjects' sympathetic and parasympathetic nervous activity. These are two bodily states that happen when you're stressed or relaxed. From the baseline, they found that subjects who looked at pink roses had lower sympathetic nervous activity (stress) by 25 percent. They also found those subjects' parasympathetic nervous activity (relaxation) rose by 29 percent.[3] Bottom line: seeing flowers relaxes the human body. This is why a bouquet of flowers is lovely for more than just its color and scent; it's a gift of healing love.

It's also a good argument for spending the $15 to $30 it costs to create a sensory-rich bouquet. If you take the time to visit it every day—and by "visit" I mean see it, smell it, touch it, and hear it—the bouquet helps to clear the worry from your mind, lower your heart rate, and relax you. And if the water is changed every few days, the stems should last for almost two weeks. Here are some great plants you can use to make a sensory-rich bouquet. They are usually available at nurseries, supermarkets, or floral shops. (Note: If you're feeling ambitious, you could plant a sensory-rich pot of plants on a balcony with a gerbera daisy, daphne, lavender, mint, and New Zealand flax, which all like similar conditions.)

SENSORY-RICH PLANTS

Sight: dahlias, roses, gerbera daisies, sunflowers, lilies
Scent: eucalyptus, roses, lilies, lilacs, daphne, rosemary
Touch: lavender, lamb's ears, Jerusalem sage
Taste: mint, lemon balm, cilantro, thyme, chives
Sound: New Zealand flax, bamboo

You may be thinking, *Well, I live in the middle of a giant dense city and the closest nature preserve is a day's drive away.* Well, Scandinavian researchers found a trip through a virtual forest produced similar, though not as potent, results as seeing the real thing. You don't, of course, get the full sensory experience as much as when in person, and subjects reported feeling a loss at not being in the true environment, but the fact that a virtual experience still lowered stress was impressive.[4] So go find a tree, leaf, or flower or the image of one and have a relaxing gaze!

Smell

By now, you may have heard that inhaling the scents of certain herbs can be restorative. In one study, middle-aged women who inhaled lavender's essential oil reduced their insomnia. In another study published in *Phytomedicine*, German researchers found that lavender oil was as effective at reducing anxiety as the drug lorazepam.[5] Similarly, some studies show inhaling rosemary oil can reduce cortisol levels, which rise when we're stressed. (Now don't go off and do that without talking to an experienced herbalist.) Many herbs have a host of healing properties, and several reputable books have been written about them, like *The Herbal Apothecary* and *The Modern Herbal Dispensatory*. But there's also some interesting evidence that shows natural herbs lower stress and aid in your body's ability to fight illness.

For instance, take forest bathing, or in Japanese, *shinrin-yoku*. It's the ancient act of walking slowly through a forest to mindfully take in the sights, sounds, and smells of the natural space. No surprise that it started in the Buddhist tradition and was later adopted by Japan's forestry agency as a way to help overworked, stressed-out city residents. Japanese immunologist Qing Li was curious as to how exactly forest bathing helped people destress. He conducted studies involving our NK cells, the white blood cells in our bodies, which fight off disease and illness. What he found was that walking in the forest for two hours every day for three days raised NK cell counts by 40 percent and then lasted for several days afterward.[6]

In further studies, he found that the essential oils (or phytoncides) emitted by the evergreens, most dominantly in Hinoki cypress trees, were a significant restorative factor. In an experiment in which subjects merely slept near a humidifier emitting Hinoki cypress oils, he found that they experienced a considerable increase in NK cells as well.[7]

Biochemist Diana Beresford-Kroeger says these powers derive from a complex mixture of aerosols that have evolved in forests during the past 450 million years. "Out there in a healthy native forest there are simply millions of beneficial biochemicals released into the air as aerosols. Some of them are too complex to be manufactured in a modern organic lab." One, however, is an odor compound called beta-ionone. "This molecule is like half a vitamin A," she says. It passes through the membranes of the cell walls and is able to shut down rogue genes in DNA. "This has a waterfall effect on a man if he happens to be carrying prostate cancer cells in his body. These cancer cells are switched off. They are also put in the off position in the liver, heart, colon, lungs and brain."[8] All from the common forest? How cool is that?

Just as inhaling the scent of tree aerosols can be restorative, so can inhaling the scent of soil. British oncologist Mary O'Brien injected a harmless bacteria common in most soils, *Mycobacterium vaccae*, into seriously ill cancer patients. Afterward, they reported feeling happier, more alert, and less pain.[9] Not long after in 2007, scientist Christopher Lowry found that mice injected with *M. vaccae* showed higher levels of serotonin, the depression-fighting chemical in our brains.[10] They displayed less stress when run through a series of tests. In the end, it seems soil bacteria acts as a kind of natural antidepressant.

So, should you go wild and inhale essential oils and dirt? Probably not. However, a long walk in the woods every other weekend would be beneficial. If you can't physically get to the woods, consider tending a potted plant, in which you handle the moist soil. Some plant nurseries even sell Hinoki cypress bonsai, which offer the scents of both soil and the tree's oil. If you're really ambitious, you could try your hand at growing a gardenia or jasmine inside, which would not only provides the soil's scent but a pleasant flower's scent. Its attractive greenery also reduces stress.

Sound

In 2021, American, Canadian, and New Zealand researchers examined thirty-six studies on the health benefits of hearing the sounds of nature and found some astonishing results. Hearing the sounds of wind, rain, birds, and water improved cognitive ability and mood and decreased pain, blood pressure, and heart rate. Accounting for the variance of study samples in certain studies, the researchers were able to conclude that those who listened to the sounds of nature reduced their stress and annoyance by 28 percent. (Annoyance is what it sounds like: being irritated by noise-polluting sounds.) They found water sounds to be the most effective at boosting mood and cognition, while birdsong reduced stress and annoyance the most.[11]

As I write this, I'm outside on a warm spring day. Birds swoop and tweet and the oak tree leaves ripple in the wind. But I can hear the traffic behind the woods in my yard. The constant swish of commuters rushing to get home is persistent noise pollution. To be totally honest, it annoys me. Unfortunately, I can't escape it. More and more Americans can't. So I urge you to do what you can to silence the noise. If you can get away from the city on the weekends, do it. If you have a quiet room in your apartment, spend time there. If you can afford the $30, treat yourself to a little indoor fountain whose trickle will mask the noise outside your window. Or use headphones to listen to recorded birdsong from an online site. Finally, if you can go for even a half hour to a nearby public garden, park, or nature preserve, do that. We all need a break from civilization's noisy race.

Touch

At first glance, touch doesn't seem like a very powerful destressing strategy, but a couple key scientific studies show otherwise. In Japan, researchers asked young men to stroke or pet a common pothos houseplant. If you know pothos, you know it's unremarkable: smooth, spade-shaped leaves, not much in the way of fuzziness, roughness, or any other stimulating texture. Despite this, subjects who stroked a real pothos leaf with their eyes closed experienced peaceful and pleasant psychological feelings while their physiological state relaxed.[12] Overall, they experienced an unconscious calming reaction when touching plant foliage.

Similarly, in 2012, American and Polish researchers found that touching the earth's surface, or "earthing," whether it be by walking barefoot, sitting, or working outside, had definitive healing effects. These healing effects also transferred to test subjects whose electrical impulses were aligned with the earth's magnetic fields in a process they called "grounding." They found people experienced reduced pain, improved sleep, reduced inflammation, and lower stress after engaging in any of these activities.[13] Participants in the grounding study fell asleep faster and had lower cortisol levels the morning after, proving touch's value as a destressing strategy. So if you can walk in the grass barefoot sometime, do it!

Taste

What does it mean to "taste" a plant? Well, when you eat a salad, you taste a bunch of leaves and veggies, right? That has a distinctly green and watery flavor. Oftentimes, it's cold and snappy on the tongue. Maybe sweet. Crunchy. Have you ever grown mint and impulsively plucked a leaf and chewed? That's a fun experience. The cold, strong taste hits your tongue, probably causing you to perk up, maybe even smile. Of course, not every plant is edible, but I think taste is important to address because when we taste a plant—I mean *really* savor its crunchy, juicy, sweet qualities—we eat in a mindful way that produces a more fulfilling, pleasurable experience. We want to taste food as fully as we can so that we can have the most enjoyable eating experience possible.

My advice is to slow down when you eat. Slow your children down. Be intentional. Remember, every time you taste a vegetable, you're tasting a plant. Honor that. Maybe even try an organic taste test. Buy a conventional banana and an organic banana, then try a bite of each. I'll never forget the first time I ate an organic banana. I thought, *This is sweet and juicy and delicious! No odd aftertaste.* It was so simple and silly but amazing.

Similarly, consider a homegrown tomato. When my kids were little, they used to argue about who got the most tomatoes in their salad. Why? Because the Juliet tomatoes from our garden always burst with sugary flavor and juiciness. One time, when we were at our usual restaurant for dinner, my older daughter, who was about eight at the time, ate a tomato off her plate and asked me why it tasted like sour water. She wasn't judging; she was genuinely perplexed about why the tomato on her plate didn't taste like the tomatoes she knew from home.

I don't mean to make anyone feel guilty for not growing their own tomatoes. Sometimes these things aren't possible. I don't grow thirty varieties of tomatoes like some gardeners I know do. But I do the next best thing: I shop for organic heirloom tomatoes at a quality grocery store. Bigger chain grocery stores sell conventional tomatoes that are bred so they stay fresh longer and don't split. That means they sacrifice taste. Smaller grocery stores are more likely to sell locally grown organic varieties. And there's always the local hippie co-op or organic food store chain. Whatever you can afford, I encourage you to buy organic produce. If nothing else, you can't go wrong avoiding pesticides.

Researchers seem to agree. A study conducted by Australian and European researchers found that those who consume nutrient-poor foods experience more weight gain and negative health outcomes like diabetes. They found that although we all have innate tastes—for instance, babies generally prefer sweet to neutral tastes and dislike bitter tastes—we also form our tastes via environmental factors.[14] If fatty, salty foods are all around us and cheap in cost, we're more tempted to eat those. But when we're focused on health, we read food labels and make better choices. When kids are surrounded by healthy food, they're more likely to eat healthy food. It's a matter of exposure and what parents allow on the table. Whatever you do, try to make your choices with intention. Mindfulness can disentangle us from stress-inducing stuff, including unhealthy habitual or automatic thoughts, habits, and behavior patterns.

WHERE DO YOU START?

Now that I've fire-hosed you with scientific information, you may be wondering what the heck you should do. To be honest, I get overwhelmed by all of this great science myself. There's so much exciting data out there, this chapter could have been twice as long. The bottom line is, if you can make time for even a short nature experience today, you'll relax your mind and heal your body. If you're not sure what to do, check out the activities below.

ACTIVITIES

Five-Minute, Five-Breath Fractal Meditation

Rating: Clean hands, no tools, outdoors, no cost

A five-minute fractal meditation is an easy, quick activity. It can be done in an office or home or even out and about in a park or on a hike.

Position yourself in front of a leaf or tree or photo of one. Though I discourage it, it even could be a computer wallpaper photo. Set your phone's timer for five minutes. Take five deep breaths. Gaze at the pattern of the tree or leaf, allowing your eye to follow the trunk through the tree's structure, from the larger branches to the smaller branches and so on. Again, breathe deeply for five breaths. Let go of your thought. If you need to repeat "leaf" or "tree" to ward off distractions, do that. Examine the leaf again. What new characteristic do you notice? What branching pattern did you not notice before? Follow the elegant path of the leaf's veins or the tree's branches. Breathe five more deep breaths. Now look at the overall shape, the edges. Breathe five more deep breaths. Close your eyes. End by saying, "Thank you, Ms. Leaf" or "Thank you, Mr. Tree," and shift your attention to what's next in your day.

A Sensory Nature Stroll

Rating: Clean hands, no tools, outdoors, no cost

Take a stroll through a natural space. It can be your own garden or a local park. After you're awake and dressed for the day, go to a natural area. At the gate or entrance, pause and take a deep breath. Take in the visual picture of the park or garden with your eyes. Scan it all around. Don't judge, just look. Observe. Breathe deeply again. Notice there are no neon signs, no discounts or deals. Just grass and trees. Feel the fresh air on your face. Feel the wind on your skin, the rain on your shoulders, the crispness or warmth. Let it be what it is.

Now look at what's just beyond your feet. What's growing? What's green? What's brown? What has huge foliage? What is tiny? What's tall and what's short? Take an inventory of all that's there, how the objects lead into one another, how the foliage layers and changes. Enjoy the scenery.

After you've done a lap through the natural space, look up. What's on the horizon? A row of tall buildings? Electricity lines? A train? If so, that's okay. Civilization needs those things. But the garden or park is what it is. Imagine if you weren't there. Nature would do its thing anyway, wouldn't it? Soak in this precious moment with all of your senses.

To do this activity with kids, create A Nature Day list. If you stroll with children, ask them to play naturalist and record what natural things they experience. Take notebooks and pens or clipboards (kids love clipboards). Ask them to create a list: wind in the trees, birds tweeting, flowers, clouds, ants or bugs, squirrels, etcetera. You could also add in scents and surfaces. Ask for details like color, sound, and so on. But while you're doing this activity, do what our family called "The Quiet Game." See who can stay silent the longest. After fifteen or twenty minutes, break the silence and compare notes. Share who found what. You might be surprised by how engaged and excited the children become. It might even launch a closer examination of a particular location or topic of nature.

Neighborhood Tree Photo Time-Lapse

RATING: Clean hands, no tools, outdoors, no cost

City trees always impress me. I can't believe they survive despite our attempts to hem them in with concrete and noise and dirty air. Despite that, they grow and bloom and show off fall colors for us. They even drop their seedpods, hoping for offspring, onto the hard surfaces we've made. Oftentimes we only see the tree for a few seconds before moving on. What if instead you honored that tree by regularly visiting it? Experience its year-long journey with your five senses. See it, smell it, listen to it, touch it. If it fruits, you could potentially taste it. You need only a bit of time and your smartphone.

Remember in chapter 3 when we created those windows of green leisure time? This could be an ongoing activity you do every week or every other week. So first, pen it into your schedule. Every Thursday evening, every Sunday morning, etcetera. Then choose a tree in your neighborhood to visit. I'd choose a tree that's about a fifteen- to thirty-minute walk so that it feels like you've journeyed somewhere. Ideal trees would be maples, elms, oaks, redbuds, katsuras, stewartias. Don't know what those are? Then choose any deciduous tree that's distinctive to you.

The tree I walk to is a crape myrtle a few blocks south of where I live. In fact, there are three of them in a row. Although I have a crape myrtle in my garden, I like to walk to this tree in particular. It's on a side street that slopes down to Lake Washington. So I get to not only admire its current state but see the personality of the lake on that day as well. Sometimes it's cloudy and cold and the lake's a dull silver; sometimes it's warm and sunny and the lake's cobalt blue; and sometimes it's a bland slate with choppy waves. Once I get to the tree, I always touch it. Crape myrtles have beautiful smooth but mottled bark that begs to be touched. In late summer, it sports bold, dark pink flowers. And its graceful branch structure—well, it's a textbook fractal pattern.

After you've decided on your tree, take a leisurely walk there and photograph it. Try to stand in the same place for each photograph. Some weeks it will look the same, but some weeks it won't, especially if it flowers. When it's winter, remember the tree's need to sleep until spring. When it's flowering, remember that's for its fruit, which is coming in summer, and when it's fall, remember its leaves turn color and shed so it can safely weather the cold. It's all part of the natural cycles of life. If you're tech savvy, after you've taken about twenty photos, you can create a time-lapse video that shows the tree changing, a reminder that it's alive and giving us its gifts. How fun!

Chapter Six

Idly Playing in the Plant World

It takes courage to say yes to rest and play in a culture where exhaustion is seen as a status symbol.—Brene Brown, researcher

In February 2014, my friend Angela convinced me of the importance of play. The day before, nothing had gone right in my life. In the morning, a broken rake had forced me to leave a fussy client's yard unfinished. Then my special needs child had had a meltdown at school. In the afternoon, the cat had gotten into the leftovers we'd set out for dinner. The plumber had rescheduled an appointment to fix our leaky shower, and I had to prepare a lesson for a new teaching gig for which I had no experience. Worse, a few days before, I'd agreed to open my garden for our local garden tour, but my garden was a tangled mess. This had all sent me to bed with a jumble of anxiety.

As I'd lain wide awake, I kicked myself for agreeing to the tour. It was a high-profile event, but my yard was hardly impressive. I had no original sculptures or multilevel terraces or distinct arbors. I worried everyone would see what a fraud I was. I was a horticultural professional with more than an acre of an eyesore. Afterward, who would want to hire me? Plus, I now had a mountain of work to do in a short time. I needed to trim broken branches due to the snow earlier in the season, plant large costly perennials to fill in gaps, scrape the moss off the patio, weed, smooth out the molehills, and trim overgrown monster shrubs. I'd been invited on the tour because a local city councilwoman had seen the front yard, which happened to be tidy that day, but, overall, neither my garden nor my life felt very tidy.

I tossed and turned. The wind picked up and rain poured. I fretted because I had to get up early the next morning. Angela was scheduled to visit. Angela and I had met in horticulture school, where we bonded over our desire to build perfect garden sanctuaries. (Oh, how naive we were in our youth.) Since then, we'd both become gardening professionals, me as a design and maintenance landscaper, she as a container designer. For almost two decades, we'd spent many afternoons, sometimes entire days, helping each other design and plant our own gardens. Over the years, she and I have debated and planted and replanted and talked each other off the ledges of frustration and indecision. We're partners in domestic horticulture crime. The following day, she would come for her regular visit to help with my garden as I'd helped her with hers two weeks earlier. But on three hours of sleep, all I wanted to do was stay rolled up in blankets and hidden from the world.

After I hauled myself out of bed and drank my tea, I cringed at the sight of the backyard. Everywhere, along the long fence and in the large island bed, chest-high weeds. God, did I have weeds. I thought about canceling. I didn't have it in me to show my closest gardening friend my screwed-up garden. Too late, she'd already pulled into the driveway. Bleary-eyed and beaten down, the last of the previous night's rain dripping from the trees, I led her around the yard, showing her all the work. I said, "This . . . and oh, this, and look at this, and this," until I threw up my hands, admitting I felt crushed by it all and didn't know where to start.

"Hmm. . . ." she said. Her petite frame was dressed in a huge fleece pullover and bulky waterproof pants, her black curly hair in a ponytail. Her brown eyes scanned the area. "How about we do the usual?"

That meant starting with the most noticeable problem and randomly choosing what to do from there. "But I need a plan," I said. "No, no plan, no goals today. . . . Let's just see what comes up."

THE POWER OF POINTLESSNESS

Figuring it was best to see what we were dealing with in the yard's biggest focal point, the island bed, we decided to weed. As we worked, we yakked about her latest container designs, our personal lives, and on and on. After a half hour, it was clear that a decorative, glazed terra-cotta globe I had in storage would punch up the bed's interest. So we considered the potential positions. Should it be hidden behind a low weigela, whose smoky purple leaves would pop against the light green of the orb? Should it be near a grass, whose wispy stems would soften the shininess of the art's surface? Or should we nestle it in the lady's mantle, whose round creamy green leaves recalled the round creamy green shape of the sphere?

We debated, stepping around to varying angles, crouching, standing to imagine the views. After deciding to place it between the weigela and grass so it would pop in color from one angle and from another it would soften, we went to the garage. The globe was big and awkwardly shaped, and the driveway sloped. How would we, two not-brawny women, move it? After some debate about carrying it, we shimmied it onto a slightly broken hand truck. Inch by inch, with me slowly pulling while she steadied it, we rolled it out of the garage and up the driveway. Hitting one loose rock or dip in the asphalt would send the globe flying, probably to crack on the asphalt and blast a hole in the garage door like a giant bowling ball.

Soon, we crested the drive and crept into the lawn, joking that, in our rubber boots and funky knit hats, we looked like two decrepit gnomes crawling in the grass looking for four-leaf clovers. Wait, no, leprechauns looked for clover. What were leprechauns anyway? Were they related to gnomes? Not sure. Leprechauns wore derby hats. They were like gentleman gnomes, who lived in the city, right? Our giggling hindered our progress.

Finally, we reached our spot and placed the orb. As we stood and assessed our work, Angela noticed a small leafless tree nearby. "What's the deal with this?"

"It's a chocolate silk tree. I was waiting to see if it came back."

She frowned at the branches. "Yeah? When did the leaves drop?"

"July."

"Uh-huh."

That uh-huh meant she knew I was in denial about it being as dead as a doornail.

"Are you going to hang Christmas lights on it and call it a special feature?"

I sighed. "Alright, dammit. Let's take it out."

We removed the silk tree, which led to questions about the bed's other focal point, the birdbath fountain, which we cleaned and washed and got bubbling again. While we did, she praised the health of a nearby viburnum, which led to talk of an overgrown viburnum I needed to transplant. Soon we were digging out the ten-foot shrub and dragging it on a tarp to its new home. When the tarp nearly ripped and the shrub rolled down the lawn, we chased it, bumbling around, swearing and laughing, mud spraying our faces.

As we slid it back on the tarp and heaved it up the slope, I noted I was sure that there weren't other moms who chose to spend a winter day like this. They were smart enough to day-drink in a warm café and gossip about the PTA. As we shoveled soil and tucked the viburnum into a better home, we debated between burritos and tuna salad for lunch, the depression and stress I'd felt earlier completely absent from my soul, replaced by animated joy and a bright hope that everything would work out.

Now, as I write this story, my heart buzzes with the exhilaration I felt that day. I feel a fond warmth as I relive the ridiculousness of it all, which, in a way, is odd since Angela and I worked so hard physically. And we didn't solve the whole "mess" of the yard, just some of it. But I wouldn't trade the experience for anything. Why? Because we had so much *fun*.

THE PARTS OF PURPOSELESS ENJOYMENT

Angela had convinced me to play my way out of stress. We ignored my desire for accomplishment and instead focused on idle play. The result was pure, exhilarating fun. Being idle in play is the third strategy of destressing, the *I* in green leisure. An activity that researchers say reaps enormous mental health benefits but that Americans are getting less of every year. Play is about setting aside goals, which we Americans aren't terribly good at. We like setting and achieving goals. We like to have a purpose and make a difference. That's fine but what it doesn't bring us is happiness. And when we don't have happiness, well, we have sadness.

In contrast, when we play, we indulge in a lightly directed activity that has little purpose and inconsequential outcomes. This, in turn, launches creativity and joy. In playing, we stimulate our brains, but we don't strain them, which leads us to lose any self-consciousness and sense of time. That process, psychologist and play therapy expert Charles Schaefer says, "elevates our spirits and brightens our outlook on life. It expands self-expression, self-knowledge and self-actualization. Play relieves feelings of boredom, connects us to people in a positive way, stimulates creative thinking, regulates our emotions and boosts our egos."[1]

This explains a lot about why Angela and I had had so much fun. Though I started the day feeling stressed and overwhelmed, my mood completely changed. We hadn't planned; we'd allowed things to unfold randomly. We faced several puzzles and solved them. We mused and imagined the possibilities, engaging our minds with hope that we could improve the situation. After we physically struggled for hours, releasing the endorphins that accompany exercise, we both beamed with the satisfaction about our changes. I felt optimistic and exhilarated. And in the end, we created a shared memory we both remember with fond humor to this day. A textbook example of play and its benefits.

HAVE YOU LAUGHED LATELY?

When's the last time you enjoyed a hearty laugh? Laughter is like a natural antidepressant. And the coolest part? It's free. During the pandemic, our family struggled through our share of losses and sadness. Worried about our kids, my husband and I started not-terribly-regular game nights on Fridays. We played easy stuff like Uno, Pictionary, and Trivial Pursuit. Well, I'll tell you what, we never laughed so hard as a family. Even those who initially were reluctant broke their icy hesitancy and let go. Yes, there was competition, teasing, and self-deprecation, but it was all in good fun and we felt a buzzing joy. I consider these game nights just as fun and happy and freeing as the family vacations we've taken, maybe more because game nights cost nothing and don't require planning or stress.

Researcher Robert R. Provine called laughter a universal part of the human vocabulary. "It's a very curious business because we don't consciously decide to do it. . . . It's an involuntary action." He found social laughter is thirty times more frequent than solitary laughter and the relationship between individuals was key, not the jokes. It is a way we bond and denotes a safe situation. He found that females laugh more than males, and kids more than adults. "At ages five and six, we tend to see the most exuberant laughs. Adults laugh less than children, probably because they play less. And laughter is associated with play."[2] So get outside and play!

FIVE KEY BENEFITS OF LAUGHTER

1. Lowers stress by lowering cortisol and altering epinephrine, dopamine, and serotonin levels (similar to antidepressants)
2. Releases endorphins, those brain chemicals that lower pain and increase euphoria
3. Stimulates your body, giving your muscles a brief workout, increasing oxygen and circulation.
4. Distracts you from anger, fear, depression, and other negative emotions.
5. Bonds you to others, strengthening friendships and deterring conflict.

Doctor and researcher Stuart Brown, author of the fascinating book *Play*, has found even more direct physiological benefits to play. He says play fires up the cerebellum and puts impulses into the executive area of the brain. It allows contextual memory to develop. Without play, he says, "we don't have humor, no flirtation, no movies, no games, no fantasy."[3] Consequently, our brains shrink from deprivation, bringing about sadness, depression, and even deviant behavior. Brown discovered this when he studied the psychological profiles of murderers. Through his research with thousands of people, he found that people who were deprived of play as children couldn't problem solve and behaved in lonelier, more dangerous ways.

So if you don't want to become a murderer, you should play? Kinda. Let's put it this way: if you want to stave off sadness and stress then play. And play can happen in nature. I'll wager beneficial play doesn't have to take place in a big garden with globes and birdbaths and unwieldy shrubs. It could happen with a few plants in an apartment or a nearby park or on a trail in the woods. In the last chapter focusing on experiencing, we talked about how mindfully enjoying plants relaxes our minds and heals our bodies, so if we're actually *playing* in nature, we'll buzz with joy while feeling an intense sense of tranquility. That combo could make for a lot of chilled-out, gleeful weirdos!

WHEN WAS YOUR LAST PLAYDATE?

When was the last time *you* had some fun with a friend? When was the last time you had fun, period? Do you feel like having fun is something you'd like to do but can't afford the time to do it? Maybe your job demands a lot of time, so much so that all you can do at night is plop in front of the TV. Maybe you're tied to small children, in which case, having fun seems like an adorably cute dream for childless people or empty nesters. I get that. I've lived the chaos that is multiple children under the age of seven. Maybe, for whatever reason, you don't feel justified in setting aside the time and money to have fun. Playing and having fun is something you'll do right after—fill in the blank—you get a bit more money, a bit more quiet, a bit more space, a bit more energy, etcetera.

Well, a *lot* of Americans feel this way. A 2016 Chase survey of Americans found that although 97 percent believed that play and having fun is important, about 58 percent didn't feel like they could work it into their schedules.[4] We certainly work video games into our schedules, with 214 million people playing them at least an hour a week, according to the Entertainment Software Association,[5] but we don't play outdoors as much. In fact, the Outdoor Foundation found that about half of the US population doesn't participate in *any* outdoor recreation.[6] Worse, the trend of recreating outside is weakening.

The main part of the problem is time. Researchers at the Families and Work Institute for the Department of Labor found 66 percent of workers say they don't have enough time to be with their children and spouses or to spend on themselves. They suffer from what psychotherapist Bryan E. Robinson calls "time famine." He says, "We've come to believe that panic and frantic are the only ways to get everything done."[7] And we miss out on the present moment.

The other deterrent is cost. A 2019 Bankrate study found that 68 percent of Americans chose to skip a fun event because of cost; in 2020 the percentage rose to 84 percent. In 2019, about 32 percent said they'd skipped concerts or live arts events. About a quarter didn't visit amusement parks, zoos, aquariums, and the movies due to cost.[8] US researchers studied the economics of national forest visits and found the cost of recreational activities and gasoline reduced the number of visits to the forests.[9] Now with the financial squeeze from the pandemic, I'll bet that trend worsens, too.

Of course, on that winter day when Angela and I had our "playdate," we didn't spend any money. We both set aside the time, and I know setting aside time can be tricky, but according to Robinson, we actually have plenty of time but only for whatever we *really* want. As he says, "You always have a choice to take charge of your life when you ask whether time is using you or *you're* using time."[10]

One telling sign is in that Chase survey. About 75 percent of women reported feeling better mental health when they had more fun. And 57 percent of people said having fun had a positive effect on how they felt physically. Charles Schaefer agrees. As he's famously said, "We are never more fully alive, more completely ourselves, or more deeply engrossed in anything than when we are playing." That's the best argument I know to fit more playtime in your life.

AN AMAZING DAY STARTS WITH A MORNING ALTAR

Several years ago, artist Day Schildkret had just gone through a heart-crushing breakup. "I was grief soaked," he said. One morning while sitting under a eucalyptus tree, he noticed amazing amber-colored mushrooms. On a whim, he started arranging them in a geometric pattern with eucalyptus bark and seed capsules on the ground. "An hour went by in a second. It was the first time in four months that my grief wasn't weighing me down. . . . I made a challenge to myself. Could I return to that spot for thirty days and make something beautiful?"[11] Day met his challenge, foraging daily for objects before creating his unique natural designs, circular arrangements of twigs, leaves, berries, rocks, feathers, and whatever he could find to make stunning works of art. Works he calls "morning altars." In time, creating morning altars became his new calling as an artist.

Day says creating morning altars is a way of honoring his creativity, his relationship with the earth, and the process of life. Because he creates his work in open spaces on the ground before leaving it to erode from wind, rain, or the elements, he sees the work as a temporary ritual that lives in the moment. Perhaps most powerfully, Day says the most important skill he uses when creating his morning altars is *play*. "I play as a way to loosen my tight grip on how I think things should be, and I let myself relax and witness what is born from that very place."[12]

In his gorgeous, inspiring book *Morning Altars*, Day offers guidance on how to play to create your own natural designs. It's easy and relaxing. (You can check out his website for more details at www.morningaltars.com.) In the spirit of play, I've modified the morning altar activity for you. See "A Day's Plant Design" activity for playing with natural objects to destress your soul and create beautiful art.

How to Be Idle and Play with Plants

So let's talk possibilities. As I said, you don't need to break your back dragging around weird garden stuff. You don't even have to be in a garden or outside. However, you do need to figure out what activity best sends your spirit soaring. What sounds fun for your playtime? Remember in chapter 3 when we explored your childhood memories of nature? Well, this is the perfect time to put those to use. Draw on what you listed. Review your green leisure mission statement. If you didn't create one, ask yourself how an early love translates into a present-day activity.

To be honest, the process can be simple. If you grew your own plant as a kid, consider growing a favorite now. Search for what enchants you at the plant store, buy it, and give it a little home with lots of light. Talk to it quietly. Dust its leaves. (Growing info is in chapters 11, 12, and 13.) See how long you can keep it alive; make counting the days a game.

If you liked to draw flowers with your mom, consider visiting a nearby park and drawing whatever's in bloom there. Can you draw your mom *with* a flower? (Mine would be a stick figure.) If your memory's related to the woods, create your own solitary treasure hunt. Make a list of objects like a pinecone, a black rock, a broken but still intact branch, leaves bigger than your palm, and so forth, and see if you can collect them. Whatever you do, don't put pressure on yourself. No goals here. Do something that *you* find interesting.

What's more, to double the fun, get in touch with good friends. Is there someone you're fond of but haven't seen in a while? In a post-pandemic, post-lockdown world, I'm pretty sure the answer is yes. Call them up. It might feel awkward at first but I'm sure they'll be glad you reached out. They may have been too shy or feeling too lonely to call you first.

Make a date. Schedule it. Remember the calendar we created? Those blocks of "Me Time"? See if one of your time slots matches up with your friend's. Avoid catching up at lunch. Lunch is nice but engaging your bodies in an activity together changes the visit from pleasant to flat-out fun.

If you're still stumped, here are some ideas. The point is to enjoy yourself. Feel free to make substitutions. Experiment. If you get an idea about how to make it better, funnier, weirder, do it! And let me know (www.karenhugg.com)! But remember to play and have fun. There's no plant play police.

ACTIVITIES

A Day's Plant Design

RATING: Soily hands, scissors or pruners, outdoors, no cost

What you'll need:

- 25 to 50 natural objects
- a small, cleared space

1. Go to your nearest park or preserve—or your own outdoor space—with a bag or basket and cutting tool.
2. Walk for a half hour and see what you can gather. Think small twigs, fallen leaves, flower heads, rocks, shells, seed heads, petals,

feathers, rocks, pebbles, berries, etcetera. I've noticed Day collects objects of similar sizes with one or a few large, central objects as a centerpiece.

3. Once you have 25 to 50 objects, find a space. Clear that space of detritus. Day uses a small broom.
4. You can arrange your objects in a geometric pattern, which I find incredibly soothing. The symmetry really relaxes me. Or you can create a fun little representation: a laughing face, a dog with crossed eyes, a smiling snake, a flower waving hello, a cat with a top hat, a sunshine that says, "Yo!" or any other image that makes you smile.
5. Allow your impulses to guide you. Relax. Don't worry. Breathe into the fun.
6. Stand up and take a look at what you've created. It doesn't matter if it's silly or rough. Thank the objects for what they've given you.
7. Take a photo of your fun design and send it to me through social media or my website (www.karenhugg.com).

A Smiley Face of Succulents

RATING: **Soily hands, gardening tools, indoors, moderate cost ($60–$80)**

If you have a sunny window, growing a smiley face of succulents is simple, and it'll make you smile every time you see the playful artwork.

What you'll need:

- Two heavy-duty plastic saucers, twelve inches and ten inches
- One small bag of organic cactus mix potting soil
- 3 *Sedum* Gold Leaf (or any tiny leaved, yellow sedum for yellow face; four-inch pots)
- 1–2 *Sempervivum* Dark Beauty (or any dark-leaved hens and chicks for eyes; four-inch pots)
- 1–2 *Sedum* Gold Moss (or any tiny leaved, dark sedum for mouth; four-inch pots)

1. First, poke or drill one to three holes in the bottom of the ten-inch saucer. *Be careful.*
2. Cover the bottom with a thin layer of potting soil.
3. Remove your two Dark Beauty plants from their pots and loosen the soil. Set them in the saucer, gently spreading the roots. Space them so they resemble eyes.
4. Remove your two Gold Moss plants from the pots and with either a root saw or your hands, divide the plant so you have two strips. Place them in the saucer in a curved shape for the mouth. Again, spread the roots and arrange as you need to. Don't worry, the plants will be fine.
5. Remove your four Gold Leaf sedums and divide each pot into four pieces. Then fill in the face as best you can. It's okay if there's spaces in between. You want to give the plants some room to grow.
6. Fill the gaps with soil. You can use an old spoon if you like. Make sure everything's tucked in and no roots are exposed.
7. Set the ten-inch saucer into the empty twelve-inch saucer and water. If you notice a lot of water in the larger saucer, drain it so the plants don't rot. If you want, you can fill the larger saucer with tiny gravel and the face's yellow leaves will grow over it.
8. Place in a sunny window and water every two to three weeks in summer and every three to four weeks in winter. Remember, succulents are hot weather plants, so they like to bake in heat and sun!

Retro Plant Family Photo Frame

RATING: Clean hands, no tools, indoors, low cost ($20–$40)

Let's say you like plants but you don't want to grow them. Why not keep them in your life through a family portrait frame? If you were alive in the 1980s like I was, you may remember those photo frames with multiple slots, some square, some oval. They were dorky and cute. Nowadays, you can pick one up in a thrift store for all of three dollars. Or you can buy a modern updated one at a craft supply store. Some are even shaped to represent a family tree. Buy one of those, a couple old magazines (also available at thrift stores), and cut out pictures to fit the frames. Maybe even add your own people portraits. I have nerdy famous horticulturalists in mine. Hang the "family" photo frame somewhere visible where you will notice it and smile. It might turn into a conversation starter with friends!

Pretty Plant Bingo

RATING: Clean hands, art supplies, indoors, no to low cost ($0–$20)

If you're looking for a plant play activity to do with kids, try making plant bingo cards. Each child can make his or her own. On sheets of stiff paper, create a twelve-square grid. Then ask the kids to draw a leaf, flower, rock, tree, etcetera in each square. Make it colorful. If you know for sure that certain items are in your local park or preserve, even better. Afterward, go on a walk in a park with the kids and see who can find the goodies in the pictures first. Later, if you want to give out a prize, consider a tiny cactus, jade plant, or air plant. They're all easy to grow.

Chapter Seven

Supporting a
Little Green Life

She said she wanted to see beautiful things. So I took her to where I planted my seeds.—Darnell Lamont Walker, filmmaker

THE PROUD MOM OF A SEVEN-YEAR-OLD . . . PLANT

One morning in 2021, I came across a post in an online plant group that piqued my interest. A member named Crystal wrote: "Are plants dearer when you start them from seed?" She posted a picture of a snake's head fritillary, or *Fritillaria meleagris*, that had taken seven years to bloom. Seven! This got me thinking. Was Crystal more attached to this plant because she'd grown it from a seed and nurtured it for years rather than a more mature potted plant from a nursery? I'd done both approaches and had to admit plants from seeds had a special place in my heart. If we spawn a plant's life from that amazing teeny thing called a seed and foster it for years, does that make us happier than instant gratification?

Back when Crystal decided to grow this fritillary, she'd planted the seed in an open tray pack with regular potting soil and a touch of steer manure and pumice. She'd wanted a loamy mix (potting soil) with nutrients (steer manure) and good drainage (pumice).

Once the plant grew into a seedling, she transplanted it into a pot and nurtured it for three years before setting it in a marked spot in the ground. From there, she monitored the plant each year as its leaves, resembling grass, emerged and died back. She made sure to lightly fertilize the plant so as not to overwhelm it with nutrients. And she didn't overwater. During Pacific Northwest winters, bulb perennials can often become waterlogged and rot.

Well, seven years later, the plant's signature drooping, speckled cup emerged. Bumblebees visited. Since it blooms early, fritillary provides nectar for pollinators that emerge early in spring. Delighted, Crystal felt immense pride in her accomplishment. "Seedlings are just a level down from raising a kid. The right soil, light, warmth (or chill) is incredibly important. Doing all things right brings me tons of happiness!"

Crystal continued her care as the fritillary grew and naturalized over the next few years. Soon, she was separating the bulbs and sharing the plant. "These are also called chequered lilies and the pattern on each is amazing," she said. "Sharing gives me a lot of joy."

Crystal succeeded in nurturing a life that wouldn't have existed without her. She also provided food for bees when nectar is scarce in the early spring season. Most impressively, Crystal destressed by supporting another life. When she grew the seedlings, she liked feeling the weather around her, whatever it was. She loved hearing the birds. Each time she went to work, she'd start out wearing gloves but at some point always wound up with the gloves in her pocket, her hands in the dirt. Without fail, she said, tending to her seedlings took her mind off her problems and helped her relax.

"I glow as they grow," she said. "There is a very strong connection between me and my plants." What's more, her relationship to her fritillary is even more special than her other plants, almost as if she'd raised a child whose trajectory required more time, care, and love. Its success gives a parent extra satisfaction and pride. When Crystal tends to her seedlings, she says she feels three words: "Focused. Happy. Content."

SUPPORTING OUR WAY OUT OF STRESS

What Crystal had done was employ the fourth strategy to destressing: supporting another life. The S in green leisure. "Supporting" is really my term for caring, for being kind, altruistic, or nurturing. Experts say when we're kind to another, we gain a whole array of positive psychological effects. Here are a few.

First off, distraction. When we're distracted by another's situation, we set aside our own problems for a while. That "another" could be a person, a pet, even a plant. This matches what researcher Stephen G. Post found in an overall review of the scientific literature in 2005. Altruism offered a "distraction from personal problems and the anxiety of self-preoccupation, enhanced meaning and purpose as related to well-being, a more active lifestyle that counters cultural pressures toward isolated passivity, and the presence of positive emotions such as kindness that displace harmful negative emotional states."[1] That's a lot of bang for the buck of being kind!

Second, our perception of others improves. We view them in a more positive light and with more generosity. We are reminded of our interdependence within a community. For instance, researcher Francesa Borgonovi found that people who support others through volunteering reported having better health and more happiness than people who didn't. She also discovered volunteers are equally likely to be happy whether they have high or low socioeconomic status.[2]

This reminds me of the poet Ross Gay. One day in 2007, he was riding his bike around his new home of Bloomington, Indiana. Noticing some folks working on a public garden project, he stopped by to find out what they were doing. That inquiry soon led to him helping with the project, which led to an interest in gardening. Later, he attended a meeting to create a community orchard program, where he didn't know a soul in the room. "Those people have become some of my dearest, beloved friends," he said in a podcast interview. He credited his involvement with his fellow volunteers in caring for trees, some of which may not produce their fruit or nuts for decades, as changing not only his poetry but his ethical orientation on life.

"This thing of working with people who you did not know before you were working on this thing, for the benefit of people who you may never meet," he said, "who you may well be long dead by the time they're able to eat the fruit of this gathering, was some of the most profound, meaningful, life-changing work that I've been lucky enough to be a part of."[3]

Third, positivity. When we care for others, we take a break from the guilt or distress we feel at other people's difficulties and remember how good our lives actually are. Psychiatry professor Emily Ansell studied seventy-seven adults aged eighteen to forty-four, whom she asked to perform small acts of kindness throughout their day and week. She found people who helped others more reported higher levels of positive emotion. What's more, their behavior impacted how they responded to stress. "On days when participants reported fewer instances of helping others than their average," she wrote, "they had a more negative emotional reaction to stress; when they held elevators and opened doors more than usual, it sheltered them from the negative effects of stress. They reported no decrease in positive emotion that day and lower than their average negative response to stress."[4]

Lastly, and perhaps most importantly, when we support others, we're lengthening our life. Stephanie Brown and her team of University of Michigan researchers found that mortality rates were *significantly* reduced among older adults who provided key support to friends, relatives, and neighbors. Even those who merely supported their spouses emotionally had better mortality rates than those who did not.[5] So be nice to your neighbors, friends, family, and sweetheart. You'll live a longer, happier life.

TAKING CARE OF PLANT BABIES

Now, is all of this going to happen to the same extent if you take care of one plant? Not quite, but you'll still take your mind off your problems and relax. Stress will lessen if not disappear. Plus, when you take care of a plant instead of a pet or child, you'll commit to a low-stakes, low-cost endeavor that offers a low-pressure introduction to caretaking.

Like Crystal, millions of people have been trying their hands at lowering their stress through nature. Take the pandemic. We were all blasted by loss and so much uncertainty. More of us than ever turned to nature for solace. In 2020 during the pandemic, twenty million more people tried their hands at gardening, bringing the number of American gardeners to sixty-three million.[6] Also, from 2019 to 2020, 87 percent of independent garden centers reported an increase in sales, and 68 percent reported more than a 15 percent increase.[7] Similarly, people in the United Kingdom bought 322 million more plants in 2020 than in 2019.[8] The Royal Horticultural Society reported that 67 percent of Londoners bought a houseplant in 2019.[9] Being a plant supporter is a growing trend across most adult age groups in the United States and United Kingdom.

The science seems to agree. For instance, in her research on caring for plants during the coronavirus pandemic, sociologist Giulia Carabelli learned that people "discovered a need to appreciate plants." She conducted a survey, and the majority of her respondents said gardening or tending plants was therapeutic. She told me, "Some lost their jobs, others lost people, all lost their daily routines. And plants were crucial in healing from the pain/suffering/pessimism about the future. For some, it was seeing plants growing/flowering/ bearing fruits, which acted as a reminder that life goes on. For others, it was the reward of seeing that their work as gardeners was paying off (the beauty of plants or what they offered could be eaten/used)."[10]

Her respondents also said they felt a new responsibility toward their plants because they more fully appreciated the companionship that plants brought to their lives. Those who were more extroverted finally found time to keep their plants alive and wanted to make the plants feel appreciated. They found caring for green lives gave them a healthy sense of purpose.

It's almost like caring for a pet or child, right? Caring for an innocent wee one that needs you. Or, in the case of a tree, a not-so-wee one. We love and care and sacrifice our time for it. In return, it cleans the air and provides pleasant greenery, but when it grows up and goes off to college (sniff)—I mean, becomes a blooming or mature plant—we can take pride in knowing we "parented" it as best we could.

Along these lines, I've given each of my three kids a plant to grow in their bedrooms. My two daughters each have a pothos and my son has a snake plant. They vary in how well they care for their wee ones, but they all successfully keep them alive. When I gave my son his plant, I gave him straightforward care instructions: "Put this on your nightstand in front of the window. Water every three weeks so the stream floods the soil surface. Goodbye." He set a reminder on his calendar and waters the plant. In return, it's healthy and happy.

Of course, you may be thinking, *Well, I've killed every plant I've ever grown!* Don't worry, I've killed some too. (It's still worth trying again, though, and in upcoming chapters, I'll help you.) Take my umbrella plant (*Schefflera*). I bought a perfectly grown, perfectly pruned umbrella plant that thrived in a perfect space in our lounge room. In a large pot, its three-foot bulk happily hung out for more than two years and put out shiny new growth often. Then my cat Maddie got sick. With a urinary tract infection, she used the container as a potty. Despite my best efforts, the bushy verdant creature I adored so much gradually dropped most of its leaves. One of its trunks withered away, and after several weeks, I was left with a second browning stem. I could see the wide dark streak in its green trunk traveling upward day by day. Soon, the rot would travel up to the tiny tuft of live growth at the top and kill that, too, unless I intervened.

I took drastic measures. I cut off the tip, which was still hard and green, and stuck it in a glass of water. I waited, checked on it every day, shifted it closer to the window, changed the water every five days. After a couple weeks, just when I thought the stem would give up the ghost, I saw the tiniest, most delicate root in the water. I changed the water again, encouraged. Several days later, two more roots appeared. When it had several thicker white roots, I planted it in a tiny pot. Umbrella plant lived!

Now, umbrella plant has grown several new branches, added a dozen whorls of leaves, and topped out at one foot thus far. I can't tell you how proud I am! It hung in there. It survived. My beloved little guy is on its way to becoming a glossy green beauty again. This endeavor gave me a huge sense of accomplishment. After several houseplants perished under my watch over the years, I managed to nurture this one. I'd actually kept it alive.

What was it about this experience that gave me such a rush? It was something more than just the satisfaction of being kind. It was a changed feeling inside me that I think Crystal shared as well. By getting the plant to thrive again, *I* thrived again—not just in my feelings, but in my entire identity. I proved I was a good houseplant mom after all.

This scans with what happiness researcher Sonja Lyubomirsky found. She discovered that one of the biggest consequences of being kind to another has a considerable impact on self-perception. When we do good acts for others, it often helps us view ourselves as altruistic and compassionate, which can boost our confidence and optimism. We may even discover hidden talents or expertise we didn't know we had.[11] Like Crystal and the fritillary. Finding those abilities helps us feel more secure in our identity. We feel more accomplished, and therefore our identity changes and grows positively. By preventing umbrella plant from biting the dust, I'd taken on the new identity of superhero houseplant mom.

This also confirms what Lyubomirsky and her team discovered about parenting and happiness. Unlike what the media has reported in the past, she found parents evaluated their lives more positively than nonparents, felt relatively better on a day-to-day basis, and felt more positively because they cared for children. Overall, subjects reported higher levels of happiness and more meaning from life than nonparents.[12] So even if you don't have a child, I'm sure you can gain some happiness from caring for plant babies.

As Michael Merzenich, a California neuroscientist, believes, "When you deliver kindness, it's exercising the same reward machinery in your brain as when someone is kind to you."[13] So don't be shy about being kind to a person, pet, or plant.

WHAT GREEN LIFE CAN YOU SUPPORT?

So what can you do to support a plant? Well, let's take a look at the options. If you own or rent a home and have a patch of outdoor space, you're golden. Get out there and at least take an inventory of what you've got. See what's brown and might be dead. Give it a water and see what happens. If a plant is sagging, give it a bit of all-purpose fertilizer and wait a couple days. See if it perks up. If it blooms, you'll enjoy the satisfaction of feeding a little bee, butterfly, or maybe even a hummingbird. If you want advice on what to grow, check out "A Mini Hummer's Habitat" activity.

If you don't have a garden but have an apartment, you're also golden! Try growing a houseplant or two. If you've always killed your plants because you forgot to water, check out my secret special

advice in the "Anthropo" activity below. You'll never forget to tend your plant if it's staring you in the face.

If you don't want to grow any plants, what about getting out and helping at your local botanical garden, public food garden, or park? You could volunteer to get involved in the garden tours or front office. If you don't want to formally volunteer, you can go to your favorite public park, put on gloves, and just pick up trash. I'm sure there's plenty. Don't feel disappointed by humanity's thoughtlessness but rather take pride in helping the plants grow in better soil and providing a pretty space for your neighbors.

Whatever you do, consider what psychology professor Patrick Raue at the University of Washington recommends for destressing: "Do things that give you a mood boost and make you feel like you've accomplished something."[14] Pretty simple, huh?

ACTIVITIES

Raising a Green Beanie Baby

RATING: Soily hands, basic tools, indoors, moderate cost ($30–$50)

If, like Crystal, you want to try your hand at becoming a seedling parent, start with bean seeds. Bean plants don't require special soil or time-intensive care. They also sprout quickly! For beginners, growing seeds that are larger and more solid, like seeds that you can hold in your hand and easily see, makes the experience more satisfying and pleasurable. Once the seeds become sprouts, you can cut them off the seedpod and eat them or let them grow into a plant. To grow actual beans later on indoors, you'll need to pollinate the flowers by hand, but for right now, why not enjoy the simple fun of watching seeds emerge from their little shells? They're so dang cute!

What you'll need:

- an egg carton or Dixie cups
- packet of organic bean seeds
- one small bag of seed starter soil
- light source (window or light with a grow bulb)

1. Fold six to twelve seeds in a damp paper towel. Leave on a plate for five to seven days, making sure to keep the paper towel wet.
2. After the beans sprout a tiny white stem, fill the egg carton cups with seed starter soil to about a quarter inch from the top.
3. Set each bean seed on the soil cup and cover with a light layer of soil.
4. Water with a sprinkling watering can if you have it. If the seed becomes exposed, cover it again.
5. If you have a low-humidity home, you can slide the carton or cups into a large plastic bag, leaving the end open. You'll also need temperatures 70 degrees or higher so if it's winter, set atop a refrigerator.
6. Water lightly every other day until you see growth. When you see growth, remove from the bag, place in a sunny window, and continue to water. If you have an outdoor ledge, you can transplant the seedlings into larger pots and grow outside for lots of beans.
7. Remember, you're honoring the fresh wholesomeness of life by growing your own plants, so don't forget to enjoy the process!

Anthropo Your Planty Friends

RATING: **Clean hands, art supplies, indoors, low cost ($20–$30)**

This exercise helps you see your plant as more than just a green structure in the background of your life. It anthropomorphizes your plants so that you can view them as living beings. The eyes, the mouth, maybe a nose, will stare at you day and night, reminding you that they need your care. Plus, they'll look like a nerdy little gaggle of friends. A great activity to do with your kids!

What you'll need:

- a plant of your choosing
- face stickers, like Sticky Lickits or Bluecell sticker decals

1. First, name your plant. It can be as simple as calling it by its common name, like "Umbrella Plant." My youngest daughter called her plant "Greenie," which worked great! She often talked about "Greenie" like it was part of our family and her personal pet, which it actually was. You can even call it a cute, old-fashioned name like "Walter" or "Wilhelmina."
2. Make a nameplate with a marker and popsicle stick and put it in the soil.
3. From your collection of stickers, choose a set of eyes, nose, and mouth. Stick those on the main trunk or a prominent leaf of your plant. Have fun. Nerd it up. I like the eyes with glasses sticker along with buckteeth and a teeny nose. This reminds you that your plant is not only alive, but your pal!

A Mini Hummer's Habitat

RATING: **Soily hands, basic tools, outdoors, higher cost ($60–$120)**

Let's say you've got a balcony or back porch. Great! You can plant a mini hummingbird habitat with just one container. Each plant provides food for each season. If you're lucky, some hummingbirds may even set up a nest and have babies the following year.

What you'll need:

- an eighteen- to twenty-two-inch clay, ceramic, or plastic container
- one large bag of potting soil
- red columbine (*Aquilegia formosa*), spring perennial (quart or gallon)
- hardy fuchsia (*Fuchsia magellanica*), deciduous summer shrub (quart or gallon)
- Oregon grape (*Mahonia X. media*), fall/winter evergreen shrub (quart or gallon)

- bee balm (*Monarda*) or salvia (*Salvia nemerosa*), summer perennial (quart or gallon)
- saucer for water
- hanging hummingbird house, usually made of grass (optional)

1. Pour the potting soil into the container so it's three-quarters full. Lay out the plants with the fuchsia at the center, red columbine to the right, bee balm at left. Oregon grape can go behind the fuchsia.
2. Place your saucer of water at the front but nestled into the foliage so the bird feels safe when stopping to drink.
3. Hang your house from the sturdy branch of the Oregon grape so that it's secure and hidden.
4. Wait and watch for the hummers to zoom in. Hummingbirds return to the same places for food, so you may get yearly visitors!

A Teeny, Free Food Farm

RATING: **Soily hands, basic tools, outdoor, higher cost ($60–$120)**

This container of vegetable plants can be set out on a sidewalk or on front steps with a sign to encourage passersby to take whatever food they need.

What you'll need:

- a twenty to twenty-four-inch ceramic, clay, or plastic pot
- a three-foot-tall trellis
- one large bag of potting soil
- one Juliet tomato plant (quart or gallon)
- three romaine lettuce plants (four-inch pot)
- a burpless cucumber plant (four-inch pot)
- a bush bean plant (may be grown from your seeds or four-inch pot)
- six-pack of carrots
- six-pack of onion plants
- two-pack of marigolds (to deter pests)
- wooden craft sign

1. Fill your pot about three-fourths full with potting soil.
2. Place your trellis in the back center of your pot.
3. Remove your plants from their containers and arrange them with the tomato at the front of the pot, the cucumber under the trellis, beans at the left side, and the carrots on the right side
4. Plant the onions around the pot in a circle, about three inches apart
5. Plant the marigolds on either side of the tomato plant
6. Write "Free Food" or "Take What You Need" on your wooden craft sign in permanent marker or paint and insert at the front of the container.
7. In July, after vegetables have matured and ripened, set out in a semipublic place so people can harvest as needed.

Water the pot every few days, and every day in hot weather. With your fresh potting soil, the plants shouldn't need fertilizer. Also, the marigolds should deter pests, emitting a scent that's unattractive to insects. In the end, don't forget to enjoy your own fresh food!

Chapter Eight

Uniting with Like Nature Minds

Our ability to reach unity in diversity will be the beauty and the test of our civilization.—Mahatma Gandhi

In 2010, Ron Finley made an ordinary move that created an extraordinary movement: he grew a vegetable garden. Sometimes called the "Gangsta Gardener," he lives in South Central Los Angeles, where access to healthy food is either minimal or nonexistent. As Ron has said, he was "tired of driving forty-five minutes round trip" just to buy an organic tomato or apple, so he started growing his own food on the parking strip or "parkway" by his home. Parking strips are the stretches of land between the street and a sidewalk. They're technically owned by a city but maintained by homeowners. Since Ron's was a patch of weeds and trash, he and a group of volunteers started growing vegetables and fruit trees there. But the city of LA gave him a citation for not trimming his "overgrown vegetation." Ron decided to ignore it, since the city had done nothing when the strip had grown weeds with trash. Plus, he'd left room for drivers to exit their cars. Instead, he continued growing what he called his "food forest," and because he grew more than he could eat, he allowed passersby to harvest whatever vegetables they needed.

Meanwhile, the city of LA turned his citation into a warrant for his arrest. But Ron and his fellow gardeners started a petition to give him the right to grow food and thereby help the community. They were fighting city hall, so to speak. Because they gathered nine hundred signatures, they actually had a shot, albeit a long one, to win. Then Steve Lopez, a local reporter from the *LA Times*, covered Ron's story, shining a light on the city's review of the petition and thereby gathering even more support. Who wouldn't want a guy growing free vegetables that fed his neighborhood? In the end, the city—maybe because it had been shamed, maybe because it believed in the cause—allowed Finley to continue growing food on his parking strip. What's more, a city councilman endorsed his project.

As Finley notes, planting vegetables became more than just growing his own food. It beautified his neighborhood and lifted up his community. With LA Green Grounds, a community organization dedicated to helping homeowners grow their own food, he helped install fifteen to twenty parking strip gardens. Urban gardening is about people, he's said,

> you're exchanging food, you create responsibility and you create a relationship in the community. . . . Now you have people participating in growing their own food. They have skin in the game. The air is better, the biodiversity of the soil in your neighborhood. You're bringing in pollinators, you're bringing in bees, butterflies, hummingbirds. You're changing the ecosystem when you put in a garden. We're part of the ecosystem so that garden is changing us. And the beauty factor. You get to walk outside your door and experience nature every day. That's going to change you. I don't care how jaded you are.[1]

Ron Finley did change people. He changed their minds and he even helped change the city's law. By creating one garden, he created a whole movement and brought together dozens of people. Gardeners from, as he says, all walks of life, worked side by side. Friendships formed. A nonprofit organization was born. Now through the Ron Finley project, he works to educate and encourage people to create their own edible gardens.

How Uniting Leads to Lower Stress

When we come together for a common cause, we're practicing the fifth strategy of destressing: uniting, the *U* in green leisure. When we unite, we build relationships based on a mutual interest. We interact. Cooperate. Come together. Bond. That can happen in passing, like when we work alongside someone for a day or on a deeper, ongoing basis, like when we make a more intimate, long-term friend who shares our interests and opinions. Or maybe somewhere in between. The bottom line is when we unite, we foster feelings of togetherness, which in turn make us feel empowered and not so alone in life.

As our schedules have become busier and more technology oriented, we've lost our in-person connections, and of course, the 2020 pandemic put that phenomenon on steroids. In 2018, a Cigna survey found about 47 percent of Americans reported feeling lonely. In early 2020, that number jumped to 61 percent.[2] Men were slightly lonelier than women, younger folks were lonelier than the elderly, and those in rural communities were lonelier than those in urban communities. Ironically, those who heavily used social media reported feeling lonelier than those who didn't.

Marta Zaraska, the author of *Growing Young*, says loneliness raises cortisol (our stress hormone) levels and increases inflammation.[3] American researcher Julianne Holt-Lunstad and her team have even found loneliness can be as bad for your health as smoking.[4] Recent UK research says it can increase stroke and coronary artery disease by 30 percent.[5] So gathering together is the antidote. It heals us in important ways.

In my own life, attending horticulture school and belonging to nonprofit gardening organizations has given me the satisfaction and pride in accomplishing not only the improvement of actual gardens, but lifelong gardening friends whom I can lean on for inspiration, plant knowledge, and joy. Generally speaking, gardeners are nice people, and they accomplish things! Members of nonprofit organizations not only improve actual gardens, they organize events, workshops, parties, and plant exchanges. Plus, participating in a plant organization can be plain fun! The annual Plant Amnesty Halloween party in Seattle comes to mind. People dress up like trees and bees and other weird things from nature and play bingo. It's a whole thing.

SIX WAYS TO SOCIALLY CONNECT VIA PLANTS

If you'd like to get your hands in the dirt but don't want to grow your own plants, you can meet people through a variety of ways.

1. University extension and master gardener programs offer long-term classes on growing fruits and vegetables, ornamental horticulture, container design, and so on.
2. Nonprofit organizations are clubs where folks learn about particular plants, get to know each other, volunteer on public garden projects, and host plant sales and exchanges.
3. Nurseries offer one-day classes in houseplant care, potting bulbs, tree trimming, and so forth.
4. Floral shops and craft stores offer workshops in flower arranging and wreath making.
5. Neighborhood community centers may post about volunteering at community food gardens, park border renovations, rain garden work parties, or parking strip tree plantings.
6. High school, middle, and elementary schools usually welcome parents or neighborhood residents to visit and lead vegetable and ornamental plant projects on school grounds.

When volunteering at a local botanical garden years ago, I grew acquainted with a young man named Daiki who'd traveled all the way from Japan just to learn about horticulture in the Northwest. As a two-person team, we discussed pruning cuts and shaping strategies for shrub roses while growing acquainted with the culture and landscape of the other's country. Though we were both limited by language, we still managed to bond over our deep admiration for the garden and love of flowering shrubs and to laugh at our past growing fumbles. It was a gentle warm friendship I cherish to this day.

When not volunteering in person, I've even gained support from acquaintances I've made through social media. Especially when we share a personal interest. For instance, I met a gardening pal online because he was a fuchsia nut, gardening on 1/92 of an acre in Manhattan. These long-distance friendships have helped me solve plant problems and given me a sense of solidarity when I'm struggling with my garden or have general questions. Some folks have even turned into real-life acquaintances. This is why I don't recommend completely ditching social media. It does have a place. Just keep in mind that overall, one in-person interaction creates a way stronger bond than one hundred online interactions.

FIVE EASY SUCCULENTS TO SHARE IN PLANT GROUPS

If you belong to an online plant group or neighborhood email list, you can share succulent starts as a way of getting to know fellow plant lovers and nearby residents. Here are some easy ones you can propagate via leaves, stems, or pups. All prefer a cactus mix soil.

1. Hens and chicks. Red, green colors. Remove baby plants with roots from the mother, plant in soil.
2. Prolific echeveria. Blue-green color. Break off the leaves, let dry until roots form, plant in soil.
3. Purple aeonium. Purple color. Cut stalk at desired height, dry for three days, plant in soil.
4. Jade plant. Green color. Cut small branch off at node of larger one, let dry for five days, then plant in soil.
5. Aloe and agave. Orange, green colors. Remove baby plants with roots from mother, plant in soil.

WHY DO WE NEED OTHER PEOPLE?

What is it about interacting with another human being that helps us? Is it the actual exchange of information, the mere presence of another person? The shared experience of our time together? Or perhaps the reassurance that we're not alone? What is it about being with another person that makes us so happy?

Well, it seems we're hardwired to be social. It's innate. Neuroscientist Matthew Lieberman says we know we're innately social because when we're born, we're born helpless. We rely on others to care for us so we can survive. "Mammals are born immature, incapable of taking care of themselves." Each one of us survived infancy, he says, "because someone had such an urge to connect with you, that every time they were separated from you or heard you cry, it caused them a pain that motivated them to come find you and help you over and over again."[6]

Additionally, millennia ago, humans realized that working together in groups increased our chances for survival. We cooperated to find food, to build shelter, and for safety. As our brains became more complex, we began sharing tools and resources. We bonded over genetics and language. Over thousands of years, we've joined to solve problems, whether it be avoiding a saber-toothed tiger in the grasslands of ancient Africa or creating a new space for food crops in modern-day Los Angeles. It's just how we're built.

What's also interesting is Lieberman has found that although we think of the pain we experience when social connections are severed as metaphorical or intangible, his studies show that social pain is actual real pain. He's monitored it via brain scans. During an experiment in which subjects played catch virtually with two other people via a computer game, he found an interesting result when subjects were excluded from the game. "The same brain regions that register the distress of physical pain were also more active when people were left out of the game compared to when they were included." This makes sense. Ever been the target in a grade school game of dodgeball? It sucks. When we experience social rejection or exclusion, we *physiologically* suffer.

"You might think that our tendency to feel social pain is a kind of kryptonite," Lieberman says, "but our urge to connect and the pain we feel when this need is thwarted is one of the seminal achievements of our brain that motivates us to live, work, and play together. . . . You can't build a rocket ship by yourself."[7]

Similarly, researchers have found that people who have strong social connections live longer lives. A study published in *PLOS Medicine* reviewing 148 studies found that people who had fewer social relationships died earlier than those who had more.[8] Essentially, a low number of social relationships created a mortality risk. American and European researchers found close family bonds and church attendance are common traits among those aged ninety and older in Italy's Cilento region.[9] Educator Dan Buettner cited strong family bonds and social connections as a key to longevity for residents of Ikaria, Greece.[10] And lastly, researcher Stephen Post, in a review of the scientific literature, found that elderly subjects who volunteered often had a 63 percent lower likelihood of dying during the study's period than those who did not volunteer.[11]

We are more social than any other animal species on the planet says biological anthropologist Michael Platt. Although primates, which he studies, are a close second, nothing matches humans' capacity to be social and to organize. We are particularly cooperative and have a greater interest in sharing resources. More than any other mammal, we divide and distribute our skills and labor.

One fascinating upshot of being social noted by Platt and other researchers is that when we look into another person's eyes, the hormone oxytocin is released. Oxytocin is the positive brain chemical some call the "love hormone." In Platt's studies on oxytocin and macaque monkeys, he found when making eye contact, dominant monkeys became more relaxed and submissive monkeys became more confident.[12] One study out of Japan even found that staring directly into your *dog's* eyes releases oxytocin in both your brain and your dog's.[13] (Is that why doggos have the kootest eyes in the whole world?) The next time you want to boost your well-being, try making eye contact with a partner, a friend, or even your pup. Your early evolutionary self will thank you.

PARKING STRIP SPRUCE UP AND SOCIAL HOUR

When I renovated the parking strip at my last house, I often talked with neighbors who stopped by while walking dogs or strolling home from work. Neighbor kids, bored with summer, helped plant. I even attracted a cat who adopted me, our little Aleksy. (Don't worry, I'm not suggesting you get a cat!) But working on your strip opens the door to casual, aimless interaction that, like studies show, eases loneliness and boosts happiness. What's more, brief conversations can turn into long ones, which turn into friendships. Gardening on the street is like having office hours. You might as well hang up a sign that says, "The Gardener Is In. Come Chat."

Here's what I did for my parking strip project. First, I dug out the lawn with a digging fork until I had bare earth. I turned those dug-out chunks of lawn over so they created a berm and filled cracks with topsoil. Because I'm a design weirdo, I fetched boulders from the rockery and, with Angela, set them at the corners. They were ginormous and heavy. We backed my truck to the curb, removed the tailgate, and with our feet, pushed the boulders off the edge. They hit the dirt with a loud thump! Then we shimmied my digging bar (a long piece of iron that looks like a giant nail) underneath and inched them into shallow depressions we'd dug. That way they looked like they'd been there forever. The boulders added a rugged beauty, their stony humps hidden by coneflowers before reappearing when plants went dormant in autumn.

Second, I planted a mix of tough, sun-loving trees, shrubs, grasses, perennials, and groundcovers. Memorable choices were Kanzan cherry, rockrose, New Zealand flax and blue oat grass, Russian sage, and pink coneflowers, yellow thyme and sedums.

For existing parking strips, here are some small tasks that go a long way: Top-dress with compost and/or bark mulch. Plant ferns, carpet bugle, or brass buttons in bare spots. Cut back overgrown groundcovers. Fish out trash from foliage. If plants have brown leaves, trim dry foliage and water well.

Is Social Gardening a Thing?

What's also amazing is that our innate need for social interaction goes even more swimmingly when combined with gardening or nature. For instance, German researchers studying prosocial behavior in children tracked a group of sixth graders' emotional states during a window of time when they learned science and worked together in the school garden. Not too surprisingly, they found gardening together promoted cooperative behavior and boosted self-esteem and confidence.[14] When you get to digging in the dirt, good things happen.

Similarly, in 2020, an Australian senior living facility partnered with a local high school for an interesting experiment. They brought in teenagers regularly to plant and tend vegetables with the elderly residents. It was a smashing success. The seniors, many of whom kept gardens in the past, were able to pass on their gardening knowledge to the teens, and the teens in turn were able to assist with the more physical aspects of the work. The teens also learned about growing healthy food and giving back to the community. The seniors, some of whom had no nearby family, benefited from the companionship and vigor of the young people as well the fresh air and sunshine of the outdoors. Plus, self-confidence and outward compassion were boosted all the way around.[15] (If there were an award for sweetest community project ever, I think this one would win.)

More broadly speaking, it seems gardening isn't even necessary when combining social interaction and natural settings. Take this impressive Canadian study of more than 550 public schools. Researchers from the Toyota-Evergreen Partnership found that when the schools "greened" their grounds—meaning that they replaced asphalt and grass with trees, shrubs, artwork, water features, and gathering areas, student behavior changed drastically for the better. Check out these stats: "Study participants reported that when students were learning and playing on a green school ground, they were being more civil (72%), communicating more effectively (63%) and were being more cooperative (69%)." Now, how do we moms bottle *that* behavior?

Plus, these kinds of improvements weren't limited to students. Interactions between students and teachers were enhanced as well. Also, "Just under half of the study participants (44%) reported that student discipline problems had decreased on the green school ground and an almost identical percentage (45%) reported that

incidents of aggressive behavior had decreased."[16] You don't even have to garden to enhance social behavior and boost happiness—just hang out and talk with other people in a gardenlike setting. I could do that all day long!

WHAT IF I'M AN INTROVERT?

As easy as it sounds, chatting with another person in a garden may not feel natural to an introvert. Chatting with a daisy might feel better. It doesn't talk back, and you don't feel the pressure of entertaining or speaking coherently around a daisy (you might with a fancy rose). If you're not familiar with the term, introverts tend to be more comfortable around fewer people because large numbers of people drain their energy. Conversely, extroverts *gain* energy by being with people. I used to be more introverted but in recent years I've become more of what social scientists call an "ambivert." Ambiverts like more meaningful social interaction with a few people in smaller doses. I don't want to sit home alone, but I don't want to go to a huge loud party, either. Just a small gathering of good friends.

If you do think of yourself as an introvert but dread the idea of forcing yourself to get out and be among people, don't fret. There's good news. To boost your mood, social interaction doesn't have to be intimate or last for very long. In 2019, researcher Jessie Sun and her team found that social interaction, even small brief doses on a train or while waiting in a line, boosted participants' happiness. Her team also found that both extroverts and introverts benefited, though introverts benefited more when the interactions were more substantial.[17] This is a strong argument for making the effort to appropriately chat up a stranger. Next time you're at the coffeehouse or deli waiting for your order, you may want to make eye contact with the person beside you and mention that ol' standby, the weather. Or, if you admire someone's dress or bag or cool jacket, let them know. Everyone loves a compliment. Plus, the responses might put a spring in your step.

One note, of course, is to remember safety. Don't creep on people. If you're a man and the only person to talk to is a woman, maybe hang back unless she speaks to you first. If you're older, like of the gray-haired variety, joking around to a teenager might be met with an annoyed stare. But commenting to a waiter about that night's busy restaurant crowd or whether a pregnant lady would like a seat on the subway seems appropriate enough. The bottom line is you know what's appropriate; you can feel it in your bones. Read body language, check people's facial expressions, be kind, and be safe.

PUTTING YOURSELF OUT THERE

Let's say you're ready to try something new and meet people. What should you do? Well, the easiest activity for me has always been to volunteer. Because I love nature, a gardening or plant-oriented organization makes the most sense. For instance, volunteering at a botanical garden is a healing way to spend an afternoon, especially if you don't have your own outdoor space. It's a nice, finite activity where you show up for a limited time, don't worry about costs of plants or future maintenance, and then leave for the day. Plus, it's a great way to unite with others in the name of the common good.

But if a public garden isn't available to you or not your thing, you can always find other organizations that need help. Many city and county governments sponsor tree plantings, public artwork projects, and park renovations that could provide an opportunity to spend time with your neighbors and plant-loving friends.

For instance, a few years ago, I served on my local tree board. I live in a densely forested suburb near Seattle. While serving, I met some wonderful folks I didn't know existed in my hometown. I even connected with my old horticulture professor (and by "old" I mean "former," so don't worry, Tim). During my time with the group, we studied whether our forest canopy was growing or shrinking, and volunteered for small jobs like street tree care, ivy removal, and various beautification projects. During our meetings, it was fun to dream of a better future for the natural areas in our small town, hammer out ideas together, and bond over shared experiences. And all in the name of trees.

What I suggest is first to figure out your comfort level of social interaction. Do you want to work with a lot of other folks? In an organized, structured situation? On a project that benefits an entire community? Or with a few folks on a more informal project? Or with one familiar friend in your own garden? All are fine choices. The point is to get out there somehow and have a chat. And maybe even, as they say in the United Kingdom, "have a laugh."

Things can be informal. Take my friend Raj. He likes to garden and has recently been planting plants near the piñon tree in his front yard. Every day when he's out there working, a neighbor inevitably passes by and often stops to chat. They talk about what he's growing, how everyone's health is, the latest work news, car projects, the weather. Sometimes kids hang out and ask about the plants. They're incredibly curious and that gives him a chance to evangelize about nature and its benefits. Sometimes he gives the neighbors' toddler "knux," little knuckle fist bumps. Raj is a friendly guy, but he doesn't have time to volunteer, so these front yard social calls give him regular, short interactions that build affection and friendships over time.

Also (and as mentioned in chapter 6), Angela and I help each other informally with each other's gardens. She comes to my house for an afternoon and helps me with whatever projects I've got going on and sometime the next week or so, I do the same for her. We don't do it every week or even every month, but often enough and for almost twenty years now. Gardening together is an activity we love. We design our borders and focal points and sitting areas. We haul plants, we dig, we weed. We definitely talk for hours. On some days, we're actually clean, with washed hair and soil-less clothes and dry shoes, and on those days, we shop, we lunch, we impulse buy. On other days, we plant, we transplant, we chase giant shrubs as they roll down a hill. Sometimes, we do a bit of all. What you do doesn't matter as much as that you interact with friends in nature.

If you've figured out what social interaction level you're comfortable with but need some ideas about what to do, check out the activities that follow.

ACTIVITIES

Plant Watching in the Semi-Wild

RATING: Clean hands, plant identification app (see appendix), outdoors, low cost ($20–$50)

You know how birder people get together for outings at their local park or nature preserve and watch for birds? (You know, the stereotype of a person with a hat and binoculars.) Well, why not gather a few fellow plant-interested friends or a group from a gardening club and go to a public park or botanical garden to identify plants? Public gardens are great because they often provide wide, paved walkways and benches for those in wheelchairs or folks who need to stop and rest now and then. You could even go to a local plant nursery, especially good for those who like houseplants. In a nursery, of course, the plants often have tags, but there's lots of information that doesn't fit on those teeny plastic spikes.

The first thing to do is download a free or low-cost app onto your smart phone. Then, you simply launch the plant identification app on your phone and point it at the plant in question. The app usually identifies the plant accurately. Then you can deep dive into the plant's needs and history before getting ideas and feedback from friends. Write down your favorites in your Escape-to-Nature notebook. Then when you're good and tired from walking around, share lunch and yak endlessly about your dream garden or houseplant nook.

Houseplant Stuff Swap Party

RATING: Clean or soily hands, maybe garden tools, indoors, moderate cost ($30–$70)

If you collect houseplants, do you have friends through an online or real-life group who do, too? One fun activity is to host a plant stuff swap party. It's the perfect event for anyone because you don't need experience or even to have grown a houseplant before. What you do is host a party of five to ten people with drinks and snacks to exchange all of your extra plant stuff: houseplants, moss balls, cuttings, bulbs, tools, soil, pots, whatever you don't need. And if you don't have any of that stuff, spend $10 and contribute a small plant to the mix. Lay out the offerings on a table with a sign to take one and leave one. Then eat cheese, maybe drink wine, and break the silence by talking houseplant life. Later, after the plant stuff is exchanged, you can give away the leftovers to a charity or other folks in an online plant group.

Shared Space Beautification

RATING: **Clean and soily hands, garden tools, indoors or outdoors, moderate cost ($30–$80)**

If you live in an apartment building, do you have a common space? A lobby where the mail comes, a front stoop outside the entrance doors, a courtyard of plants, a roof garden, or even a parking strip? If so, post a notice that you'd like to beautify the space with a plant (or plants) and ask people to stop by on a Saturday morning to chat about it. If you put out free coffee or donuts, people will show up for sure. Exchange ideas about what to plant and ask for donations in a jar. Will one or a few people shop with you to buy the plant, pot, and soil? Would anyone like to help by watering the area? You never know who might live in an apartment now but had a garden in the past and misses it. Don't be shy. Chat 'em up.

Turning over Earth Together

RATING: **Soily hands, garden tools, outdoors, low cost ($0–$30)**

If you have some outdoor space and your neighbor or friend also has an outdoor space, what are you waiting for? You both need help. You both love plants. You both already dig in the dirt. So call her and see if she'd like to turn the earth together. Garden while getting to know each other. Or catch up. Tell her you're looking for a partner to exchange help for your balcony containers or garden a couple hours every month.

I like this activity because there's a lack of pressure. Neither of you needs to know much about plants. Half of gardening is trial and error anyway. Plus, you'll be focused on the task of taking care of the plants, which means there's no pressure to continually carry a conversation. There's no need to fill the silence between you. And the best part? You might make a friend as you both accomplish a little project whose tangible results you can see and enjoy in plain sight afterward. Hopefully, you won't have to chase a giant shrub down a slope, but you might have a good time.

Chapter Nine

Recognizing What
We've Grown

Gratitude is my bulletproof vest.—Pam Grout, writer

THE "NOT-SO-BAD" NOOK

In 2002, my husband received a medical diagnosis that blasted through our young adult lives. Cancer. Stage 4 of the colon that had spread to his liver. After we dealt with the shock and severity of the situation, not to mention canceled an enormous road trip, we embarked on a new life phase young people aren't usually familiar with: urgent, intense medical treatment. Meanwhile, I'd just begun horticulture school. Though I considered dropping out, a steady, optimistic professor encouraged me to stick with it (thanks, Tim). And so while my husband struggled to work a nine-to-five day without losing his lunch, I slogged around in the rain, studying the leaf arrangements on a privet or the size of fir cones. Every day, as I drove the ten miles to the college, I'd cry in a blackened fit, then park the car, wipe my mess of a face, and spend five hours examining plants before sobbing the entire drive home. It went on like that for months.

One day, not long after a CT scan showed my husband's cancer had thankfully shrunk some, I guessed a correct answer during an impromptu quiz in my plant diseases class. The reward was a free plant. Its common name, ironically, was dead man's fingers (*Decaisnea fargesii*). It fruited in huge beans that were dark blue, bulbous, and fleshy. It was strange and rare and wonderful. You may think it a macabre sign, but I saw it as the opposite. My husband had made incredible progress over the last several months and I'd guessed correctly in a *diseases* class about a *dead man's* fingers. I felt like we were leaving our disease behind, and the only dead man's fingers would be on an exotic plant. So I took it home and decided to call it by its other common name: blue bean plant. At a loss for where to put it in my garden, I kept it on an old table near a window in a cooler nook in my house. As it sprouted soft new leaves, it reminded me that my husband was still alive and with me.

Not long after, I met Angela. Our class was studying plants at Seattle's Woodland Park Zoo. While most of the students took turns smelling the lovely scent of a daphne shrub, she quietly approached me, said she'd heard about my husband, and told me how strong she thought I was. If I needed anything, she was there. *What?* We barely knew each other. I collapsed in tears. We ended up holding hands as we wept, dropping behind the class and entering the zoo's aviary together, watching in silence as the birds flit from branch to branch. Later, when I came home, I realized a good luck charm that my husband's chemotherapy nurse had given us was still in my pocket: a rustic silver medallion embossed with a winged guardian angel.

I set the good luck charm beside my blue bean plant. That July, after my husband's liver surgery, which showed no cancerous cells in the removed tissue, I searched the closet for my father's old eyeglasses. As I mentioned, my father died when I was four. He didn't survive cancer, but my husband had. I felt grateful that I hadn't lost my husband but wanted to honor my dad, that other important man in my life, so I set the glasses alongside the plant and medallion. That way, I could remember our good fortune and the years I'd spent with my father, who was a funny, loving dad.

Later in December, my husband's CT scan showed no sign of cancer. After more than fourteen months of chemo and two major surgeries, he was cancer free. We went to Hawaii to celebrate, his wavy, regrown hair blowing in the wind every day. Later, I came home with one of those plumeria sticks in a bag you get at the airport. Plumeria are smallish, tropical trees whose scented pink or white flowers are used for leis. Grateful that he'd recovered, I planted the plumeria branch in a pot and placed it on the table beside the blue bean plant, the angel medallion, and my dad's eyeglasses. It occurred to me that I had a photo of my grandmother with a white flower behind her ear. So I set that against the plumeria pot. Grandma Pearl must have blessed it with some botanical magic because the plumeria grew. And not only grew but flowered. The scent was almost as sweet as a daphne.

My husband has been well for twenty years (knock on wood). Nowadays, his biggest challenge has been raising three teenagers and working too hard on too many evenings. Mine has been to remember what I'm grateful for. Whenever I complain that life isn't going well enough, he squeezes my hand and says, "It's not so bad. We have this house, we have the kids, we have the pets. We've got enough money. It's not so bad." He doesn't say, "Life's great!" or "Buck up!" Just a simple, tender refrain: *it's not so bad.* No, it isn't. We're lucky to be here on this earth with the people, animal, and plant souls we love, along with the inanimate comforts of every day. As for the ones we've lost, we were lucky to have had them in our lives for a time. My heart almost breaks as I write it. *Our lives aren't so bad,* my husband, the survivor, always says, and wow, isn't it true?

RECOGNIZING EVERY "GET" YOU GET

One thing a life-threatening illness teaches you is how to savor each moment. (Not that my husband ever needed that lesson.) Life slows down into these prolonged stretches of fear, hope, and endurance. You go on, simply because you can't *not.* Every day, you wake up and ask yourself, "Well, what do I *get* today?" Then you take those small "gets," the gifts, and enjoy them as fully as you can. That ledge, my "Not-So-Bad" nook, represented what I was grateful for during that era. The people I'd loved and who were gone, the friend I was beginning to love, and the most important partner in my life who I was "getting" to love day to day.

Having the nook in my visual sight grounded me every day during those years. The green leaves, the tiny medallion glinting in the sun, the intimate token of my dad, and my grandmother's smile all calmed and reassured me. If I was upset, I'd wander over and study those objects, touch them, sometimes even speak to them. They reminded me of what I was grateful for and helped me to recognize the goodness in my life.

Now we live in a different house and the nook has morphed into a gratitude cabinet. It's a bookcase with glass doors holding a collection of emblems of our "not-so-bad" life. (To make room in the cabinet, I emptied out the crystal vases I inherited, which aren't my style and I've never used.) Atop my gratitude cabinet are two plants, a variegated African violet from a special friend, and my porcelain flower vine. (I'll tell you how I keep these alive despite not being near a window in chapter 11.) Inside is a faux saguaro from our time in Tucson, a beloved photo of my favorite stairwell in Paris, pivotal books, a cement orb mosaicked with plants, the ashes of our beloved pets, the cutest Halloween picture of my kids, old photos of my sister and relatives, my mother's vintage jewelry, and a fake plumeria plant (because, let's face it, the first one bit the dust and life's not perfect).

I love this cabinet for three reasons. First, throwing off the chains of displaying what I'd inherited instead of what was important to me enormously empowered me. I felt alive and free and finally able to semipublicly share who I truly was with whoever I invited into my home. Second, the cabinet provides a quiet, steady reminder of where I started in life, where I've been, and where I'm at now, which in turn strengthens the gratitude in my heart. And lastly, it's an awesome conversation starter! Friends inquire about the various plants, photos, and memorabilia. The objects remind them of the people, experiences, and objects in their own lives for which they're thankful. This shoots straight past small talk into intimate, fun, and even emotional conversations, which ends up bonding everyone closer together.

SCIENCE SHOWS FIVE BENEFITS OF GRATITUDE

Unknowingly, I had coped with this enormously stressful era by engaging in our sixth strategy of destressing: recognizing, the R in green leisure. Noticing the good in our lives may be the *most* powerful means of destressing. It's about recognizing the positive and embracing it wholeheartedly. When we recognize the people and experiences we're grateful for, we appreciate how fortunate we really are. We feel gratitude for what we have and distracted from what we don't. And when we do that, regardless of how much time we have left, we live our lives with full and total engagement.

Different researchers count the benefits of gratitude in different ways, but all commonly cite five throughout the literature. It's a complex subject because one can always "find" more benefits to gratitude depending on how you sort them. We have at least five scientifically proven ones to discuss. How cool is that?

First, gratitude helps us savor our experiences and live them fully. Psychology professor and foremost gratitude expert Robert Emmons, author of *Thanks*, says that when we truly recognize the ins and outs of an object, person, or experience, we notice the various aspects of it and therefore extract all the benefits of those moments. Because of this, we're engaging in life with our utmost presence. As he says, "In effect, I think gratitude allows us to participate more in life. We notice the positives more, and that magnifies the pleasures you get from life. Instead of adapting to goodness, we celebrate goodness."[1]

Second, gratitude boosts self-esteem. Robert Emmons offers this explanation, "when you're grateful, you have the sense that someone else is looking out for you—someone else has provided for your well-being, or you notice a network of relationships, past and present, of people who are responsible for helping you get to where you are right now."[2] In 2014, researchers Chen and Wu studied athletes and found that those with a higher sense of gratitude increased their levels of self-esteem over a six-month period. They also trusted their coaches more.[3]

Third, gratitude helps us cope with stress and trauma, deters negative emotions, and staves off depression. Psychologist Todd Kashdan and his team studied gratitude in Vietnam War veterans. They found that vets who felt higher levels of gratitude had lower rates of post-traumatic stress disorder.[4] An Italian study of more than four hundred participants examined the tendency for gratitude, depression, anxiety, and three ways of relating to one's self (criticizing, attacking, or reassuring the self). "Gratitude predicted less depression and anxiety symptoms, and . . . is a protective factor against psychopathology not only due to its association with improved relationships with others, but also because it is connected to a less critical, less punishing, and more compassionate relationship with the self."[5]

Similarly, British researcher Alex Wood and his team conducted two studies of students who'd just transitioned into college. They found gratitude led to lower levels of stress and depression, in addition to fostering and perceiving higher levels of social support. They also found gratitude reduced the frequency and duration of episodes of depression.[6]

Fourth, gratitude encourages social bonding and nurturing others, and deters aggression. University of New South Wales–led research found simply thanking a new acquaintance makes them more likely to want an ongoing social relationship with you.[7] (That's easy!) It strengthens the "find, remind, and bind" theory first proposed by researcher Sara Algoe. It suggests gratitude motivates people to develop new relationships (find), nurture them (remind), and ultimately maintain them (bind).[8] As her study noted, gratitude signals a communal relationship and may feed mutual behaviors that build friendship among folks. In other words, kindness begets kindness.

This matches what University of Miami researcher Michael McCullough and his team found. Gratitude supported this kind of "reciprocal altruism." When people feel grateful about a kindness done for them, they're motivated to repay that act of kindness back. In fact, the behavior extended to third parties, causing a looping network of kindness and positivity.[9] People didn't feel indebted to others, just thankful and happy to pass on the good vibes. So call it what you will, reciprocal altruism, upward spiral, love fest. Whatever you call it, it's all good.

FIVE WAYS TO SAY THANKS WITH PLANTS

Though it dates to ancient times, expressing emotions by giving flowers became popular in nineteenth-century Europe. Back then, sharing emotions was considered coarse behavior, so they used flowers. Certain flowers symbolized certain emotions. For instance, red roses delivered upside-down represented anger. Yellow carnations symbolized dejection. To express your gratitude to someone, why not go beyond flowers and offer a fresh approach with plants? Here are five ideas:

1. *A thank-you plant.* Do you have a friend who's recently helped you out? Or a client who keeps your business afloat? Maybe a relative who's in need of a visit? How about showing your appreciation by giving them symbolic plants? Bamboo represents luck. Aloe vera encourages healing. A Chinese money plant brings wealth. Peace lily represents sympathy. Prayer plant represents gratitude. Plus, the giftees will think of you every time they see or care for the plant.

2. *A homemade herb bouquet.* Invited to dinner? If you grow herbs (or even if you don't), you can create a small cluster of rosemary, thyme, chives, and basil to say thanks for the invite. In addition to looking lovely, the host can use it in future dishes.

3. *A jar of extras.* If you garden on your balcony or backyard, do you have any extra flowers, vegetables, herbs, or baby plants to share? Set in a recycled food jar and pass on to a relative, friend, or whoever helps you in small ways every day (librarian, grocery clerk, waiter, bank teller, etc.). You'll brighten that person's day and get that good altruistic buzz.

4. *A houseplant cuttings cluster.* Have new neighbors? You could help them explore houseplant choices by giving them a cluster of leaves on stems from your collection. If you place them in a used bottle with water a couple weeks in advance, some will probably root. Or simply present in water as is. Your giftees can either toss later or root the plants themselves. Either way, they'll appreciate your lovely green efforts.

5. *A frame of nature photos.* Nowadays with sophisticated phone cameras, we can easily collect nature photos. What are your favorites? At your local drugstore or using a home printer, print five nature photos and put them in a multiple photo frame or booklet. If you or the giftee is in the photos, even better! You'll not only show gratitude but highlight fond memories and calm images sure to warm their hearts.

As if that weren't enough, UK researcher Nathan DeWall and his team reviewed five different studies related to gratitude and found that it reduced aggression across the board. It's as if gratitude is an antidote to it. People with daily grateful moods showed lower daily physical aggression. People who experienced more gratitude showed less anger when insulted and fewer hurt feelings in daily interactions. His review concluded, "Gratitude is a positive emotion that has a built-in feature of enhanced generosity and sensitivity to others' concerns."[10]

Fifth, gratitude helps us remember our blessings and not yearn for more. It deters feelings of envy and resentment and foils our predisposition to hedonic adaptation. Hedonic adaptation is our natural tendency to adjust back to a set level of happiness after a new experience or circumstance. When we feel the thrill of buying a new car or making a new friend or earning a bonus at work, we feel atop the world. But that happiness is short-lived. We adapt to it and the feeling fades. But if we practice gratitude and count our blessings often, that excited, buzzy feeling returns. We relive the thrill and feel a pure contentment inside.

GIVING GRATITUDE A GO

Right now, you might be thinking, *Yeah, but if we're always thankful for what we have, aren't we ignoring our problems? Aren't we in denial about the suffering of the world?* Well, when psychologists have studied survivors of severe trauma, like Holocaust survivors, for instance, they've found they often have a *greater* appreciation of life. They feel happy to simply be alive here on earth.

Also, you might wonder, *Doesn't gratitude kill our ambitions in life?* If we practice gratitude, we'll float around like dreamy, happy zombies à la Kenneth from *30 Rock* or Brian from *Office Space*. We'll never work to make our careers or personal lives better. We won't fight and move forward with societal change. Not the case, says Emmons. "We found people are actually *more* successful at attaining their goals if they are also keeping a gratitude journal at the time."[11] Apparently, gratitude actually leads to action.

So, what do you do to give gratitude a try? Well, outside of a gratitude cabinet (see activity below), I have a few good ideas based on happiness researcher Sonja Lyubomirsky's findings.[12] First, you can practice gratitude by keeping a gratitude journal, which is the most common approach. You also can opt for a more personal experience by writing a thank-you letter to someone for whom you're thankful. If you're more socially inclined, you can call that person or even pay them a visit and take them a plant. The point is to make that recognition. The last option is to simply set aside a few minutes of downtime or to meditate every week and mentally count your blessings.

I keep a gratitude journal. I try to write in it every week though sometimes there are lapses. Interestingly, it seems to occur during times of stress, probably when I need it most. But I've found that not only writing in a gratitude journal but rereading past entries boosts my spirit. In reading entries from 2020, I remembered that, ah yes, in February I was feeling at my most optimal health (hilarious because the pandemic later destroyed that). My eyes watered with warmth when I read about how in June my writing friend Natasha picked me up and dusted me off during a terribly low career point. I laughed out loud when I read about how I'd finished an enormous excavation project of lava rock in my garden that had plagued me for ten years! It involved digging up soil, sifting it, and wheelbarrowing the rocks to a huge pile in my yard before giving them away on an online group. Finally, I smiled so hard when I read about how in November my editor friend Gretel had helped me brainstorm and shape this very book.

But life's not all unicorns and rainbows, right? Well, it's true. In fact, neuropsychologist Rick Hanson has said we have a natural negativity bias. "The brain is like Velcro for negative experiences, and Teflon for positive ones."[13] That's an evolutionary survival thing. But he also says the gradual accumulation of good experiences literally changes our neural makeup. By having good experiences and then truly enjoying them, we can soften our negativity bias. So reliving the unicorns and rainbows instead of—what? the cockroaches and storm clouds?—in a gratitude journal can lift your level of happiness.

Robert Emmons has studied gratitude journals—a lot. For *decades*. He says that the act of writing translates our thoughts into concrete images and statements, which makes us more aware of what we're thankful for. We also can make sense of our life events, which in turn makes our life more meaningful. Another upshot is if we've had lives of severe trauma or missteps, we can find great redemption and hope for the future by journaling our gratitude.

WHAT YOU GAIN FROM A GRATITUDE JOURNAL

Over several studies, Emmons has found that those who kept a gratitude journal gained an amazing slew of benefits. First off, people experienced more positivity overall. They were more alert and enthusiastic, more determined and attentive. Participants also said they'd helped someone else with a personal problem or gave them emotional support. Also, some people experienced longer and higher-quality sleep. And lastly, some folks were more likely to make progress toward personal goals.[14]

If you'd like to try your hand at a gratitude journal, Robert Emmons has some recommendations. One of his overall tips is to look at what you're grateful for as a "gift" and refer to them as such in your writings. If the word "gift" feels too strange or woo-woo, you could call them the "not-so-bad things."

First, motivation is important. You can't go through the motions. You have to *want* to become happier and improve your life. If the exercise is done out of obligation or halfheartedly, its impact is greatly diminished. I relate to this. When I tried it with a friend's child who was not into it at the time, she went through the motions as quickly as possible to finish it. Don't worry about getting it over with, make time and relax into the experience.

Second, describe fewer things in greater detail rather than listing as many things as possible. Don't make a grocery list. Grocery lists are boring. Well, unless you buy amazing stuff like shark sushi or avocado cereal. Wait, ick. Anyway, what describing in detail does is help you to relive your wonderful experiences. It's as if you're dreaming an awesome movie all over again, and by dreaming it, you're reexperiencing all of the awesome aspects.

Third, Emmons found focusing on the people rather than the things in your life provides greater impact. I mean, which would you rather have? Your children or the new car? Hopefully, you answered your children, though on certain days when they're being little jerks, you might rather have a new SUV, right? But most days, I bet you'd choose your children. This attachment to people makes sense, since, as we learned in chapters 7 and 8, we're hardwired to take care of each other, and we thrive when we interact with others.

Fourth, so you know how in *It's a Wonderful Life*, George Bailey gets the opportunity to see what the town of Bedford Falls would have been like had he never lived? And, of course, what happens? He sees how poorly things turned out and recognizes the numerous positive effects he had on all of the people and situations in his life. He ends up sliding around on the snowy bridge with those wild eyes, his hair all messed up, begging to live again. Well, subtracting the positive experiences you're grateful for and musing on what your situation would have been like had they not happened is enormously helpful. Consider it the Bedford Falls exercise.

Fifth, Emmons says focusing on the unexpected or surprising events you're thankful for has more of a positive impact as well. I get this. How do you feel when your spouse comes home with flowers or dinner or even ideas for a new vacation destination? Wait, what? He hasn't done that lately? Tell him to get on it straightaway! The thrill of a surprise is really unmatched in terms of the buzz you get in your mind and heart.

Sixth, writing in a gratitude journal once or at most twice a week is more effective than writing daily. Apparently, this relates back to that concept of hedonic adaptation. If you list the things you're grateful for too often, you'll adapt to the emotional reaction that comes with it. It's as if you'll become a bit numb to its impact. So, keep it regular but to a minimum. You don't want to write, *My daughter's so adorable and sings like a little diva* 846 times. Snore.

A GREEN GRATITUDE RITUAL

What day and time would be good for you to write in a gratitude journal? Can you review your calendar for "Me Time" and block out five minutes, fifteen minutes, one whole hour? And could you write with nature in mind? Don't be too ambitious. I've found starting out with the smallest of goals is best because they're achievable. For instance, I journal for fifteen minutes right before bed, usually on Sunday nights. If your goal is short and sweet, you'll probably achieve it and feel like you're actually accomplishing something, as well as making a positive change.

If you're still unsure what gratitude ritual is right for you, check out the following activities. They vary in time, commitment, and style. See if one of them resonates with you. Good luck recognizing your gifts!

ACTIVITIES

Your Gratitude Cabinet

RATING: Clean hands, no tools, indoors, low cost ($0–$30)

As I mentioned, when I decided to create a display space for my gratitude, I began with an old table by a window. After we moved, the collection landed on the buffet in my dining room, kind of haphazardly, until I realized I didn't have to store the not-so-antique crystal I inherited from my grandmother. I could better honor her by displaying a sweet photo of her plus her retro pointy glasses and a sprinkle of 1920s costume jewelry. Storing the crystal away in a closed cabinet was the best choice I ever made. It freed up the most noticeable area of my dining room. Now, the bookcase stands right in my line of sight during dinner. I feel like I'm actually sharing a meal with the souls I cherish most but who can't be physically with me.

Do you have a cabinet or shelf or table where you can collect representations of what you're grateful for? What piece of furniture might you be overlooking? What's stored away in your drawers because it's so sentimental you can't part with it? Reclaiming a piece of furniture to display all that you are thankful for is a wonderful way to make a conscious practice of your gratitude, reminding you every day, especially when you're not thinking about it, of your "not-so-bad" life. And for the top of your gratitude cabinet or altar or nook, do you have any meaningful plants? Even fake ones or photos that remind you of special places or people will do. The greenery will soften the objects and relax your heart.

A "Not-So-Bad" Notes Pot

RATING: **Clean hands, no tools, indoors, low cost ($0–$30)**

1. Place a houseplant on your nightstand or a table not far from your bed (near a window or grow light). Arrange it so it's within the sight line of your pillow. Every morning, when you roll over, you'll open your eyes and the first thing you'll see is a green friend. Say hello. Resist the urge to check your phone. Instead, check your plant. This small act reminds you that your true home is the natural world and you have another opportunity to relish it. Breathe deeply and sink into the quiet. Appreciate your plant's elegance and grace. How it probably grew while you weren't watching. Like humans, plants need the darkness of night to rest. Then open the shade or curtain and provide the light it also needs. Thank your plant for sharing its life with you. Smile and go on with your day.
2. Every night before bed, jot down on a sticky note one event that happened during the day that you're grateful for. A "not-so-bad" moment. Post it on the plant's pot. In the morning, you'll not only appreciate your plant's beauty, but the first thought in your mind will be something positive you're thankful for. Later that night, repeat the ritual. Do this until you have seven sticky notes on the pot. On Monday morning, remove all notes and start fresh for the week.

A Twenty-One-Day Nature-Grateful Text Exchange

RATING: Clean hands, no tools, indoors, no cost

If all of these activities feel like too much of a commitment, then try what leadership expert Conor Neill did for twenty-one days. During brief windows of downtime, like during a coffee break, he'd take out his phone and tap out three things he was grateful for in that moment. "I noticed over the course of a few days, I shifted my mind from being anxious and irritated and frustrated to being more aware of what was happening around me."

When Neill committed to this exercise by not only taking a note on his phone but actively texting these things to his friend and siblings, his experience became even richer and more of an ongoing loop. It turns out his friend and siblings were grateful too and texted him back with three things for which they were grateful.

Instead of texting three things, I've found that simply recognizing one moment of nature I'm grateful for is almost as helpful. Can you either jot down a note or take a photo of a moment in nature you're grateful for every day for the next three weeks on your phone? If you saw a bee nestling in a flower, a cute dog romping in tall grass, or noticed the broad beauty of trees over your head, record it and share it. You can exchange this bit of recognition with a friend or family member or even post on social media with the hashtag #greenleisure. You can also send it to me via my website (www.karenhugg.com) or social media handle (www.instagram.com/karenhugg) and I'll post it!

Chapter Ten

$\mathcal{D}$

Exercising Outside without Trying

There is no such thing as bad weather, only inadequate clothing.—European proverb

When I left my last tech job in the early 2000s, I learned a vital lesson about my body that's stayed with me through the years. It's not complex or mind-blowing, but it drastically changed my life. It affected not only how I eat but how I move in the world—literally. First off, before I tell you this story, I want you to know I want you to celebrate who you are. Be happier. Enjoy life. Appreciate your body no matter what it looks like for the miracle it is. That's what this book is all about. But if you're feeling like your health and your body aren't where you want them to be, then read on. My story might help you.

In chapter 1, I told you about how I lived inside a small white screen. How I built content for the web while sitting in a scentless office under bright lights without any natural sounds. What I didn't tell you was while I was working, I sat a lot. I mean, a lot. I sit now, by which I mean, right now to write this, but back then I sat for *nine hours straight*. I got out and walked maybe a few hundred steps to get lunch and back but that was it. Maybe a few hundred more before bed. The next day, I'd get up and repeat the pattern. This went on for about five years.

Well, it's no surprise that I gained about thirty-five pounds. I went up two pant sizes. No big deal, right? But anytime I'd lift something, my back would hurt. When I walked a little further, my ankles ached. About a year later, I crept up two more sizes, then another two. I managed okay because I was busy. But with an avalanche of work constantly crushing me, I ate late dinners at restaurants with my husband, both of us too tired to cook. With limited time and zero energy, I didn't exercise and indulged in a bowl of ice cream before bed. Walking the dog around the block was the best I could do.

Meanwhile, my pants were getting tighter. By the time I flew to France on a work assignment, I felt heavier and slower than I'd ever felt in my life. I had a hard time getting out of chairs. My knees hurt. Every time I went down steps, pain pricked at my ankles. Whenever I lifted a heavy box, my forearms wobbled. After a couple months, I returned to America exhausted and burnt out. In France, people didn't eat gigantic meals like those served at the restaurants in America. And they didn't really exercise; they just stayed active and walked everywhere. So I bought a book about a low-carb diet and vowed to join a gym.

But there was a problem: I could hardly walk. I was thirty-two years old and I could *barely walk*. I'd leash up my dogs and head up a mildly sloped, uphill street near our house, but after one long block, about a tenth of a mile, I huffed. My legs moved like two cumbersome logs. I'll never forget how exhausted I was when I reached the local park. I had to get a drink from the fountain. On a cool rainy day.

After I arrived home, I felt like I'd run a marathon. While my dogs happily lapped up water, ready for more play, I plopped on the couch, in need of recovery time. My back ached. My knees creaked. Feeling regretful, I berated myself for letting things get so out of hand. What was wrong with me? Other folks at the office worked as hard as I did but were slim and agile. But I couldn't scrape up the self-discipline to eat right or exercise. I felt like such a loser.

Not too long after, my husband convinced me to quit my job and look for a saner, more fulfilling one. "There's no point in two of us being stressed," he said. "We'll cut corners and get by on one salary for a while." He urged me to spend a few months painting our old fixer-upper of a house. So I did. I threw myself into painting the house and renovating our tiny backyard.

The yard renovation required walking a little bit every day. Because the space was a short rectangle, about forty feet by twenty-five feet, I often walked from one corner to another to another. I'd walk a brief thirty feet from the front driveway and to the backyard countless times a day. Excited to learn about plants, and during that sweet spot when I'd fallen in love with my butterfly bush but didn't know much else about gardening, I started researching plants. I dug up old grass and made new plans for the borders. Gardeners from my neighborhood and local email groups shared their divided plants with me. I spread fresh soil and compost. Planted plants. Watered. Mulched. Weeded. And I did it all over and over again.

Spring and summer passed. Every day, I'd put on my jeans and head out with my tools. There was always weeding or planting or trimming or even transplanting to do. If I'd recently planted a blue hosta with a yellow Japanese forest grass and a purple Heuchera, I'd worry about their water. So I'd walk the hundred steps to the hose reel, drag the hose to my new colorful collection, and water. When I'd noticed the soil around the rose bushes was dry and gray, I'd haul bags of compost from the car through the backyard and rake it through the bed. And if a large shrub had overgrown its spot by the porch and couldn't grow any higher, I'd slowly dig it out before dragging it to a more spacious home. And at the very least, I walked. Always walked.

The idea of "steps" wasn't a thing back then, but if it were, I would have exceeded ten thousand by midday. I was on my feet for hours, zigzagging across a brief patch of land. I carried hefty bags of compost from the car in front to the yard in back, then squatted and stood, squatted and stood, as I cut the bags open and spread the compost. With pointed shovels, I dug in the dirt and squatted some more before lifting plants into wheelbarrows and lifting them

out again and planting them and shoveling soil over their root balls. Generally, I dragged around plants, tools, and bins of weeds in circles. With my lack of gardening experience and snail-like pace, it seemed like I wasn't really accomplishing anything. Later I realized I was crushing a new garden.

Though a garden is a work in progress, I did transform a junky, neglected space into something pretty and inviting. I even installed a teeny pond that a silly raccoon messed with all the time. I got a small greenhouse. I built muscle. In the end, it felt absolutely fricking fantastic. But the most important lesson I learned was spending time with plants helped me to lose all of the weight I'd gained without trying. I didn't *try* at all. Only *did*. Like Yoda says, "There is no try, only do." Well, only "doing" was like magic. Moving around among plants was the healthiest thing I'd done in years for my mind and body. I didn't think. I didn't plan. I didn't diet. I just moved my body in nature.

EXERCISE, A MIND AND BODY ELIXIR

Without realizing it, I was practicing the seventh strategy of destressing: exercise, the *E* in green leisure. By simply staying active, I was dropping weight pound by pound while gaining strength. I won't say I didn't feel tired or achy. I totally felt tired and achy, but hot baths and occasional ibuprofen fixed me right up. And the best part? I felt *happy*. Satisfied. Content. Like I'd spent the hours of my day in a way that mattered to me. I'd done honest work that had boosted my spirit and, in doing so, honored my life.

Am I saying that everyone should just quit their job and take up gardening? No. Definitely not. That's not realistic. But the lesson to remember is that gardening is exercise. I didn't change anything else. I still ate until I was full. I still had the occasional glass of wine. I even ate cake during birthday celebrations. Gardening was part of an exercise routine in which I made a lot of progress through smaller habits. In fact, to this day, whenever my pants start to feel tight, I make sure to get out in the garden for a couple hours every day. When I can't do that, I walk, I ride a bike. The key is to move your body in nature.

Health experts of course are all over exercise as a cure-all. Psychologists call it a natural antidepressant. Physicians call it the best medicine. I don't have to lay out all of the reasons we need to exercise because it often dominates the news. Plus, you know how energized you feel after a vigorous walk or pick-up game of basketball. We're high from the endorphin rush, and the rush stays with us well after the activity is done. But as a reminder, I'll give you a quick overview of its basic benefits.

First, exercise keeps your weight in check and prevents diseases like cancer. When we're too overweight, we're putting more pressure on our heart, organs, and bones. But when our weight is in a good spot, we avoid type 2 diabetes and hypertension. We also are less likely to develop breast, colon, and lung cancers.

Second, exercise reduces heart disease and prevents high blood pressure. Being active boosts your good HDL cholesterol and decreases unhealthy triglycerides. Your heart and cardiovascular system are integral to good blood circulation and disease prevention. Plus, if you exercise, you reduce your risk of stroke.

Third, exercise increases our muscle mass, strength, and power, which helps in literally navigating through life. In the past, I've found when I don't at least get out for a daily walk, my knees hurt and I have more trouble with stairs. Ironically, doing squats strengthens knees! Exercise also helps with osteoarthritis and joint problems. Falls and fractures are less likely when we have strong muscles and bones. We can simply balance better and navigate whatever obstacles come our way.

Lastly, exercise strengthens our brain and reduces stress. It curbs short-term anxiety and improves cognitive functioning. It reduces the stress hormones of cortisol and adrenaline while stimulating endorphins. Our mood improves. We feel more positive, and the more we do it, the more confident we feel. Plus, we sleep better. At this point in my middle-aged life, I can attest to the power of sleep. If I don't sleep well, my tendons and joints feel it the next day.

All of those benefits of exercise are pretty cool, right? What's even better is a person only needs to be physically active for about 150 minutes per week to lower mortality risk by 33 percent.[1] That's a daily walk or light weekday workout. You don't have to go full throttle with running stairs or pumping massive amounts of iron. Just get off the couch, onto your feet, and do stuff. Researchers say even small things like changing the laundry or watering plants helps.

BUT WHY EXERCISE IN NATURE?

If light exercise can strengthen your body, fight off disease, lower stress, and boost your spirit, why not just do it at the gym? Well, a mountain of studies show that exercising while outside is even more effective. One, you're more stimulated by all of the sights and sounds of the outdoors. Your mind's more engaged because of small obstacles and issues you must navigate in an uneven, slightly unpredictable environment. Also, your senses are at one with your natural evolutionary home. You get those benefits we talked about in chapter 5: seeing natural fractal patterns, smelling trees and soil, hearing birdsong, etcetera. Also, you get the sunlight and vitamin D effect. And lastly and maybe most importantly, exercise deters that negative mindset bias.

According to physician Eva Selhub and naturopath Alan Logan, the coauthors of the highly informative book, *Your Brain on Nature*, when we don't regularly exercise, we're likely to make up excuses to blow it off. But with a lower-stakes, easier exercise like, say, walking in the woods, we're less likely to focus on the negative. "The key is to magnify the positive emotions, particularly during the early 'no pain, no gain' period. . . . This is where green exercise can work its magic, amplifying positive thoughts, tranquility and cognitive refreshment."[2]

That's an interesting term, "green exercise." University of Essex researchers coined it in 2003 to give the concept of exercising in nature a more formal term.[3] So where should you start with green exercise? Well, like I said, I walked a mostly forty-by-twenty-five-foot space for months and it never felt like a chore. So, yes, you can garden. If you have an outdoor space, go for it! If you don't have an outdoor space but want to garden anyway, volunteer at a community garden. They need you.

In fact, a 2020 meta-analysis of nineteen studies reviewed by Thai and UK researchers found that participating in community gardening lowered one's body mass index significantly.[4] Also, Dutch researchers at Wageningen University and Research Center studied thirty allotment gardeners. They gave people a standard psychological puzzle to perform and found that those randomly assigned thirty minutes of outdoor gardening versus indoor reading between tests were less stressed and more refreshed afterward. Cortisol levels went down and mood was restored.[5] What's more, gardening increases longevity. In a University of Hawaii study of centenarians in Okinawa, researchers found that most residents gardened.[6] In fact, gardening was common to centenarians in Japan, Greece, Italy, Costa Rica, and the United States. Gardening benefits the body, mind, and life expectancy.

TEN OUTDOOR ACTIVITIES IN YOUR NEIGHBORHOOD

Are you a social sort? There are a plethora of outdoor activities organized by the local parks department, community organizations, and private trainers and instructors. They include:

1. Yoga in a park or at a rural retreat center
2. Birdwatching in local parks and preserves
3. Lawn bowling events
4. Tai chi classes in the park
5. Guided urban nature walks
6. Personal trainer bootcamps
7. Outdoor dance classes
8. Croquet and bocce ball clubs
9. Slack line groups (tightrope walking that's low to the ground)
10. Good ol' college hacky sack

BEYOND THE GARDENING GATE

If you don't want to or can't garden, what then? Well, there are several options.

One of the easiest is walking in nature. In chapter 5, I touched on the term "forest bathing." It's got a fancy name but it's really just taking a long walk in the woods. Researchers have found this simple act gleans enormous results for the body and mind. Japanese researcher Qing Li and his team found that walking for two, two-hour segments every day in a forest setting versus urban walking lowered blood pressure and cortisol, and suppressed the sympathetic (fight-or-flight system) and enhanced the parasympathetic nervous system (relax-and-rest system).[7] In other words, that last part means it reduced stress. He also found that participants slept much better as well. You can find more details in his outstanding, easy-to-read book, *Forest Bathing*.

Similarly, Japanese researchers from Hokkaido University conducted an experiment with type 2 diabetes patients. They measured blood glucose levels before and after walks in a forest. Predictably, the blood glucose levels lowered after walking in the woods. However, they also studied a group who simply sat in the woods and didn't walk. Those folks' blood glucose levels were lowered as well, though not as much.[8] So if you're unable to walk, merely sitting or rolling along in a wheelchair in nature still matters. The bottom line is being outside is beneficial.

In a UK report on ecotherapy, University of Essex researchers conducted an interesting study on the psychological effects of walking in a natural setting. They found that people who walked in nature felt much better than those who walked in a shopping center. For instance, 90 percent of participants felt their physical health improved. They saw a reduction in fatigue, increased agility, less joint stiffness, and weight loss. What's more, 90 percent also reported increased self-esteem. Conversely, 44 percent of participants felt reduced levels of self-esteem after the shopping center walk. Also, 71 percent of outdoor participants had lowered levels of depression whereas feelings of depression *increased* 22 percent for indoor participants. In terms of anger and tension, 53 percent of outside walkers reported feeling less angry as opposed to 33 percent of indoor walkers. Lastly, 71 percent felt less tense after the outdoor walk versus 50 percent who reported less tension after the indoor walk.[9]

If you're a bit more ambitious, you might try jogging in nature. Swedish researchers found that runners who jogged in parks with trees and greenery reported less anxiety, depression, and anger than those who ran in urban settings.[10] Some studies have found, including an oldie from James Pennebaker,[11] that people who run on wooded trails versus open, nonwooded places complete their courses faster and with more enjoyment. Being able to focus on your outdoor surroundings seemed to lessen the pain runners felt.

Got a mountain bike? If not, you might want to get one. First off, riding a bike of course is a great low-impact exercise. The British Medical Association studied ten thousand people and determined that bike riding twenty miles a week lessened the risk of heart disease by 50 percent.[12] That's incredible! If you bike in the country or woods, you'll get an even bigger boost to your health. Mountain biking with its rough terrain builds strength in the back, arms, legs, and core muscles. It lowers stress and offers fresh air, a serotonin boost from sunlight, an antidepressant effect from the inhalation of soil, and the healing phytochemical scents of the forest.

And if you're a water lover, consider kayaking or canoeing on a lake or calm river. Lots of places, like city parks departments, rent kayaks and canoes. (Sometimes they even rent pedal boats.) In general, paddling gives your upper body and core a workout. You strengthen not only arms but chest, shoulders, and your abdomen. It's of course great aerobic exercise for the heart, and good for the mind, too. Take Scotland's Nick Ray. He's struggled with depression for years and credits sea kayaking as key to his survival. "Being in nature is very here and now . . . . Nature doesn't judge me. . . . If I'm paddling and I'm against the tide, I know that in a few hours' time the tide will turn and the paddling will get easier. And that's true for my depression as well."[13]

WHAT ABOUT WINTER?

I know you're probably thinking, *Yeah, right, it's 17 degrees as I read this right now. How am I supposed to get into nature in January?* Well, the University of Essex researchers found some interesting information. Researcher Carly Wood and her team learned that study participants who exercised on a treadmill for thirty minutes while watching a video of a natural setting lowered their stress more than those who watched a video of a "built environment."[14] I ride an indoor bike where my favorite poster of a cat in a garden hangs on the wall. My eyes often land on the image of the sweet kitty resting amid the lush flowering plants.

What's more, winter affords us the opportunity to tend to our houseplants. I often use the postholiday January season as an excuse to repot and clean up my houseplants. Hauling them from their various rooms in the house all the way down to the basement for repotting definitely circulates my blood. Hauling them to the bathtub and spraying off dust from leaves with the showerhead is exercise, too. Even watering each plant in each room gets me some steps. Afterward, for being such a good plant parent, I reward myself with a visit to the nursery and sometimes purchase a dreamy new plant. By the way, shopping also counts for steps!

FINDING YOUR PASSION ACTIVITY

In the end, the key to getting good green exercise is engaging in an activity that *you* like. That way it won't feel like a chore, and you'll do it more often. Take my friend Gretel. She encountered her first mountain bike at twelve years old when her dad got one, and they tooled around on bikes together. Later in college, she got her own mountain bike and rode occasionally with a friend. One day when they saw a group of boys happily race down off the road and along a creek bed, they got inspired and followed their fun lead. A lifelong passion was born.

For Gretel, mountain biking is about getting away from the noise and crowds of the city to breathe fresh air. "My favorite thing is how the juniper and pine trees smell like honey. Once you get a few miles from the trailhead, you see fewer people. The sound of my breath and the tires on the dirt is all I can hear, along with the birdsong." On one ride alone, she passes through a variety of biomes: "dry wildfire-burnt areas, dense aspen groves, towering pine forests, subalpine elevations, creek side trails covered in the white seed heads of cottonwoods, and stunning meadows of wildflowers. When I stop to catch my breath, I hear the enchanting sound of fluttering aspen leaves."

No matter what you choose, remember the point is to get outside and smell the fresh air, check out the sky, listen to the wind, and remember you're alive. Your body has blessed you with another day to enjoy, so check your green mission statement. Can you slot in your preferred activity during a "Me Time" window on your calendar? If you don't have or want a mission statement but want to get outside, check out these ideas.

ACTIVITIES

Three Nature Activities You've Never Tried (Spring/Summer)

Rating: Clean hands, no tools, outdoors, low cost ($0–$50)

A surprising quote on the green exercise website caught my interest. A man who'd participated in one of the University of Essex's studies said, "I didn't even know there was a nature reserve near where I lived."[15] That reminded me of how many opportunities there are to explore that we may not know about. For instance, I recently learned about three activities in my area. A lakeside park in my neighborhood rents paddleboards. I've never tried that. Also, there's an easy mountain bike trail twenty minutes away from my house. Lastly, outdoor yoga classes meet in summer at our local community center. This year I'm going to try all three of those and see which one I like best.

What activity have you been curious about? Have you ever canoed in the woods? Or played badminton or this new sport called spikeball? (Spikeball involves spiking a ball off a trampoline in an outdoor setting, which is great for families with kids.) What about picking apples during an open weekend at a private orchard? Harvesting a live Christmas tree from a farm? Any of these activities provide exercise, fresh air, and the sensory benefits of plants. See if you can try three new activities you've never tried before this year.

Geocaching Treasure Hunt (Spring/Summer/Fall)

Rating: Clean hands, no tools, outdoors, low cost ($0–$50)

Geocaching is a recent trend among outdoors lovers. You register an account on a geocaching website, and it gives you a list of things buried or hidden around the world to find. Those objects can be educational, historical, or personal to the person who hid them. Regardless, it's a fun challenge because you're engaging your mind to figure out the object's hiding place and getting outdoor exercise. Once the object's found, you can share your story of finding the object in a log attached to the object. And if there's no geocached objects near you, you can create your own trail of hidden objects for someone else. (See appendix for more information.)

Fall: Fast and Furious Raking (Fall)

RATING: Clean hands, rake, outdoors, low cost ($0–$50)

Maybe you have leaves in your own garden and you're tired of them. I've got a giant oak that does its huge thing every year. Well, why not make a game out of how fast you can rake those leaves? Give yourself an hour. Yes, *one hour*. Put in some earbuds or headphones and play energetic tunes or your favorite podcast. Then rake away, raising your heart rate a bit. You're inhaling that beneficial antidepressant bacteria, seeing fractals, and gaining an upper body workout. Plus, vigorously leaf raking actually burns almost three hundred calories per hour. Not bad for tidying up!

Spooky Stroll through a Cemetery (Fall)

RATING: Clean hands, no tools, outdoors, low cost ($0–$30)

Fall, of course, is spooky Halloween time, so why not get some exercise by taking a long stroll through a cemetery? Cemeteries may house the dead but they're also about love, remembrance, and honor. There are lots of beautiful and unusual tombstones to visit, especially in older cities. Plus, mausoleums often have ornate cement inlays. Pretty flowers are always within sight. You might even find inspirational quotes. And if there's a loved one who you'd like to visit, make it a meaningful spiritual occasion by laying flowers or having a picnic.

Animal Tracking in the Snow (Winter)

RATING: Clean hands, no tools, outdoors, no cost

A few days after the snow falls, we often see little critter footprints in our parks and natural areas. Bundle up and take an aimless hour out to see if you can follow bird, squirrel, cat, racoon, or deer tracks. Where do they lead? Can you identify the footprints and match them to a particular animal? Don't worry about spotting the animals but have your camera or phone ready to snap a photo if you see them. You never know when that crow whose footprint you were following is suddenly cawing in the tree above you.

While you're outside in the cold, observe the silent landscape and how the snow softens its shapes. How the snow clings to bare branches. It's often so quiet. Breathe that in. Feel the crunch under your feet. Take in the sight of the leafless trees and their elegant structure. Don't forget to look at the sky. The sky's light, even when cloudy, will replenish your vitamin D levels and refresh your mind.

Indoor Spinning with Outdoor Scenery (Winter)

RATING: Clean hands, no tools, indoors, low cost ($0–$10)

If researchers found that riding an indoor bike while looking at nature lowered stress, then why not dial up a calming nature video online and watch that? I've tried it. It works. You don't have to spin fast, just enough to get your heart rate up. Make sure the video includes greenery. Waterways combined with plants is even better for reducing stress.

Part Three

================ ✑ ================

BLOOMING WITH JOY

Now that we've discussed the seven strategies of green leisure, ideally you have an idea about which strategies and how many are right for you. Most likely, it will be a combination. Remember, whatever you decide is based on your preferences and needs, not anyone else's. The point is to destress through nature, not put more pressure on yourself. If you're interested in destressing through plants by bringing nature to your home, read the next chapters. I think I can help.

This section addresses the healing power of houseplants, creating indoor and outdoor green leisure lounges, and maintaining nature's magic. We'll address why having plants in the home is a mentally healing endeavor and how that healing can happen even with artificial re-creations or plant representations. We'll also focus on creating plant refuges, or "green leisure lounges," both inside your home as well as outside, if you have an outdoor space. We close with how to maintain the healing magic through positive green leisure habits.

Chapter Eleven

———— ✍ ————

The Healing Power
of Houseplants

A beautiful plant is like having a friend around the house.—Beth Ditto, musician

When I was in my early twenties, I had my first serious relationship with a houseplant. No, we didn't date, we didn't go to dinner, we didn't move in together to "see where things went." But I did indeed fall in love. I'd just moved to Seattle into a rental house that I shared with three women. On my first day there, I noticed a variegated vine on the windowsill above the kitchen sink. It wasn't a big healthy plant, only a couple of stiff strings with a few rubbery leaves. But those leaves interested me. They were waxy, green and white, with a pink blush on the edges that brilliantly brightened when the sun shone through. The plant sat in a small pile of dirt inside one chunk of cracked glass block on an old plate. It seemed dry. When I asked my roommates what kind of plant it was, no one knew. When I asked who watered the plant, they laughed and said no one really did. It was mine if I wanted it. So I decided to at least water it now and then.

We had fun in that house. We all got along well enough and were struggling to get ahead at our entry-level careers, figuring out who we were and what we wanted to do with our lives. It was Seattle during the grunge era, where music dominated, and everyone knew everyone and going to club shows on the weekend was the norm. All the while, my plant, whose name and variety I still didn't know, grew slowly over the months. About a year later, when I was packing my things to move out, I noticed the plant had grown a fresh new leaf. There was something about that leaf that resonated with me. Like a fresh leaf, I was creating a new life in a new city with deepening roots. On impulse, I tossed the plant in a cardboard box.

That plant stayed with me for almost two decades. It saw six homes, two careers, a quick divorce, a long marriage, the agony of cancer, a grateful recovery, three kids, two dogs, two cats, and one long stay in France. Or should I say it *survived* all that? In particular, when I was in Europe and my husband was in charge of watering, he kinda forgot. The plant survived anyway. Years later, what it didn't survive was my cat Aleksy. He chewed the poor thing down to a nub, and despite watering and sweet-talk, it didn't grow back. Losing it crushed me. That era of my life ended.

Still, there was no reason why I couldn't replace my *Hoya carnosa variegata* "Tricolor." (When I turned into a plant geek, I found out the name.) So I did. For me, it wasn't just the plant itself, but what it represented: experiences and memories, which, through its lovely presence, I keep in my heart every day. But for this new *Hoya*, I call it by its prettier common name, a name that matches its beauty and denotes its preciousness: porcelain flower.

Why was I so attached to this plant? Because my first porcelain flower was my first pet. Before dogs or cats. It was an easy pet that I, a young unattached woman, could manage. It represented the potential of my future. Seeing it every day, still on my shelf, still alive, despite all of the angst, fear, disappointment, loss, and even occasional depression, was like a mental salve. It didn't judge me or abandon me. It offered a steady presence when I needed steadiness. A way to relax. It was like a lovely green pet whose beauty congruously locked into my innate disposition to be among plants.

Of course, I know I'm not alone. In talking with other Gen X women, and even some millennial women, I've since learned many had plants that they bought or were gifted in their twenties, which have, in some cases, survived twenty-five years of house moves, marriages, births, divorces, severe illness, and more. My friend Kimberly named her enduring corn plant Herman, a plant she says has always been a "reflection," healthy or not, of her own well-being. My friend Sara potted dozens of baby plants that she gifted to friends and family over decades from her single ivy plant. And my friend Liz hauled her umbrella plant, a plant given to her mother when Liz was born, across the country three times. These plants traveled through life with these women, offering a reassuring presence, biophilic companionship, and the overall healing power of a houseplant. Like a dog or cat or other pet, they'd become part of the families these women had built throughout their lives.

SHOULD YOU PET YOUR PLANT?

A few years ago, my daughter conducted a revealing science experiment. She grew two small rubber tree plants and petted one every day for about a month. She gently stroked the stem in an upward motion with her fingertips for thirty seconds twice a day. Interestingly, the plant she stroked grew almost an inch taller and visibly stouter than the plant she hadn't touched.

While other, more formalized scientific research has proven that stroking a plant helps it grow, it's unclear if a human caress is actually what a plant prefers. I mean, do they like it? Are we annoying them, like when we humans hug our dogs? Scientists tell us dogs feel trapped by hugs and they're simply tolerating our human expression. Do plants feel the same way?

Science isn't sure. We do know that when a plant detects a vibration like wind or the stimulation of a hand petting it, it triggers the tongue-twister thigmomorphogenesis. The plant releases hormones that spur growth. It toughens up and grows stouter in response.[1] Think windswept pines on an ocean beach. So petting a plant may not make it happy. In the meantime, I'd say if you'd like to pet your plant to show your love, just be brief and gentle.

SHOULD YOU SPEAK TO YOUR PLANT?

I admit, I do talk to my plants. Sweet-talk. I like to have a little conversation with them whenever I visit. But my voice, or any noise, including music, produces vibration. And when the plant senses that vibration, it again triggers thigmomorphogenesis. Although a variety of studies show that plants do sprout earlier and grow more quickly and more stoutly when exposed to music and sounds,[2] I'm still not convinced that this is because it's actually healthy for them. They may not *like* the vibrations. So if you want to tell your green baby how nice it looks that day or ask if it'd like a little cleanup, I'd do it in a quiet, soothing voice.

What Houseplants Do to Our Bodies and Minds

These stories of a plant showing its power in psychologically healing us corresponds to the science. In a study that supported Roger Ulrich's study of hospital patient recovery (see chapter 5), researchers at Kansas State University found lower rates of pain, anxiety, and fatigue in patients who recovered with live plants in their rooms than among a group that didn't. They felt more positively about their environment and reported lower levels of stress.[3] Similarly, researchers from Washington State University (WSU) found that study participants were able to tolerate more mild pain if in a room with plants. "We found that more subjects were willing to keep a hand submerged in ice water for five minutes if they were in a room with plants present than if they were in a room without plants."[4] I find that amazing. They also found that other kinds of colorful objects didn't distract patients from their pain as well as plants did. That shows the power of plants to soothe our pain.

There's also a slew of studies examining the effects of houseplants on workers in office situations. For example, Taiwanese researchers found that office workers with a window view of nature had lower anxiety. Workers who had *both* a window view of nature and indoor plants in the room gained the most anxiety reduction benefits.[5] Similarly, Andrea Dravigne and her team in Texas conducted a survey among 450 employees. They found that workers in offices with plants rated their job satisfaction as higher. Their outlook toward their bosses, colleagues, and work overall was more positive. It seems that 60 percent of people working in offices without plants reported feeling happy but 69 percent of people working in offices with plants reported feeling happy. Interestingly, 82 percent of people with both plants in the office and a window view reported feeling happy.[6]

Also, WSU researchers found that in a windowless, college computer lab decorated with plants, participants were more productive (meaning they had a 12 percent quicker reaction time) while completing a computer task than when they completed the task in a room without plants. Even though their systolic blood pressure rose in both environments, it rose less in the room with plants. It also returned to baseline levels more quickly.[7] What's also fascinating is that those plants only had to be placed within the participants' *peripheral* vision, not direct sightline. Wow. You only need to catch a *glimpse* of a plant for it to help you.

Lastly, in a collection of studies on the interiors of offices, hospital work areas, and schools, Norwegian researcher Tove Fjeld found twelve symptoms like fatigue, headaches, stuffy noses, and coughs were 23 percent lower when participants had plants in their offices. Complaints of coughing were reduced by 37 percent and fatigue by 30 percent. In a hospital workroom, reports of headache decreased by 45 percent, fatigue by 32 percent, and coughing by 38 percent.[8] In a later study, they found that workers reduced their symptoms with just one plant on their tables. Hopefully, corporations will consider all this compelling information when planning future office layouts.

Schools reflect this as well. Researcher K. T. Han took small trees into a high school classroom in Taiwan to compare academic achievement and behavior among students. He learned that the students in the classrooms with small potted trees had higher scores in the areas of comfort and friendliness. Also, students had fewer absences and better behavior in terms of punishment than those in the control classrooms.[9] Jennifer Doxey and her team in Texas found significant improvements in student interest and enthusiasm as well as instructor organization when university classrooms had plants. Class participation was also higher.[10] It seemed the plants simply made the students (and teachers) happier.

Have you ever seen a plant, either real or fake, in a hotel room? I haven't. That's a shame, but hotels are catching on. Some major chains have realized plants make people happier. They're incorporating more live indoor plants into their lobbies to attract travelers. And more travelers are demanding plant and plant-oriented décor. In an Orbitz survey, 63 percent of millennial travelers wanted to see more plants in hotel rooms. And 61 percent said plants boosted their overall mood. Almost 50 percent said they'd be more likely to book rooms at hotels that decorated with plant photos.[11]

These are all convincing arguments for the inclusion of plants in indoor spaces. I mean, it makes sense, right? Humans have spent hundreds of thousands of years in nature, and now in the last two hundred years, we've been forced into a lot of natureless, indoor spaces for extended periods of time. It's forced both our bodies and minds to cope. It makes sense to vacation in plant-rich settings and advocate for more plants in our offices, schools, hospitals, and hotels. And if nothing else, you can always decorate with plant images or grow houseplants to help you recover from plantless, indoor settings.

GROWING YOUR OWN GREEN PET

In fact, growing your own houseplant is really the easiest form of green leisure, right? You're bringing the healing power of plants inside instead of going outside for it. All you need is one: one porcelain flower, one Herman, or whichever plant enchants you. Having a plant pet eases stress and helps you relax. So where do you start?

Remember that journaling exercise in chapter 3 where we examined positive plant memories from childhood? Can you go back and look at your writing and pull any ideas out? Do you have a plant in mind? Do you already have a plant, like me, that you grew during a special time in your life? If not, brainstorm some plants that you like or particular features of plants that you like. You can write "plants with big leaves, easy-care plants, plants with little flowers, a plant like the one I see at the doctor's office." Whatever comes to mind.

Now narrow down your ideas to five plants. Keep a list of those five handy. It will play an integral part when you shop for plants (see "Houseplant Shopping Tips") and when you create your indoor green leisure lounge in the next chapter.

HOUSEPLANT SHOPPING TIPS

To source your plants, it's best to buy at a local plant store or nursery. Avoid a big box store if you can, as they sometimes source from growers that use pesticides. At least inquire beforehand. Also, buying online can be tricky. Some retailers don't divulge that you're ordering from faraway countries that don't have strict laws about checking for insects and pests. You don't want to accidentally import more murder hornets! Shopping locally helps keep local businesses healthy.

When shopping in person, if you don't have a magazine or online picture of what you want, ask the clerk for the plant by *botanical name*, not common name. That's the more official scientific name given to a plant, usually rooted in Latin words and made-up horticultural ones. Common names are called "common" for a reason. Several different plants may be known by one common name. If you can't pronounce the name, just scribble it on paper and take the paper with you to show the shop clerk.

When deciding among plants, here are some things to keep in mind.

1. Look for plants whose leaves are fresh and green all the way to the tips: no holes in leaves or webbing between leaves or yellow or brown leaves. This ensures it's been raised in healthy conditions.
2. Check for free soil space between the emerging plant stems and the edge of the pot. You don't want a plant that is overgrown, rootbound in the pot, and has been neglected.
3. Also, brush the plant a bit with your hand. Do bugs fly out? If so, pass on it. You don't want to bring home insects.
4. If selecting a flowering houseplant, choose one that has buds and not full flowers, since already blooming flowers may fade a few days after you get it home.
5. If you're on a tight budget, choose a smaller plant over a larger one. If you care for the plant well, it will grow quickly and make a statement soon enough.

WHAT IF I CAN'T GROW A PLANT?

What if you like plants but the upkeep of a plant isn't right for you? Well, consider buying an artificial plant and positioning it somewhere where you notice it often. Yes, artificial plants can be tacky, but studies show that seeing a rendering of a plant—even a plastic imitation—helps reduce stress. The good news about artificial plants is you can set them anywhere that looks attractive! Inside a bookcase, on a corner shelf, on a coffee table, even atop a fridge. I have both live and fake plants in my house and it looks great. Real plants near the windows and fake ones in darker areas. It's your home, so buy a fake plant and be proud!

The other great news about artificial plants is they're widely available secondhand. Have you been to a thrift store lately? There's always an aisle or table with fake potted greenery waiting to be dusted off and taken home. Similarly, discount home and craft stores often sell new fake plants. If you want to go for a more expensive, vivid imitation, see the appendix for sources for more sophisticated-looking faux plants. Whatever the fake plant, it will still soften the straight lines of your home and soothe you.

FIVE SOPHISTICATED PLANT SUBSTITUTES

First, let me say this. Fake plants are most often made of polyester, which is a kind of plastic. We're learning more about the dangers of plastic, so to add more plastic to the world is not the best choice you can make. However, because plastic does last thousands of years, a plastic plant can last a lifetime and then be passed on to someone else. Arguably, it's recyclable if well cared for. So for those whose lifestyle or abilities preclude them from growing live plants, artificial plants are a solid alternative. (For sources, see the appendix.) But avoid plants that have noticeable stems like fiddle-leaf fig, eucalyptus, and vines. You'll see the plastic scaffolding, which looks tacky. The obvious trickery will take you out of a serene moment. Alternatively, here are five faux plants I've found that look more chic than tacky.

1. *Grasses.* At home discount stores, you can find hip fake plants that don't look like gaudy roses shooting out of a fake watering can with a rooster on it. (But, hey, if you're into roosters, that's cool.)
2. *Boxwood.* Live topiaries have a neat dense appearance and fake ball-shaped boxwoods are no different. I suggest going with trimmed orbs or natural renditions. Traditional yet formal.

3. *Succulents.* Cacti, euphorbia, and other succulent plants already resemble rubber so subbing them for the real thing isn't a stretch. Plus, most visitors won't notice the difference. With their rosette forms, succulents offer a variety of color and structural interest. Modern and hip.
4. *Ferns.* Ferns are graceful and evoke the forest. Their fronds add a warm architecture and the overall bushiness softens surfaces with a sophisticated presence. Plus, their low profile won't block a dining table view.
5. *Air Plants.* With their long stiff leaves and slow still-life growing patterns, air plants also look artificial. So muted green *Tillandsias* work as a cool calming statement. They offer a wisp of plant material to make your décor playful while carrying exotic, delicate appeal.

If you can't bring yourself to decorate with an artificial plant, how about a *picture* of a plant? Studies show that simply viewing *images* of plants lowers stress.[12] Again, thrift and discount home stores sell lots of paintings and photos of plants and greenery. Local artists sell original paintings of plants in galleries or online. Regardless, don't be fooled by cold images that are white or tan or gray—go for green! The point is to evoke nature in your mind, so decorate with a rendering that reminds you of the real thing. Leaf portraits, green forests, botanical drawings, vintage bouquet paintings. They all work.

My house is an example of plant imagery, or plantery, on steroids. In my living room, I have fake ivy sitting high on a bookshelf to soften its lines. I have living plants by the windows. I have pillows woven with flower and leaf images. Storage boxes printed with irises and violets. Vases on the fireplace with bouquets of grass and baby's breath. A framed photo of a garden. A hummingbird and lily ceramic. A faux tree branch lamp with a shade embroidered with yarn leaves. A vintage liqueur bottle with yellow roses. An antique tray with white peonies. A midcentury watercolor bouquet painting. Even my stone coasters have antiqued images of hydrangeas. Yes, I'm weirdly into plants.

I know that seems like a lot, but when you toss in a plain couch, plain armchairs, rug, books, simple tables, curtainless windows, and a large fireplace, I actually have several decorative planes without plant imagery, which serve as an anchoring foil to the leafiness. Of course, a balance is ideal. You don't want a look that's messy, busy, or overwhelming, like a jammed shop of junk. In fact, incorporating just a few plant-related items will help you destress. Even wood helps. Let's say, in addition to the candles on your coffee table, you keep a small pot of fake grass. Or a used gardening book whose cover displays a beautiful garden. Or a print with a portrait of a leaf on the wall. What about a giant fake ficus tree in the corner? I love giant fake trees in corners! You can't grow a live tree in a corner anyway! It makes so much sense to decorate a dead dark space this way. If you do it, make sure to use a dense, lush tree, which I talk about in "Five Sophisticated Plant Substitutes."

TEN GOOD CHOICES FOR CUT GREENERY

Another way to relax with plants without growing them is to evoke greenery with cut stems from live plants. The trick here is to choose green stems, not cream pampas grass stems or curly brown twigs. You need that green color to fulfill your natural visual yearning for nature in order to relax. Also, bundling cut greenery so that it appears full and lush will boost its impact. Your brain will register it as a growing, live plant and not as a few anemic leaves and branches. For sourcing, seek out friendly neighbors and see if you can cut these from their garden or shop at grocery stores and florist shops. They're all widely available. To help them last, display in a vase with cold water.

1. Eucalyptus stems (fresh scent, waxy stiff leaves that last)
2. Olive branches (pretty leaves with dark surfaces and light undersides)
3. Baby's breath (delicate stems and tiny white flowers)
4. Lavender stems (fresh scent, flowers dry elegantly)
5. Curly willow (great structural interest, small leaves)
6. Flax swords (bold deep color, tough and lasting)
7. Holly branches (glossy sculptural leaves, some berries)
8. Conifer branches (cedar/spruce/juniper, fresh scent, lasting color)
9. Bay tree branches (spicy crushed scent, good for flavoring soup)
10. Palm fronds (bold statement, tropical look)

A CLEAN, MODERN LINES APPROACH

At this point, you might be thinking, *Yeah but I'm not frou-frou, I don't like curvy things, I like "clean modern lines."* I'd like to address that. I mean, for thousands of years we decorated with plant and flower imagery on everything from civic buildings to hairbrushes, but then from about the 1950s to the 1970s designers like Charles and Ray Eames, Pierre Koenig, and Ludwig Mies van der Rohe departed into architecture and décor that featured long straight lines, geometric shapes, and cold materials like steel and glass. (Nature was sometimes incorporated via views.) Most people saw the style as reflective of the future, technology, and industry. It solidified into people's personal identities. But ultimately, I wonder if we've been brainwashed into straight geometry. Yes, the look is modern and chic, I suppose, but I wonder if that means the curves of nature aren't. Are they passé? Too romantic? Is a square pond somehow more refined than an irregular, curving one more akin to nature? I'm not sure. It is interesting to note that there isn't a lot of New Brutalist architecture being built anymore.

Anyway, I don't mean to offend. If you're truly a clean, modern lines kind of person, that's cool. If that's what sends your heart soaring, then consider adding greenery in that style. You can use square pots, solid color containers, single large plants, or pot collections in gray, white, or black. Streamline your choices whenever possible. Some more drastically sculpted plants include the ZZ plant, fiddle-leaf fig, and Krinkle Kurl plant. With those, you can make a modernist statement while helping yourself destress from a busy life.

YOUR HOUSEPLANT STYLE

If you're interested in trying your hand at growing a plant, your first task is to decide what plant's right for you. You could grab an alluring orchid from the grocery store and grow that, but I don't recommend it. Orchids need incredibly particular conditions to grow. I don't even grow them. I mean, do you have a tropical rainforest

in your house? Probably not. So re-creating that will be tricky. Of course, if you're more experienced with plants, go for it! Orchids are so sexy and exotic. But beginners might want to consider an easier plant. In my first activity, I suggest the one plant I would grow if I couldn't grow any other plant.

If you've decided that an artificial plant or cut greenery is right for you, then explore what kinds match your personality. In "Five Sophisticated Plant Substitutes" I offer choices for fake plants that don't look tacky and in "Ten Good Choices for Cut Greenery," I list cut greenery that evokes live plants. What are the plants or plant imagery that you want to make your own? Don't worry about arranging, we cover that in the next chapter. For now, the point is to figure out how to create a nature-enhanced home sanctuary that reflects *your* personality while providing a refuge from the stresses of the day. Honor yourself with that. And have fun exploring!

ACTIVITIES

The Easiest Pet Plant to Grow

RATING: Soily hands, garden tools, indoors, moderate cost ($30–$50)

Even if you didn't have a decades-old attachment to a plant pet, you can always start one. Though that porcelain flower was my special coming-of-age plant that holds deep sentimental value, it's not actually my favorite plant. My favorite plant is easier for beginners to grow. In fact, everyone needs one! It's fuzzy and colorful and fun. I love it so much I actually wrote a whole novel (*The Forgetting Flower*) based on an imagined one. It's an African violet.

African violet (*Saintpaulia ionantha*) is the beginner's best pet plant for a few reasons. First, it matches most of our indoor climates. African violets like heat and indirect bright windows. Second, they're drought tolerant, surviving for almost a couple weeks without water, so if you forget to water, they'll forgive you. Third, they have cute fuzzy leaves. Fourth, your cat won't chew those fuzzy leaves; the texture is too strange. Lastly, they flower! In deep violet, bold magenta, pastel pink, lavender, and white and with plain petals, frilly ones, fringed, all kinds. The leaves can be variegated, too. What pretty, cheery plants. I challenge you to grow an African violet and not smile at it adoringly when it blooms!

What you'll need:

- African violet plant (four- or six-inch round pot) with bloom color of your choice
- Ceramic glazed pot with drainage hole and saucer (six- to ten-inch diameter)
- One small bag African violet potting soil (or regular potting soil mixed with perlite)

1. Fill your container about halfway with soil.
2. Snuggle your African violet plant into the middle of the pot. If the roots aren't loose in the soil, loosen them a bit.

3. Fill around the plant with soil, pressing down lightly all around so that the soil surface of the potted plant and the container is even.
4. Water the surface well. Note: never water an African violet's leaves! They'll brown. Stick the tip of your watering can underneath the leaves.
5. Place beside a limited-sun or indirect bright window. (They need four to six hours of light.)
6. Water once every seven to ten days (unless the soil's still damp and dark from the previous watering). Lightly fertilize once a month from April until August. You can set the plant on a tray of pebbles with water for added humidity.
7. When it blooms, pause a while and enjoy the lovely sight.

Sleuthing Your Green Décor Style

RATING: Clean hands, basic art tools, indoors, low to moderate cost ($0–$50)

In your Escape-to-Nature notebook, revisit your list of five plants and the activities I gave you in chapter 3 about plants and happy memories. Any clues to your style in there? If you made an inspiration collage (either a tangible one or online), study that. What did you choose? Look for patterns of color, shape, style, materials, and plants. What do you see over and over? I can tell you right now, I'm unconsciously drawn to violet flowers and I love green velvet fabric. It's almost eerie. I don't think about it; it just happens.

What are you subconsciously drawn to? Make a short list of plants, flowers, and décor items. For example, cacti in white pots, cotton textiles with circle prints, orange ceramics, rattan chairs, rustic wooden tables, large flowers but not peonies. Then keep that list handy as you assess your existing green décor. Make a list of what you want to get rid of and what you want to add. (Remember there's lots of free stuff in online groups!) Set a budget you're comfortable with and shop at nurseries, gift shops, and thrift stores with your décor profile in mind. If you find something cool, post it on social media with the hashtag #greenleisure. Keep searching until you find all the fun stuff that thrills you!

Chapter Twelve

Creating an Indoor, Green Leisure Lounge

My green thumb came only as a result of the mistakes I made while learning to see things from the plant's point of view.—H. Fred Dale, gardening writer

Five years ago, if you'd asked me where my green leisure lounge (GLL) was, I would have said in the corner of our own lounge. My GLL consisted of a big comfy chair with bookcases of my favorite books and knickknacks on the left and a huge corn plant I rescued from our local town mall on the right. With a view of three plants in the windows and the back garden, this corner has been my special spot for years. It's where I write, relax, meditate, watch the rain, play guitar, and hang out with my family. It always worked because I mostly used the space when my kids were in school and my husband was at the office.

Enter the 2020 pandemic. Suddenly, my husband and kids were all home, every day, all day. Sound familiar? It was loud. It was trying. It was nuts. Eventually, we adjusted. We figured out online school and my husband modified our home office. Life went on. But my special refuge was no longer a refuge. During the day, people streamed in continually to make food, rinse dishes, touch base about school, ask questions, head out the door, and all else. I needed a new space—desperately. I considered our office, but every day that room was filled with voices during my husband's work calls. I considered the basement, but my son sometimes lifted weights there. So I settled on our living room. Though darker and without my garden view, it had pocket doors I could close and south-facing windows where I could grow plants. I just had to figure out how to make it work.

The room is a rectangular space with a bay of three windows at the front and a fireplace on the opposite interior wall. Two windows sit at the western end, shaded by small outdoor trees, and an arch with two pocket doors are on the opposite wall. With a couch and two chairs and bookshelves, it was already set up for socializing, not plant refuge time, so I thought long and hard about how to make the space work.

After a series of changes I'll share later in this chapter, I was able to create a little refuge. Now, when I need a break from the noise of the household, I retreat there. Especially on sunny afternoons. I feel safe and relaxed. Without pressure. I don't get interrupted because I've told everyone it's my private retreat space so if they pass by, they know not to interrupt. Setting it up didn't require big changes or big purchases, just a few modifications and lots of decisions. Although it's still in a "public" area, I can at least breathe deeply, let my mind clear, open the windows, and enjoy the view of greenery. It's enough to drastically lower my stress and improve my mood.

WE ALL COULD USE A REFUGE OF GREENERY

Most of us thankfully have homes. If you are reading this book, it's likely you're fortunate enough to have a home, whether it's a traditional house with a picket fence, or a tiny apartment, a suburban mansion, city loft, or even a miniature house. In our enclosed retreats, we sleep and rest, cook and eat, raise our kids, pet our dog, and generally entertain ourselves. Homes make us feel safe and at ease and that's why they're so important. They keep the cold out and keep us warm. Even if we don't have a garden, we can at least create a green space inside to relieve ourselves from the stress of the day.

Where do you land when you come home stressed out? On the couch in front of the TV? In your bedroom? In the bathtub to escape the kids? Although I understand the need to veg out in front of the TV, I think TV's calming effects are limited. If you're watching something funny, that laughter will help you, yes, but a lot of crime dramas and action movies increase our stress. So ask yourself where you would go if you could take twenty minutes to spend alone and relax? Is there a private nook, a particular window with a view to greenery, an entire basement that gets some daylight? A bathroom with a tub? Keep this idea in the back of your mind. We're going to build a plant refuge in your home.

To do that, we can't just decide where we'd like to retreat and that's that. We have to combine our needs with our plants' needs. And although *we* like to live under a roof with walls, hard floors, artificial light, and soft furniture, plants don't. In their natural habitats, they don't grow under roofs. When's the last time you saw a plant outside growing under a roof? Maybe you'll see ivy climbing a pillar under a highway, but that ivy always grows toward the rain and light. We humans don't have a lot of rain and light inside our homes. And we don't have bare earth. Got any loose soil on your floor? I doubt it. That means if we're going to create a plant-oriented refuge, we have to artificially re-create the weather and land in which they usually thrive.

FIVE EASY HOUSEPLANTS TO GROW

If you're a beginner, consider these five plants. They all grow on forest floors, so think warmth, somewhat moist air, and indirect light. An organic potting mix should suffice for soil.

1. Pothos (*Epipremnum*) grows in a cheery mound with spade-shaped leaves that gently trail. For a bushier look, snip the strands' ends; for a hanging basket effect, let the tendrils creep. Pothos loves indirect light. Darker varieties tolerate the lowest levels. They like water once a week but tolerate less, up to two weeks. Native to Polynesia, they thrive in warm conditions, 60 to 80 degrees.

2. Snake plant (*Sanseviera*) shoots up vertically in long fleshy blades, like a grass for giants. The yellow-green cultivar is most common but for lowest maintenance, choose Black Coral. It's dark and dreamy. It grows to three feet tall with silver and light green cutting through the smokey black leaves. The dark quality means it holds more of a particular kind of chlorophyll that catches low-intensity light. So if you set it a few feet from a window and soak the soil every few weeks, you'll keep these African natives upright and happy.

3. Cast iron plant (*Aspidistra*) lives up to its name, though you won't hear a clang if you knock on it. It's difficult to kill, not only tolerating low light but rare watering. Plus, if you live in zone 7 or above, you can grow it outside. But don't expect it to grow quickly. In a way, it exists rather than grows. The Japanese native creates upright leaves from rhizomes slowly, making fuller, established plants costly. Place in a north- or east-facing window, water every one to two weeks, and let it be a delightful cauldron of inky green.

4. Peace lily (*Spathiphyllum*) sports the glossiest green leaves, which, with their corrugation and graceful fountain-like habit, makes for an enchanting sight. But the peace lily's superpower is its air-cleaning abilities. It neutralizes carbon monoxide, benzene, and formaldehyde, gases coming from furniture wood adhesives and fuel-burning appliances. It also likes indirect light and water once a week. If it gets good bright indirect light, it blooms elegant white spathes that resemble its lily name.

5. Chinese evergreen (*Aglaonema*) knows how to soften the edges of a room. Its dense habit creates a lush oval of foliage and it isn't fussy if neglected. Darker varieties tolerate lower light levels and outright scorch in direct sun. That's what makes them low maintenance! They want occasional watering, whenever soil is dry, every two to three weeks. What it really likes is warmth, above 60 degrees and avoiding drafty windows. Otherwise, brown edges appear. Wilt means you watered too much. Set them in a cozy spot and don't do much except admire their evergreen ways.

A PLANT'S NATURAL HABITAT IS A GUIDE

In the past, when clients have asked me about houseplant care, I've always urged them to imagine the native habitat, or usual outside conditions, where their plant likes to grow. What kind of climate does it like? Sometimes the answer is as easy as desert versus forest. For instance, you can't grow a happy cactus in a low-light, humid bathroom. But you can grow a fern, which is a forest understory plant. Over thousands of years, it's adapted to grow in a low-light, humid atmosphere. In fact, it *likes* that and becomes a happy, snappy fern. So, if you match a plant's indoor conditions to its native outside habitat, you'll grow a healthy happy plant. Force it to live in conditions it dislikes, and you'll grow a sick sad plant. It's fairly straightforward.

During those chats about houseplants, I learned that my clients rarely knew their houseplant's original habitat. Of course they didn't. Grocery stores and nurseries often label their houseplants with tags like, "Tropical Plant, 1 quart." That's not a lot of info. The thing to remember is that all houseplants are plants that actually live outside somewhere. It's usually someplace you probably don't live. Like Brazil or Africa or even Hawaii (aloha to Hawaiian readers!). For instance, a Kauai resident is unlikely to grow a Swiss cheese plant (*Monstera*) indoors because it's too easy to grow in a backyard. Though not native, they grow up the local trees there. In fact, they can be a nuisance. But to someone in New York, a Swiss cheese plant is a "houseplant." The word "houseplant" really means any plant that grows in a warm winter area. So if we can figure out the plant's native outside conditions, we can grow a plant that thrives.

Do you see what you're actually up against when you grow a houseplant? The horticulture industry creates and distributes millions of these warm winter plants to the consumer market, making them seem ubiquitous and therefore easy to grow. Yet they tell consumers next to nothing about where the plant natively grows and what conditions it likes. No wonder so many end up in the garbage. The industry doesn't set up consumers for success. You see a stunning begonia or orchid at the grocery store, buy it and take it home, the plant suffers, and you toss it, feeling like a failure. If you've had this experience, raise your hand. But don't blame yourself. You didn't get much help.

WHERE *NOT* TO GROW HOUSEPLANTS

Though there's a lot of dreamy online photos of houseplants on shelves, in corners, on tables at the center of rooms, these photos are misleading. They imply that you can just set up a shelving unit against your wall and grow as much as your heart desires. What they don't show is the grow bulb above all of those plants or mention that the display is temporary. I'm not saying it's impossible—each person's home is different—but if you try growing houseplants in the following areas, your plants will probably struggle to get enough light.

1. Against an interior wall
2. In a bookcase
3. In the center or far interior of a room
4. Atop a fireplace
5. In a dark corner
6. In a windowless nook

What Can Your Home Offer a Plant?

The good news is you *can* grow a plant indoors with a little preparation. So, let's determine what your home can offer. Think of this like you're adopting a plant pet and you want your home to be as equipped and ready for your pet's needs as possible. When you adopt a dog or cat, you buy a bed and set it in a sunny warm place, right? You decide where to put food and water dishes. What toys might keep them busy, what treats they'll like. Similarly, let's assess your plant pet space.

First, what kind of home do you have? Is it a multibedroom house with more than one floor that gets light from all directions? An apartment whose only exposure is to the east in the living room? What about a basement studio? Is it generally warm or cold? Drafty or airtight? Humid? How much free floor space do you have? How much do you *wish* you had? Do you want to grow one plant or three or do you imagine yourself surrounded by an indoor jungle? Whatever the conditions, jot down a little list. For example: apartment, two rooms with south light, warm upper floor, airtight, low humidity, limited floor space, want to grow baskets of vines and maybe cactus. Good. Now, let's focus on three basic conditions: light, humidity, and temperature.

Light

Light is key to your houseplant's survival. Heck, it's key to *our* survival. In terms of houseplants, the more light, the better. You can always reduce light via curtains or shades but it's difficult to gain more from a window. Oftentimes we think we have more light than we do. So take a clear-eyed examination of your home. First, tally up the potential spaces you can dedicate to a plant. How many windows do you have? What are their exposures? East, west, north, south? East light is great for part-sun or medium-light plants. It gives off a weaker morning, direct light for a few hours. West and south light is great for full-sun plants. It radiates the hottest, direct light at the hottest part of the day (even in winter). North light is the weakest. It gives off faint, indirect light all day.

HOW MUCH OXYGEN DO PLANTS CREATE?

You may have read the many articles about how plants clean the air and create oxygen. Although it's true that plants absorb carbon dioxide and eliminate toxic chemicals like toluene, benzene, formaldehyde, and xylene from the air, they don't produce much oxygen. The average leaf produces only five milliliters of oxygen per hour. We breathe fifty *liters* of oxygen per hour. So, depending on conditions, you'd need three hundred to five hundred plants in one smallish room to truly produce usable oxygen.[1] But they're still worth growing because they do somewhat eliminate toxic chemicals.

Light is a bit trickier than just figuring out your exposure. You have to figure out about how many hours of a particular kind of light a window gets. Sometimes buildings or trees block light from entering a window. For instance, you could have a south-facing window that gets direct light but it might face a courtyard and therefore get two hours of direct, south light a day. In my own house, my living room windows face south, but because of tall trees in my front yard, it receives direct sunlight for only a few hours in the afternoon. Here are a few tips to help figure things out.

On a sunny weekend day, check in on the room in which you'd like to grow your houseplant. Keep a sticky note and pen on a table there. Record what time the sun starts to come through, if it does. Are there shadows on the floor? If so, that means stronger light. Later, check in again and write down when it fades, do the math, and figure out how many hours of direct sunlight that window gets. If it gets about four hours or more, you can probably grow sun-loving plants. If the sunlight never created shadows, your window gets indirect light. This means lower-light plants will do well there. If the sunlight was direct in the morning and then faded, you have medium-level, or moderate light, which means you can grow plants that like indirect light.

Repeat this exercise for any other rooms whose light you'd like to figure out. Sometimes we instinctually know how the light moves because we've lived in a place long enough to become familiar with the sun's shifting pattern. If that's the case, write down the general light conditions for wherever you'd like to grow plants, paying special attention to that nook or room that might make a good plant-oriented refuge.

One note to remember: if you live north of I-80, the highway that cuts horizontally across the United States, you'll probably need a grow light in winter for your sun-loving plants. The most common problem I see among clients with sick houseplants is a lack of light. (The second? Overwatering.) Especially in the north, where overcast skies can last for weeks. Invest the eight bucks in a bulb and put it in either a decorative or task lamp. Turn it on for a few hours every day. That's all you really need to do to keep your plants happy in winter. My mom in Chicago keeps a pothos happy exclusively via light from a full-spectrum bulb in a decorative lamp behind her couch.

Humidity

Another factor in growing houseplants is humidity. Humidity is the percentage of moisture in the air of a room. This is a biggie for indoor homes. Most of us have dry air indoors, especially in winter. Certain plants have specific humidity needs (see fern example earlier). In my own house, my bedroom is warm and dry, since the windows are newer and airtight. We have a large vent for a smallish room. Plus, the space also is warmed from the heat rising from the entry stairwell. With unobstructed east morning light, the bedroom absolutely cooks, despite my efforts to close the vent and pull some shades. Can you think of the habitat, or even state, these conditions are similar to? Yes, Arizona. The Sonoran Desert. My bedroom is a mini-Arizona. So, what do I grow there? Two succulents: a Christmas cactus (*Schlumbergera truncata*) and Medusa's head (*Euphorbia flanaganii*). They love it!

HOW TO BEST INCREASE HUMIDITY

You might have read that misting plants is a way to increase humidity, but the truth is, the tiny droplets evaporate quickly. It's not that effective, because you don't put enough water in the air. Tropical houseplants prefer humidity levels at about 50 percent or more. Unless you live in the southern United States, you probably won't achieve that. If you did, you'd grow mold on your walls. But you can help your plants a bit with these approaches. They are listed in order of effectiveness.

1. *A humidifier.* The goal is to increase your overall humidity in the room, and a small humidifier or diffuser is the most effective way to do that. You'll noticeably change the dryness in the air. However, be careful not to overuse, as you don't want mold growing on your windowsills or walls.
2. *A terrarium.* These open glass/plastic enclosures are coming back in style, and there are lots of cool ones to choose from. You can buy at home discount stores, nurseries, or even pet stores if you want an aquarium tank. Fill your terrarium with dirt and grow your plants inside.

You'll have to keep the cover nearly closed for high humidity. Though you'll increase the humidity greatly—think mini tropical rainforest—you may rot your plants if you overwater. Also, a happy plant can put out new growth quickly and outgrow the space. Still, you can decorate terrariums with twigs, stones, moss, and even fairies. Fun for kids!

3. *Cluster plants.* Because plants transpire water through their leaves, you can cluster them so that they create their own little microclimate. It won't increase humidity hugely but takes advantage of the plants' natural ability to humidify the air and the leftover water in saucers.

4. *Wet moss in a pot.* I read about this idea a while ago and like it. It too increases humidity only by a small percentage but it's pretty and low maintenance. You need a pot an inch or two larger than your planted pot and sphagnum moss from a nursery (or craft store). Set the outer pot underneath the smaller pot. In the gap between pots, stuff sphagnum moss, then water. As the moss dries out, the vapor rises around the leaves. I also like this idea because it acts as extra overflow for watering, channeling water upward through the moss.

5. *Pebbles in a tray with water.* This is a low-cost solution with minimal effect. The vapor hangs around your plant only if you set the tray directly underneath your container. In a plant pot saucer, fill with clean rocks or glass marbles and add about an inch of water. I refill mine once a week in winter, every two weeks in summer.

Conversely, kitchens and bathrooms offer higher humidity levels. It's a bit more like Hawaii in our bathrooms. Warm and humid. Maybe bright, maybe dim. Think sunny Kona or rainy Hilo. In my upstairs bathroom, I have a lot of humidity from our shower and eastern light from one frosted glass window. It's bright indirect light in summer but weaker light in winter. What likes it there? My spotted rattlesnake plant (*Calathea lancifolia*).

Somewhere between Hawaii and Arizona is our lounge. It's a subtropical kind of place like North Carolina. Because the room is an addition, it's cooler at night and in winter but warm enough during the day. Plus, it contains ambient moisture from the sink and stove in the kitchen. With a bank of windows facing north, it gets a load of bright indirect light and enough humidity. What do I grow there? Corn plant (*Dracaena fragrans*), elephant's ears (*Alocasia*), spiderwort (*Tradescantia pallida* 'Variegata'), and umbrella plant (*Schefflera arboricola*).

Where are the Arizonas and Hawaiis and North Carolinas of your home? Do you have any? Maybe you already live in those states, in which case, congratulations! They're all wonderful. Maybe you live in a cool damp house. Maybe you live in a warm upper-floor apartment, where the heat from the lower floors rises. Or maybe your house varies in climate like the rooms in my house. Whatever the mini-climate, it's important to note them before you move a plant into those conditions.

So what do you do if you're unsure about the humidity level in a room? Well, you can try what I call the "glass sweat test." You put four ice cubes in a glass with water and set it on a table. Leave it for about five minutes. Then, see if it has condensation droplets on the outside of the glass. If it has some droplets, the air is somewhat humid. If it has a lot of droplets, the air is very humid. If it doesn't, the air is probably dry. The good news is changing humidity is a lot easier than changing your room's light. Check out "How to Best Increase Humidity" for how to change your room's humidity.

Temperature

Temperature and humidity go hand in hand. Warmer air holds more moisture, cooler air doesn't. That's why if you have a warm room, your air will seem drier. In cooler rooms, humidity tends to condense and rooms can feel more moist. That's why mold grows on windowsills and in showers and whatnot. In general, we have homes that fluctuate from the 70s or 80s during the day to the 60s at night. These fluctuations mirror the fluctuations that happen in outside habitats, and plants don't mind that. In fact, some prefer big temperature swings. It helps them go dormant, regain lost moisture, and, overall, regenerate.

It's the extremes that you have to watch out for when growing houseplants. If your house gets hotter than, say, 85 degrees, your plants might wilt. If your house drops below 60 degrees, plants might get chilled and drop leaves or rot. Within these extremes is the issue of draft. Let's say you grow a plant in a super sunny window that's drafty. This happens when people grow plants on radiators in old houses. You're cooking the plant during the day and freezing it at night. Not healthy. A better solution is to grow a hardier plant by a drafty window without the radiator. Or put plastic film (sold in kits at hardware stores) over your window to block drafts and grow a desert plant. With these solutions, the plant won't suffer from extreme fluctuations.

Now, can you tally up the locations in your home that will likely stay between about 60 and 80 degrees? Do any of these match the potential location of your green leisure lounge? If so, then bravo! You're on your way to destressing via a home plant refuge. If not, do you have a second choice that might work? It can be as simple as a window with good light or a basement corner beside a window. If you're unsure, decide based on where you, not necessarily the plant, would be happier. We'll work from there.

Preparing Your Green Leisure Lounge

For your lounge, you'll need the following: a place to sit, a place to set your book or mug or phone, and plants. Some type of boundary object (a door, a wall, a standing screen) helps, too. First, decide on which window and which room works best for you. Again, if there's only one window and one room, that's fine. And if there are more choices, well, then all the more fun. You can create two or three GLLs. Regardless of how many, if you find a window that's beside a corner or a straight stretch of wall, that's best.

What you really want in your GLL is a bounded place of rest and repose. Comfort. Joy. Restoration. Ideally, corner walls, a door to a room, doorway to a nook, a standing screen, bookcase, bay window, or even sofa and console table can suggest a threshold to your retreat. That way, when you cross it, you know it's refuge relaxation time. The boundary is clear.

To prepare your space, you must first honor it by clearing it and cleaning it. What's already there? Do you need to rearrange furniture? Clear out stuff? If so, do that first. Sort through what you don't want and give those objects away. As Marie Kondo says in her book, *The Life-Changing Magic of Tidying Up*, you can honor your past by thanking the object for serving you when you needed it and passing it on. So do that until you feel like you're finished but only finished for this particular space. If you let your clearing project grow larger, you may never get around to creating your plant refuge. After you've cleared, then clean. Vacuum, wipe down surfaces, maybe even clean the window. Ready the space for your plants as if you were creating a nursery for a new baby. How exciting!

Then, you'll need a comfortable chair, bench, or pillow to sit on. Depending on your space, you can sit directly facing your plants or you can sit at an angle beside your plants. If you have a corner, a chair and lamp and maybe even a picture on the wall will create a cozy, inviting spot. And if you can reuse or buy a small table or pedestal and place it beside your chair, even better. Just make sure the space is comfortable to sit in for long periods and the table and plants and any other décor are to your taste and no one else's. If you have all that, you'll have a green leisure lounge where you can relax and restore your spirit.

My new GLL was tricky because I already had furniture in my living room. The mini-climate was subtropical. Enough light, enough humidity, and no drafts. I had a free corner to use but that free corner wasn't big enough for a chair. I knew I wanted to view outside plants since I had in recent years installed a mixed border that was thriving in my garden. I had a long bay window nook that was a good foot deep where I had always grown plants. So instead of moving furniture around, I moved plants. I decided I could sit in that window nook pretty darn easily. If I sat in the nook itself, I could see my front border outside, so I moved most of the plants to other rooms in the house. I left a cluster of three plants in the nook, straight in my line of vision. By clearing the space of plants, I was able to take advantage of the unused prime sitting space in the room. Now, on Saturday mornings, I'm able to soak in the view of my front garden, enjoy the daylight on my face, and sit near my African violets, which bloom in beautiful shades of purple and magenta, cheering my mood.

WHAT SHOULD YOU GROW?

By now, hopefully you've determined what kind of light, humidity, and temperature your potential plant refuge area gets. If so, you now can have fun choosing your plant(s). Perhaps you've already decided based on reading chapter 11 and making the list of five plants. If you didn't, ask yourself a few questions. Will you grow one large plant on a stand? Multiple plants atop a rectangular table or bookcase beneath the window? A hanging basket with a plant? (I love those.) The choice is, excitingly, yours. If you're still stumped, though, do this very simple activity: go to a plant shop or nursery and show the clerks your notes about your light, humidity, and temperature conditions. They'll be able to help you choose the right plant for the space.

If you're inclined to grow more than one plant, I suggest you buy *three* plants. (Ha! An excuse for more, right?) But there's a good reason for this. When designing a garden, I use the rule of odd numbers. It's a standard design trick. You don't decorate your coffee table with just one candle, you create interest with three of varying sizes. In a garden, I don't plant only two hostas (unless I'm aiming for symmetry), I plant three or five or even seven. For some reason, grouping in odd numbers is more natural and appealing to the eye. So, unless you want a symmetrical look (which is totally fine, by the way), I suggest decorating your space with one, three, or five plants of varying sizes.

So, which to choose? Well, if you go with one container and one plant, go big. Make a statement. A tiny cactus can work if that's what you've got, but it doesn't create a strong focal point. A tall weeping fig (*Ficus benjamina*) or fiddle-leaf fig (*Ficus lyrata*) will remind you of its presence. Plus, large plants offer outstanding architecture, almost like a sculpture. Likewise, if you go with three plants, consider an upright, a mounding, and a trailing plant (See "Cozy Collection of Houseplants" activity). That combo offers contrasting textures, shapes, and color, and thus creates visual interest.

If you go with a cluster of five plants, you'll want two uprights; for a cluster of seven plants, then three uprights. Repeating shapes provides continuity and cohesion, making the scene harmonious.

If you've never grown houseplants before, I recommend starting with either one large plant or a group of three and see how you do. See "Five Easy Houseplants to Grow" for a list of easy-to-grow plants. Once you've chosen your plants, have fun decorating with your green babies. And if you're not decorating with live plants, see "A Green Leisure Lounge without Live Plants" for suggestions.

GIVING YOURSELF A GREEN LEISURE LULL

Now that you have your plant refuge in place, you can care for both it and yourself by creating a window of time in which to relax. A break, a breather, a lull in the action. Remember the slots of "Me Time" we created? Well, now's the time to revisit that and see if there's a recurring day in which you can spend time in your green leisure lounge.

What exactly do I do during my green leisure lull? Well, it's easy. There are two main parts. First, I visit my plants. Second, I relax among my plants.

WHAT TO DO (AND NOT DO) DURING AN INDOOR, GREEN LEISURE LULL

Do's

1. Do sit in the light, directly if you can.
2. Do breathe deeply and gaze at the greenery.
3. Do something crafty or creative.
4. Do read a physical, light book or magazine.
5. Do listen to relaxing or pleasant music.
6. Do smell healing scents.
7. Do enjoy a delicious snack.
8. Do talk to a favorite friend or relative.
9. Do write a letter or journal in your diary.
10. Do allow this simple time to be enough.

Don'ts

1. Don't keep your phone, tablet, or laptop nearby.
2. Don't check your texts, email, or groups.
3. Don't watch TV or videos.
4. Don't listen to frantic or aggressive music.
5. Don't pay your bills.
6. Don't make appointments.
7. Don't talk to someone who stresses you out (especially kids).
8. Don't obsess, worry, or think of the future or past.
9. Don't forget to feel grateful for this time.
10. Don't worry whether you're doing this activity "right."

VISITING

For me, visiting usually means checking on the plants. Seeing how they're doing. Enjoying their new growth or blooms. Rearranging or repotting. Also, watering, trimming, feeding. And so on. But not always. Sometimes I'll squeeze in an extra ten minutes of plant refuge time when no maintenance is required. But on days that it is, I start with my plant visit so my relaxation time isn't spent worrying about maintenance tasks.

PLANT CARE TIPS

If you've opted for a few easy-care houseplants to start, you'll only have to water your plants once every week or ten days. I water my plants on either Saturday or Tuesday. Tuesday afternoon if I forgot to water on Saturday. Sundays and Mondays are too busy with family and work for me. By having these days slotted for my plant care, I don't have to think about when or how I'm going to care for them. I just know that on Saturday mornings after I ride my trainer bike at about 9:30 a.m., I shower and care for my plants.

First, I get out my plant care kit, which consists of my watering can, a metal bucket, trowel, rubbing alcohol, and snips. I store it behind my biggest plant so I always know where it is. I fill my watering can with water. Always cold or tepid, never warm. If a plant takes in warm water, it's vascular system will turn to jelly and it'll wilt. So coldish water is good. Now, if it's the first Saturday of a new month, I add a little liquid all-purpose fertilizer to the water (except in November, December, and January). Then I make a round of all my plants. In my case, I have at least one plant growing in every room. I leisurely visit each one.

I look for dead flowers or leaves on the soil. I rake them with my fingers and toss them in my bucket. Then I soak the surface of each pot's soil fully but no more. I count to ten for a very large pot, to five for the average pot, and to three for small pots. After I've watered every plant around the house, I go back to the first plants I watered and check their trays. If there's no water, it means they were dry and really needed that water, so I water a bit more. This to me is easier than poking my finger or a chopstick in the soil to see if the soil's dry, though once in a while I do that. My other rule is that if it's been sunny and 75 degrees or warmer every day for a few days (think in terms of if you're thirsty, your plants are probably thirsty), I spot-check the plants on Tuesday afternoons after I'm done working and I want to get up and move around. In this situation, my elephant's ears will probably want water but my African violets won't. You can often tell by whether a plant's leaves are sagging or not.

After I water, I use my snips to cut off any brown stems or leaves on sick plants. If the plant has bugs, I cut off affected leaves and toss them in the outside compost. If the plant has a serious infestation, I treat it with rubbing alcohol. I dunk cotton swabs in alcohol and rub it over the leaves and stems. This kills whatever bugs have gotten the better of it. I toss the used swabs in my bucket. Sometimes you need to scrape off the top layer of soil to get rid of insects, but your plant will thank you by putting on new growth within weeks. And if a certain location isn't working, move the plant to another and see how it does. In the end, growing plants is trial and error. Don't be scared and don't feel bad if your plant dies. You tried. That's all that matters.

Lastly, I occasionally dust my plants' leaves. I wipe them down with a damp cotton cloth. Slowly and casually. This allows me to have a gentle bit of green intimacy with my plant, touching and stroking its leaves like I would a dog or cat's fur. During these moments, I'm able to calm down, visually absorb the beauty, and quietly ask the plant how it's doing.

RELAXING

After I've tossed the dead material in the compost outside and rinsed my bucket, I take ten to fifteen minutes to relax among my plants. The relaxation is a kind of eyes-open, green meditation. I set the timer on my phone to make sure I don't leave too soon (which is common if I'm stressed). I've already told my husband and kids that this is what's happening during my "Me Time," no debating it or blowing it off. It's important for my well-being.

First, I shut off my phone and leave it in a different room. Then I take a deep breath and cross that small threshold. In my case, it's the arch of my pocket doors. I close the doors behind me and sit in my window nook. Sometimes I light a pretty candle to denote the start of this special time. You could also ring a bell or chime. Or plug in a diffuser with Hinoki oil. Even eat a square of gourmet chocolate. Then, I position myself so the light shines on my body if possible. I breathe deeply for ten breaths. In summer, I open the window so I can hear the birds. Otherwise, I listen to whatever ambient noise is around me. I let the source of whatever it is be: airplane, car, kids, or so forth.

I take in the plants outside with intention, my eyes roaming from trees to shrubs to perennials, the sky. I note what's blooming or has lost its leaves or is being rained upon. I watch for birds, butterflies, bees, and bunnies. If I'm anxious and want to leave, I say aloud, "Relax for right now," and force myself to breathe another ten deep breaths. Sink into my own stillness. When my inner voice talks, I say aloud, "Not now. Later." Soon, my inner chatter fades away and I'm able to simply sit in silence. If that feels strange to you at first, keep doing it. You'll find that after a few months, your inner chatter will fade. Practice makes perfect! You'll have more quiet moments between the chatter, more moments of relaxed openness when you don't hear any voice in your head. Cherish those. They are healing you.

After this meditative time, I allow myself a bit more activity. But the activity is only what pleases and soothes me, nothing challenging, complex, or dark.

Remember, the reason to engage in a green leisure lull is to honor yourself. All week, you accomplish so much, so slow down during your "Me Time." Take time to enjoy no-goals *leisure*. Treat yourself well, not like the leftover errand you forgot to do, but rather the first fun activity on your agenda. Once you've restored your own attention and healed your soul, you'll feel like a whole, peaceful spirit. In turn, you'll have more patience and kindness for the people you love.

A GREEN LEISURE LOUNGE WITHOUT LIVE PLANTS

If you'd like to destress with greenery without growing plants, check out these ideas.

First, decorate with the color green. Muted or dark greens tamp down arousal. Research shows they calm stress in the brain. It's relaxing, evoking nature and growth. Studies also found that people feel optimistic when they see green.[2] Using it in fabrics, blankets, pillows, rugs, and drapes makes sense. Oddly, I rarely see it in home stores. There's a lot of taupe, putty, charcoal, cream, and brick but not green. It's interesting. We've overlooked our innate connection to this color. And it seems many décor possibilities in varying shades exist. Hopefully, in the future more folks will dial into the power of green!

Second, create a greenery space with artificial plants and plant imagery. See chapter 11 for artificial plants and image ideas. Arrange faux plants as you would live plants, in clusters of odd numbers or a mix of one vertical, one mounding, and one trailing, or different plants in same-colored pots. Decorate with plant photos and nature-related objects as you like. Together, they can form the view your eyes settle on during your green lounge lull.

Third, focus on an outdoor view. If you see trees, a park, lawn, shrubbery, a window box of flowers, or any greenery through your window, you can restore your attention by gazing at this "borrowed" natural space. To start, decide which view is best. If there's one window and one tree, that's fine. If there are a few, stand in each corner and look at the views. Which is broadest? Which makes you happiest? If the view is of a tree with a broken branch, skip it. You have to feel an "ahhh . . ." moment. Arrange a comfortable chair from which to enjoy your view. Do you have space for a small table and a drink or a book? (No devices.) The rest is simply a matter of creating your green leisure lounge lull. Resting. Breathing. Even napping. Enjoy the healing effects of nature.

ACTIVITY

Cozy Collection of Houseplants

RATING: **Soily hands, garden tools, indoors, higher cost ($70–$100)**

With this arrangement, you'll have a simple but striking collection of plant pets. Keep in mind, this "garden" can be planted together in one large pot or three separate pots, depending on your taste. If you want the plants' colors and textures to contrast and recall each other as they would in an outdoor bed, you'll want to plant all three together. One pot offers a cleaner look, but three pots can be a fun motif of color and interest. It's up to you.

In most container designs, you'll find a vertical plant, a filler plant, and a trailing plant. So, for aesthetic and maintenance reasons, I've chosen the following plants. They all tolerate indirect light by a window (think light sun or bright east/north side). Water the peace lily and pothos about every ten days (although peace lily may need a bit more) and the entire surface about every twenty days (snake plant needs less water). Together they will clean the air and create a tiny bit of oxygen.

What you'll need:

- One clay, ceramic, or plastic container, sixteen to twenty inches in diameter.
- One large bag of organic, all-purpose potting soil.
- One snake plant (*Sansvieria trifasciata*), quart or gallon pot. This is for height. You can get a dark one, a striped one, or whatever you prefer.
- One peace lily (*Spathiphyllum*), quart or gallon. This is your filler plant. A study out of Australia shows it can increase oxygen by 25 percent. Also, it produces lovely white flowers, really bracts, that will brighten your space.
- One golden pothos (*Epipremnum aureum*), quart or gallon. Not only is this the easiest pothos to grow, it also accepts lower light

conditions. It adds an interesting pop since its variegated foliage contrasts against the dark green of the peace lily.

1. Fill the container two-thirds with potting soil. Remove the snake plant from its pot and loosen the soil on the bottom, then set it near the back of the pot, spreading the roots outward a bit and leaving space for soil behind it.
2. Remove the peace lily and loosen its soil, placing it in front of the snake plant at the right, spreading roots a bit, and leaving a few inches of soil between plants.
3. Remove the golden pothos and loosen its soil, setting it in front of the snake plant at the left, spreading roots a bit and leaving space for soil in between.
4. Fill in with soil so the container's soil line is even with the soil line of the potted plants. Soak the surface until the water drains into the saucer below.
5. Position your container to receive optimal light and enjoy!

Chapter Thirteen

Creating an Outdoor, Green Leisure Lounge

When the world wearies, and society ceases to satisfy, there is always the garden.—Minnie Aumonier, artist

Several years ago, I got a call from my client James, which serves as a good lesson in making the most of your outdoor space. For years after moving from the East Coast, he'd lived in a tiny studio apartment because he'd been too busy to shop for a new home, let alone unpack all of his moving boxes. When he called me, he not only had settled into his new townhome, but he wanted an attractive, low-maintenance outdoor space he could use on the weekends. That outdoor space was a brick courtyard around his front entrance: a wide rectangular patio to the left of the door and a snug square of hardscape on the right. He had questions: Could he eat there and maybe even grow a few flowers or herbs? (He'd recently gotten into cooking.) Also, could he block out the traffic and the sight of a nearby gas station? Lastly, could the plants survive on their own (because with a busy job he had scant time to maintain them)? Most of my answers were yes.

I set about designing a plan. Since the courtyard faced east and was exposed to the south, it received strong sunlight in summer. But because a six-story building across the street blocked the east sun in winter, it would need hardier plants than usual. And since the courtyard was mainly brick and retained heat from the sun, it needed plants that were drought tolerant. And the privacy issue. And the herbs issue. And James didn't care for the few existing plants already there, "boring" grasses. This all needed to be taken into account.

I designed a garden for James that was sun loving but part shade in certain areas with a mix of shrubs, perennials, and herbs. Since he had a small patch of unplanted ground at the corner outside his fence, I planted a maroon elderberry, a yellow spiraea, and a low ceanothus. These were tough, drought-tolerant shrubs that screened the gas station and traffic. Inside the courtyard fence and along the house where only the thinnest strip of soil lined the front windows, I planted yellow Japanese forest grass, purple coral bells, blue hostas, and dark green hellebores. It was a combination that liked partial shade, could tolerate the cool temperatures of winter, and offered foliage color without the fertilizer or watering that fancier perennials required. Plus, the hellebores and grasses provided greenery and structure in winter. In between the perennials, I planted blue star creeper to create a thick mat of green and deter weeds. The plants softened the brick's straight edge and immediately beautified the front entry.

Because James had a table and chairs he used for eating outside, I created a border that was formal but low maintenance with daphnes, dwarf variegated grasses, and hebes. The daphnes, low mounded shrubs, offered a sweet fragrance that James and his guests would enjoy while dining. The grasses softened the fence and created interest with their blades cutting upward through the fence's horizontal lines. The small evergreen hebes provided formal structure, without the pain of hedging, and purple summer flowers.

The courtyard's north side was shadier. It had a Japanese maple and neighboring trees. With a few shade perennials dotting the understory, he didn't have much space to work with, about twelve by fifteen feet. So I planted a border around the snug patio with a few hostas, coral bells, and Japanese forest grasses, continuing the pattern from the south side and bringing cohesion to the entire space. But I still had the herb puzzle. There was no room on the front stoop and the two containers that flanked the door already had evergreen cypress trees he liked. What to do?

I noticed during our initial meeting that the center of the north brick patio received a lot of sun. That little square of bricks cooked in the daylight. I also noticed that he had a wide, attractive container stored along the home's side walkway. Since he liked the container (and had even grown perennials there without success), we opted to use it. I cleaned it up a bit, positioned it at the center of the north patio, filled it with fresh soil, and planted herbs. Voila! An instant mini herb garden.

Afterward, James fell in love with his courtyard. He hosted friends and told me he even enjoyed weeding and doing a little maintenance here and there. He liked having a private green space where he could read the newspaper and decompress from busy days. Plus, he loved the varying foliage of the perennials and said, "I never knew leaves could be so colorful!" I was glad. He discovered what many of my clients in the city had discovered: you don't need a lot of space to create an outdoor green leisure lounge where you can garden a bit and destress.

Two Questions to Ask about Your Outdoor Space

If you're thinking of turning your outdoor space into a green refuge, you need to ask two questions: what can my outdoor space provide and what do I want out of the space? Of course, those two things may be at odds. You may want a huge backyard in which to grow vegetables but only have a fire escape. You may want a patio with a grill and firepit but only have a courtyard. You may want a big ornamental garden of trees, shrubs, and perennials but have only a patch of lawn. You'll have to adjust your expectations. But that's okay. Believe me, a small space can be a blessing.

For instance, take my old apartment. What seems like eons ago, I had a 750-square-foot apartment in the Capitol Hill neighborhood of Seattle. It had zero outside space, no balcony, no courtyard, nothing. But it did face west. And I yearned to grow a few flowers I could cut for the table. One day, while talking with my husband, I told him how I wished the building had ledges for flower boxes like other buildings nearby. I'd always loved the colorful flower boxes that decorated the apartment buildings in Paris.

Being the smart guy he is, my husband figured out how to string up three flower boxes outside the windows. He threaded braided wire through the two drainage holes of each window's rim, wrapped the wires under the wooden boxes, and securely tied them. With a bag of soil, two six-packs of annuals, and a few perennials, I planted a tiny cutting garden. (Refer to the end of this chapter for a window box activity.) It wasn't much, but it was enough to beautify the view outside. Plus, it required only an easy, brief slice of time to care for. Its simplicity was a joy.

Every few days, I looked forward to watering those flowers. I'd open the windows wide enough to poke my head and watering can through and sprinkle my flowering babies. I loved being close to the green crowns of the street trees as I relaxed in the fresh air. My favorite memory of that time is of one sunny afternoon in particular. As I watered the flowers, I noticed my husband walking up the sidewalk. He emerged from under a tree, saw me up there and smiled, waved, and called out. I can still feel the warm breeze on my face.

TEN FAVORITE PERENNIALS

Years ago when preparing a blog post, I was surprised by the lack of a solid top-ten perennial list on the internet for most of the United States. So I compiled what I think are the prettiest but toughest workhorses in the garden.

1. Daylily (*Hemerocallis*), easiest perennial to grow, hardy to zone 3, requires little care. Blossom lasts for about a day with energetic, spear-like leaves.
2. Sage (*Salvia*) is known to be tender but 'May Night' (*salvia x sylvestris* 'May Night') is hardier to zone 4, with deep purple upright flowers that bloom most of summer.

3. Crocosmia (*Crocosmia*) is easy to grow in full sun, hardy to zone 5. Swordlike leaves and exotic flowers bloom for weeks.

4. Stonecrop (*Sedum*) has a broccoli-like appearance and emerges in rosettes before growing into a foot to a foot-and-a-half-wide stalks topped with flat flower heads. Stonecrop is hardy down to zone 4 and loves to bake in the sun in poor soil.

5. Tickseed (*Coreopsis*), yellow and sometimes orange, red, or bicolored flowers bloom all summer long, up to a foot high with little care and is hardy down to zone 4.

6. Phlox (*Phlox*), an old-fashioned mainstay, offers constant summer color in coral, red, and pink, likes supplemental water, and is hardy to zone 3.

7. Coneflower (*Echinacea*), late-emerging prairie flowers, are somewhat drought tolerant, with pink, orange, yellow, and white flowers, and hardy to zone 3.

8. Iris (*Iris*), Japanese or Siberian for beginners, with blue or purple flowers, likes water in summer, hardy to zone 4.

9. Black-eyed Susan (*Rudbeckia*) is late blooming, reliable, and hardy to zone 4. 'Goldsturm' is the classic yellow daisy-like flower with dark center; dried heads add structure in winter and seeds for birds.

10. Bee balm (*Monarda*) is a hummingbird and bee magnet with unusual flowers in magenta or pink, some powdery mildew in late summer/fall, and hardy to zone 3.

OUTDOOR SPACE CHOICES

So let's say you would like to create an outdoor green leisure lounge. If I were your designer and we were examining your home, we'd first figure out which outdoor growing space you'll use. The answer may be obvious if you have a balcony or small backyard. But you may be blessed with more than one option. So let's talk about each.

Window Boxes and Fire Escapes

Window boxes are the easiest and simplest of all. Some apartment buildings have brackets or slim balconies where apartment dwellers can keep planters. Averaging six inches by thirty inches of soil space, one window box could hold annuals, small perennials, some vegetables, or herbs. If you have a window box, you'll want to make sure you have a tray to catch your box's water so passersby on the sidewalk don't get an unexpected shower.

The next bigger area is a fire escape. Fire escapes of course are those metal balconies whose stairs connect apartment to apartment on large old buildings to give residents a way of escape in case their front doors are blocked by fire. But growing plants on fire escapes is tricky because storing containers there may be illegal, so look into your local laws. Having said that, occasionally an urban dweller will plant a container on a fire escape, leaving an open path so that a clear line of escape exists for neighbors in case of a fire. But again, look into it first. Your landlord or local fire department's website will probably have more information about what can be stored on a fire escape.

Balconies and Back Porches

Do you have a balcony or back porch? If so, you have a lot of options. Obviously, a balcony is that rectangular stretch of space attached to an apartment building designed for enjoying the outdoors. Its average size is about four by ten feet, which provides enough space to grow a very small tree, low shrubs, perennials, annuals, vegetables, or herbs, with room for a small sitting area.

Back porches are large, wooden balconies behind city apartment buildings connected by staircases. They were also used as fire escapes decades ago but were built to be larger, sturdier, and as a way for city dwellers to enjoy the outside air. (I've hung out on many back porches during my college years in Chicago.) They range from six to ten feet deep by up to twenty feet wide, giving you plenty of space for growing very small trees, shrubs, perennials, annuals, vegetables, or herbs. Porch daylight is trickier since they're always covered by the porch above or a roof, but some face south or west and grow plants just fine.

Roof Decks and Courtyards

Roof decks come in many shapes and sizes. They can be that square bit of space over an attached garage, a flat space above a neighboring apartment, or a shared space at the tippy top of a tall building. Whatever you might have, there are a lot of great options with a roof deck. They're often designed to hold more weight, making them capable of holding multiple containers, furniture, and people. If you do have a roof deck, I'd investigate what your building allows. While you might bump into restrictions, you also might be surprised to find that no one's using the roof and it's available for growing some plants.

A courtyard is usually a hardscaped area on the ground floor of a building, either at the front or back but sometimes on the side. Oftentimes, courtyards are public spaces, preplanted with trees and shrubs and perennials. Sometimes they're private with available space for those inclined to grow plants (like my client James), and sometimes they are managed by a condo association or the apartment residents. If you live in an apartment building with a common area that's planted, there may be flexibility to grow on that land or add to it with containers. In fact, like at my friend Bianca's condo association in Chicago, there may be an older garden caretaker resident who's ready to hand off the responsibility to someone younger with fresh energy and interest in gardening. By the way, because of her building's beautiful, lush courtyard and parking strips, the condominiums sell in a flash. Outdoor green refuges are a great way to increase home values!

Front Yards and Backyards

If you live in a townhome, attached duplex unit, or stand-alone house, you may have your own square of land, dirt in the ground. Huzzah! That land at the front, back, sides, and/or at the parking strip affords the opportunity to grow a wide variety of plants. If you do have land on multiple sides of your home, you'll have multiple mini-climates. This gives you a lot of flexibility in choosing where to set up your outdoor green leisure lounge.

CHOOSING THE BEST FROM MULTIPLE SPACES

Let's say you have a balcony *and* window boxes. Or you have a back porch *and* a backyard. How do you choose where to create your outdoor plant refuge? Well, if you live in an apartment, ask yourself, which space has the friendliest climate for growing plants? Which has the best exposure to the elements, the least wind, the most light, the most rain? If you don't know, go outside and look at what your neighbors on that side of the building are doing. Are they growing flowers in window boxes? Are they growing plants on their balconies? You might even ring their bell and inquire. The way to a gardener's heart is by complimenting their plants. Chances are, their choices or advice can guide you in your decision.

If you live in a townhome, duplex, or standalone home, also ask yourself, which side has the friendliest climate for growing plants? Where is it most sunny? Where does it often feel cool and shady? For instance, you may have a backyard, but it might be shaded by a neighbor's tree or garage, which might make your sunny back porch a better choice for an outdoor lounge area. Again, if you're not sure, go out to the alley and take a walk. Is anyone else growing anything on their back porch? Is anyone growing anything in their yard? If so, how is their space different or similar to yours?

If you do a bit of this fun field research, you'll know where the right place is. You'll feel it instinctually. And if you don't, don't fret. You can always change things around as you learn from experience. But for now, choose what you think is your strongest space.

Climate

Once you've decided on where your green leisure lounge will be, you'll need to assess the climate for your overall region and your particular space. You already kinda know your region's climate, because you live it every day, but for more formal information, check the US Department of Agriculture's (USDA) website (see the appendix for more information). The USDA has created zonal maps that help people decide what plants to grow according to what zone they live in. Your agricultural or growing zone denotes how well a plant will survive down to a particular temperature before it dies.

Now, remember, USDA zones aren't 100 percent accurate because they're based on average temperatures and don't get into the more granular factors of high temperatures, humidity, wind, soil types, and so forth. That said, the zonal map is a useful enough guide in determining what plants will survive a winter in your region. So the first task is to determine what zone you're in.

Once you know your climate zone, you'll need to decide your particular home zone or zones. This is based on how much light, wind, and humidity your outdoor space has. Let's take a look at each.

Light

Light, as mentioned, is the most important factor in growing plants. The first step is to figure out which way your outdoor growing space faces. When I visited James's garden, I glanced up in the sky, checked where the sun was, and what directions the courtyard was exposed to. It might be obvious which direction your outdoor space faces or not. If you don't know, you can either load a compass app onto your phone and stand where you'll be growing plants, or you can track the sun during the course of a clear day. The only drawback to tracking the sun's movement is that the sun will usually be higher in summer than in winter. Like James's courtyard, your space may have trees, buildings, or even a porch roof that blocks the sun's light. The best way to check is to log how many hours the sun hits your growing space on any given sunny day. If you're doing this in winter, factor in that the space will get even longer, stronger light in summer. You'll have an idea of whether you have full sun (six hours of sun), part sun (three to six hours), part shade (three to six hours with afternoon shade), or full shade (fewer than three hours a day). The good news is that you can grow plants in any of those light conditions!

Wind

One issue to consider carefully is wind. Those who live in tall apartment buildings may have balconies or roof decks, but those areas may be exposed to a lot of wind. In fact, a decent rule of thumb is, the higher you are, the more wind you'll probably experience, making roof decks the windiest of all urban spaces. Then again, you could have a fire escape that faces another tall building in which strong, high winds channel off buildings and blow through lower areas, creating a wind tunnel effect. To see if you have a wind tunnel effect, walk beneath or adjacent to where you're considering creating your lounge on a windy day. If the wind blows your hair back or you have trouble walking, you know you have strong winds.

Note that this doesn't mean you need to give up that space. Sturdy evergreen plants or attractive lattice can shelter your space. But it is useful to know from which direction your strongest winds usually come. If you do have a lot of wind, check out "Eight Plants for Windy Sites." Wind means your plants dry out more quickly and need more watering.

EIGHT PLANTS FOR WINDY SITES

Here are a variety of small trees, shrubs, perennials, and grasses that can take wind. They're all hardy to zone 5.

1. Prague viburnum (*Viburnum x pragense*), evergreen shrub
2. Rugosa rose (*Rosa rugosa*), pretty, tough-as-nails shrub rose
3. Creeping juniper (*Juniperus horizontalis*), low, bluish evergreen shrub
4. Daylily (*Hemerocallis fulva*), classic orange daylily, perennial
5. Yarrow (*Alchemilla mollis*), perennial flat-head flowers that attract butterflies
6. Switchgrass (*Panicum virgatum*), prairie grass with pretty bronze wands
7. Sea holly (*Eyringium alpinum*), prickly perennial with blue flowers
8. Thrift (*Armeria maritima*), cute groundcover with pink flower balls

---

Humidity and Water

Speaking of water, humidity and water are two more key areas to examine in your space. If you live in New Orleans, you already know your air is humid. If you live in Tucson, you know it's dry. If you live in Nashville, you might get both. That's not a problem, but it is helpful to know what plants like humidity and what plants don't. If you need more guidance, you can call your local extension program through a local university.

If you're *not* growing plants in the ground, you'll need to consider a regular watering schedule. Plants dry out more quickly in containers. The sun not only heats up the top of the pot, but also the sides, unlike the ground. Your plants will rely on you for supplemental water at the least, if not all of their water if grown under a porch roof. So factor in frequent water. Also, because containers require more water, they're usually in need of more fertilizing. The frequent watering leaches nutrients from the soil. Lastly, during hot weather, plants in containers can dry out within *one day* so in July and August, set a reminder to at least check the soil every day.

THE PIECES OF YOUR GREEN LEISURE LOUNGE

Now that you know what conditions you have in your outdoor space, the next question is, what kind of plants would you like to grow? Are you inclined to grow vegetables and fruits? Do you want to help pollinators like bees and birds by growing ornamentals with flowers? Do you want year-round greenery only? Or simply a shady spot in which to sit and drink a cup of tea? Well, with the right choices, all are possible.

Overall, I recommend creating a space for plants and a space for you. As we did inside, the best scenario is where you have a view with a cluster of plants and a sitting area in which to relax. The basics are the same but what you grow is different.

Containers

Obviously, the first thing you need for your space is containers. If you're growing plants in a window box, you'll want rectangular containers about the width of your window, or about a half-foot beyond the width of your brackets. If you're growing on a balcony or porch, you'll want square or round containers of varying sizes. Small trees of course need larger containers, shrubs, medium containers, and perennials and herbs, smaller containers. If you have the strength and help to haul them and set them up, consider creating fewer, larger containers with arrangements of plants, rather than a lot of pots with little plants. Fewer bigger pots makes a bolder aesthetic statement.

When choosing containers, ask yourself whether you're drawn to straight geometric styles, more traditional terra-cotta, or fancy, ornate décor. Look to the décor inside your house for hints. Whatever your style, you can find containers made of plastic, clay, glazed ceramic, or newer composite materials. Each has its own advantages and disadvantages. See "What Kind of Container?" for details.

As far as homemade containers go, remember that not everything that holds water makes for a good container. A metal bucket, for instance, will rust. A plastic paint bucket will contain chemical residue. Anything made of cloth or leather will degrade quickly. Wooden boxes or whiskey barrels will soften and fall apart (unless made of hardy teak or cedar from a specialty store). You can make lightweight hypertufa containers, which seem to work fine, but I recommend buying thick plastic, traditional terra-cotta, or glazed ceramic containers. Oftentimes, you can find these for free or at low cost on your neighborhood email lists or in online groups. Regardless, don't forget: the pot needs a drainage hole.

If you'd like to grow multiple plants in multiple containers, focus on obtaining various sizes. You can use containers of the same color but different styles or different colors but the same style. (You can also do this with flower colors.) Or you can just go nuts and buy a random collection of stuff that pleases you.

WHAT KIND OF CONTAINER?

The type of container your plants are living in can make a big difference in how well they thrive. Containers that have a hole at the bottom are meant to be set atop a tray for overflow water. Containers that don't have a hole can be used as the overflow tray. However, I've found these sometimes do not dry out quickly enough and can grow mold or attract bugs. You might have to experiment.

Here are some pros and cons to each material.

Type of Container	Cost	Attractiveness	Durability	Advantage/ Disadvantage
Plastic	Low	Obviously artificial but can be attractive	Decent to good (a few years, depending on thickness)	Variety of colors, retains water well, lightweight, may fade and crack
Wood	Moderate	Rustic and attractive	Good (five years, depending on weather)	Natural look, retains water well, can rot quickly
Terra-cotta	Low	Classic and attractive	Good (can crack in colder climates)	Classic European look, doesn't hold water well
Glazed ceramic	High	Classic and very attractive	Excellent (rarely cracks or fades)	Available in a wide variety of styles, holds water well, can break, often heavy
Fiberglass/ composite	High	Modern and attractive	Good (doesn't crack but can fade)	Chic look, holds water well, lightweight, color fades over time

Whatever the case, cluster pots of various sizes together to create a cool interesting vignette.

One important thing to remember: if you're clustering pots together, make sure the little pots aren't shaded from the sun by the larger pots. This will require some experimenting unless you already know the angle of the sun.

If you're growing vegetables, it's better to grow them in lower, wider containers. Troughs or raised-bed planters (usually made of metal, wood, or vinyl) are best. You can order reasonably priced, easy-to-put-together raised bed kits online or you can line cinderblocks closely together to make inexpensive beds. With such a setup, roots can spread out and capture more nutrients. Also, you'll want the soil space to insert tomato cages, trellises, and maybe even hoops over which to attach plastic. Depending on how many plants you want to grow, you'll need one to three troughs or raised beds.

TEN EASY VEGETABLES AND FRUITS TO GROW

1. Peas (cooler weather, early crop, needs trellis)
2. Lettuce (cooler weather, early crop, pick before it bolts)
3. Onions (cooler weather, early crop, can grow into fall)
4. Carrots (cooler weather, pick in fall)
5. Beans (sun, summer crop, needs trellis)
6. Tomatoes (summer crop, needs cage for support)
7. Cucumbers (afternoon shade, needs cage or trellis)
8. Raspberries (sun, spreads rapidly in ground)
9. Blueberries (afternoon shade, great fall color)
10. Strawberries (sun, spreads rapidly in ground)

Soil

Don't skimp on a decent soil. The minerals and nutrients in soil are what enable your plants to grow happily and your food to taste delicious. You'll want to buy a nutrient-rich, well-draining soil. Organic potting soil is fine, but if you want to boost your nutrient intake, I'd add some organic compost to the mix. About one-third compost mixed into two-thirds potting soil is a fine proportion, especially if you're growing vegetables and fruits. (You can't use only compost because that will burn roots. And messing with chicken manure and bone meal is for more advanced gardeners.) If you're growing desert plants like succulents and cacti, then you'll want a lighter soil, like cactus mix. Don't buy a prefertilized, extra-water-retaining, pizzazzy mix. Beware of those. They often contain weird plastics or additives.

When filling your containers, don't use a terra-cotta chip or stone to cover the hole at the bottom. Dirt may bleed through a couple times, but that's what you want: draining water. You don't want to plug a hole. Also, I wouldn't use Styrofoam peanuts or anything like that to lighten a pot. Roots get tangled in those peanuts and they don't add nutrients to your soil. Even with permeable landscape fabric, that situation just becomes a yucky mess. (I've detangled other gardener's pots in frustration many times.) Give your plants all the nutrients you can by filling the entire pot with soil. If it's heavy, pop for a plant dolly so you can move it around. Otherwise, put little pot holder feet under the container so air can pass under the bottom and dry it out.

ARRANGING YOUR PLANTS

Let's say you're going to go for that one-large-container arrangement. Great! The advantage of a large container is you can create a miniature garden by combining the colors, textures, and scents of various plants. You'll need a vertical plant at the back, a mounding plant or two in front, a few flowering perennials, and some kind of trailing plant. For a container that offers structure year-round, pretty flowers, nectar for pollinators, and foliar interest see the "Almost Anywhere, U.S.A., Birds, Bees, and Butterflies Container" activity.

If you're planting multiple containers, you can use crates or those black polypropylene pots turned upside down to add height if you need to, hiding them with other pots and foliage. Just make sure to place your cluster within the sun's angle so all pots receive sunlight (unless you've accounted for that by planting shade plants).

If your plants will be on a roof deck, you may need to arrange containers to protect them from wind. This is important. If you need to plant a long planter with a row of dwarf upright yews or junipers (evergreen shrubs) or a trellis with a vine to protect your plant arrangement, I encourage you to invest in that. It can make the difference between failure and success.

When choosing plants, a good rule of thumb is to investigate what gardening experts in your area have grown. Usually, they'll have blogs or books about their gardens in your town or region. If so, check those out. Local gardening experts, preferably those who advocate for organic gardening, will have much more granular information. If you're not sure whose advice to follow, call your local nursery or university extension office and see if someone there has a recommendation. See the appendix for some sites I like to read.

Sitting Area Ideas

After creating a lovely container of plants, ask yourself what you'd like to do in your green leisure lounge. If your only aim is to relax, that's great! But since you're outside, you may feel a bit more active or social. You can use your refuge for solitary relaxation as well as other activities (see "What to Do [and Not to Do] during an Outdoor Green Leisure Lull" for ideas). Do you want to drink tea with your sweetheart? Do you want a bistro table and chairs to enjoy dinner with a friend? Maybe you have the space for a couple benches or an arrangement of outdoor furniture where you and several friends can hang out. Whatever the design, having a sitting area where you can aimlessly recline and rest is key.

Once you've decided what you want, make sure to measure the space and buy accordingly. There's nothing worse than buying a big honking chair, hauling it up to your apartment, and then realizing it's too big for the space! So measure the space and measure the furniture at the store. Remember too that you don't have to spend

a lot of money. I once found an old wooden Adirondack chair on the street for free. Another time, I bought a super comfy love seat during a home store's clearance sale in August. Also, thrift stores, Craigslist, and online groups often sell or give away outdoor furniture for little money. And you don't need much. A good old-fashioned chaise lounge and a wine crate can work!

In terms of arrangement, there may be a few options. If you have a balcony, chances are you can have your planter(s) in one corner of the balcony and your sitting nook in the opposite corner. Look for hooks or rails where you can attach hanging baskets or planter boxes. On a roof deck, you may have more room to play with. For instance, you could arrange your containers in one corner and your furniture in an L shape across from it. Or create four low "walls" of plants around a central sitting area. In a courtyard, two Adirondack chairs could be angled to take in the view of a border of plants or a dining table and chairs centrally located in the middle so that everyone can enjoy the surrounding view of greenery. And if you have a backyard with a lawn, arrange your chairs to take in the broadest and most pleasant green view.

Conversely, if you can arrange your sitting area to take advantage of a larger view of neighboring tree crowns or another pleasing vista, do that. If there's a purple-leaf maple in the next property over, consider whether you can set your plant arrangements against that backdrop. A glimpsed water view? Yes, please. Conversely, if you have an unwanted view of a cell phone tower or cement plant (I have a neighbor with a bright blue garage roof), try to either screen the view with plants or shift your seating area away from that view. Seeing industrial, shabby, or obviously unpleasant views will heighten your stress, not lower it. Instead, you want to gaze on your greenery so you can lose yourself in its magic. I mean, you don't want to miss when that first bee discovers your flowers or your first tomato ripens with red color!

GIVING YOURSELF AN OUTDOOR, GREEN LEISURE LULL

Now that you have an outdoor green refuge, you might want a regular ritual so you'll take fullest advantage of it. As I mentioned in chapter 12, my own green leisure lull consists of first visiting my plants and then relaxing among them.

WHAT TO DO (AND NOT TO DO) DURING AN OUTDOOR GREEN LEISURE LULL

Do's

1. Do sit where you have the most desirable green view.
2. Do smell the scents of flowers, soil, and wind.
3. Do spend time with a favorite friend or relative.
4. Do something crafty or creative.
5. Do read a physical, light book or magazine.
6. Do listen to relaxing or pleasant music.
7. Do enjoy a delicious snack.

8. Do play an easy game with someone you like.
9. Do write a letter or journal in your diary.
10. Do relax into the greenery. Let it be enough.

Don'ts

1. Don't do outdoor chores.
2. Don't talk to someone who stresses you out (especially not-nice neighbors)
3. Don't be annoyed by everyday outdoor sounds.
4. Don't keep your phone, tablet, or laptop nearby.
5. Don't check your texts, email, or groups.
6. Don't watch videos.
7. Don't listen to frantic or aggressive music.
8. Don't pay your bills.
9. Don't make appointments.
10. Don't obsess, worry, or think of the future or past.

If you already have created an indoor green leisure lull, you can extend or exchange that time on your calendar for your outdoor experience. You may prefer to pop outside and relax for twenty minutes whenever you can, but designating time on your calendar ensures that you always make the time to treat your plants and yourself well. As I mentioned, I mark off Saturday morning. Then any outdoor gardening time is gravy. So look for that "Me Time" on your calendar and see if you can mark it with the letters "PR" for plant relaxation time or "GL" for green leisure.

As I mentioned, first visit the plants, check on them, and enjoy. Play around a bit. Then care for them. First, get out your plant care kit. The care kit could be similar to the indoor kit: a watering can, a bin for trimmings, gloves, a trowel, and in this case, pruners. First, with gloves on, inspect leaves for holes or insects. If you see bugs disperse when you brush the plant, you'll have to water less or pull the plant out into the sunlight and open air. Then snip off any brown leaves and dying or dead stems. If the plant dropped leaves, rake those up with your hands and dispose of them. If you're unsure of the plant's illness, you can use an app to try and diagnose the problem. Or you can take a photo and bring it to your local nursery person or master gardener. They can help with remedies.

Also, you may want to adjust the position of your containers if the light's changed in the last few weeks. If it's spring and the sunlight became stronger, adjust the plants to either take advantage of the light or shade them, depending on what you're growing. If it's fall and the cold wind has become stronger, adjust the container locations so they're more protected from wind. Use this time to make those small changes.

After you've tidied your plants, water them in "rounds" as I mentioned in chapter 12. After that, it's time to relax! But before you sit down, take a moment to acknowledge the effort you made. Take in the beauty you created. I mean, what a wonderful accomplishment! Look at those gorgeous plants! Aren't the green leaves lush and cheery? Remember, caring for your plants is like caring for yourself. You're snipping off the spent branches and leaves the plant no longer needs before providing the right light, water, and nutrition to help it thrive. And in your own life, you're pruning away stress so you can grow into a more relaxed, fulfilled soul.

To honor your new leisure lounge, consider doing the "Five-Minute, Five-Breath Fractal Meditation" from chapter 5. Allow yourself to sink into the moment. Look at the complex textures, the colors and shapes. Feel the cool or warm air. Listen to the sounds of your surroundings, the birds, the wind, the traffic. Don't judge. Don't think. Feel your breath rise and fall. What do you smell? If you need a mantra, think, "Hello, lovelies," or "Happy garden," or another phrase of your choosing.

After you've relaxed during your "Me Time," you can fit in other healing activities however you like. At other times you could read a book, call your mom on the phone, knit, draw, or chat with your spouse. Whatever you do, make sure it's something that charges you with good energy, not stress or worry. No debates or dread. And no random interruptions. Don't answer the phone. Don't change the laundry because you forgot earlier; try to remember to do that beforehand. Don't make a mental list of all that you have to do (my specialty). If you have small kids, don't let them overrun this time.

Tell them beforehand that you need thirty minutes of rest and unless they're bleeding, you're unavailable. They'll survive. And if you take time for this relaxation, so will you.

Lastly, when diving into creating an outdoor green leisure lull, have fun with it. Make it a meaningful activity according to *your* taste. Enjoy all the steps. What you're doing is *leisure* and that's as important as work. Don't forget to make it a priority. Feed your soul with what makes you happy. It's all about you, your beautiful plants, and the given day.

ACTIVITIES

Part-Sun Window Box Garden

RATING: Soily hands, gardening tools, outdoors, moderate cost ($50–$100)

This is a window box arrangement for locations that receive sun part of the day, but not harsh afternoon sun. If you're a beginner and want an easy bold-colored combo, try Plum Pudding coral bells (perennial), Ann Folkard geranium (perennial), Victoria Blue salvia (annual), and orange New Guinea impatiens (annual). If you want an easy herb box, plant basil (annual), lemon thyme (perennial), trailing rosemary (perennial), and oregano (perennial). Here's how.

What you'll need:

- one window box, approximately eight by thirty inches (size can vary)
- 1 large bag of potting soil
- four annuals, perennials, or herbs of your choice (four-inch pots)

1. Before you do anything else, measure. Think in terms of how many four-inch pots you'll need for one box, then multiply that number by how many boxes you're planting. For an eight-by-thirty-inch

window box, I plant four or five plants (annuals, perennials, vegetables, or herbs) from four-inch containers.

2. In the window box, remove any stickers or tags. Pour the potting soil evenly in box, leaving about an inch or more of space at the top.
3. Space out your plants evenly. If you have taller plants (like salvia), put those either at the center or spaced in varying order with the mounding plants (like coral bells), so that the plants alternate: upright, mounding, upright, mounding. For instance, basil, thyme, basil, thyme.
4. Dig a small hole for each plant with a trowel or your hand.
5. Loosen the roots on each plant, making sure to separate roots if they're bound together. Set the plants in the holes and cover with soil.
6. Tuck them in.
7. Water them.
8. Set a reminder to water every few days. If it's hot, water every day.
9. Enjoy your cheery window garden!

Almost Anywhere, U.S.A., Birds, Bees, and Butterflies Container

RATING: Soily hands, gardening tools, outdoors, higher cost ($80–$150)

Here's a full-sun container that provides bold summer color while feeding bees, butterflies, and hummingbirds. It's on the purple, magenta, and orange end of the color wheel and should visually pop but blend into a harmonious palette. Except for the petunias, all plants are hardy to at least USDA zone 5.

What you'll need:

- one clay, ceramic, or plastic container, eighteen to twenty-four inches in diameter (size can vary). A black container will create a chic dark backdrop for the bold leaf and flower colors.
- one large bag of potting soil
- six or seven plants: one tall narrow shrub (one gallon pot), one low mounding shrub (one gallon), three perennials in quart-size pots, and one or two annuals (four-inch pots)

Recommended plants:

- Blue Arrow juniper (*Juniperus scopulorum* 'Blue Arrow') for tall narrow evergreen with a bluish color
- Soft-touch Japanese holly (*Ilex crenata* 'Soft Touch') for deep green color and fall berries for birds only
- Butterfly weed (*Asclepias tuberosa*) for upright orange color and to attract butterflies
- Thumbelina Leigh dwarf English lavender (*Lavandula angustifolia* 'Thumbelina Leigh') for upright purple color and to attract bees
- Ann Folkard geranium (*Geranium* 'Ann Folkard') for rambling magenta color and to attract bees and butterflies
- Supertunia Royal Magenta Petunia (*Petunia* 'Inpetroyma') for rambling magenta color at back and to attract hummingbirds

1. Fill the container two-thirds with potting soil. Remove the Blue Arrow juniper from its pot, loosen the soil on the bottom, then set it near the back of the pot, spreading the roots outward a bit and leaving space for soil behind it.
2. Remove the Japanese holly and loosen its soil, setting it in front of the juniper, spreading roots a bit, and leaving a few inches of soil between the plants.
3. Remove the Ann Folkard geranium, loosen its soil, and place it in front of the Japanese holly, spreading roots a bit. This will eventually spill over the container's edge.
4. Remove the dwarf English lavender, loosen its soil, and set to the right of the geranium.
5. Remove the butterfly weed, loosen its soil, and set to the left of the geranium.
6. Remove the petunias, loosen their soil, and tuck in behind the dwarf English lavender and butterfly weed. These will spill over the container's sides.
7. Fill in with soil so that the soil line is even with the soil line of the potted plants. Soak the surface until the water drains into the saucer below.
8. Position your container in full sun, water every other day in summer, and enjoy the cheery colors and birds, bees, and butterflies!

Chapter Fourteen

———————— 🖋 ————————

Maintaining Nature's Magic

Nature is not a place to visit. It is home.—Gary Snyder, poet

On the island of Maui, an extraordinary botanical feat grows. I first discovered it in the early 2000s when my husband and I toured the Kula Botanical Garden. The sight of it took my breath away. A spectacular, living tunnel of butterfly bushes.* Multiple massive shrubs had grown together, intertwining to form an enclosed dome overhead that visitors could pass underneath. There was no arbor, no structure to hold the tunnel up, just a huge interweaving of branches. Jammed with yellowish-orange blossoms, the tunnel spanned about twenty feet long. Dark beneath and wildly colorful up top. Its gigantic domed girth reminded me how small I actually was in the scheme of nature.

When I came home to Seattle, I told Angela about it. A few years later, on a trip to Hawaii, she visited the spectacular dome as well. After she came home, she felt the same awe I'd felt. We decided that at least one of us had to grow a butterfly bush dome in our gardens. It was too cool not to. Angela already had a noninvasive butterfly bush growing in the perfect spot. She had wisely

———————————————

*I was unable to confirm if this butterfly bush is *buddleia madagascariensis*, which is listed as an invasive species in Hawaii. So I don't recommend growing this variety in warm weather states.

211

planted it between her front porch and a side walkway so she could enjoy it either while eating dinner or as she roamed the garden. Since it was already about seven feet tall, we decided to try the dome in her yard. She purchased another noninvasive butterfly bush and we planted it on the opposite side of the path. Then we twined a few of the tallest branches together to create an overhead arch. Nature did the rest.

Once again, we were playing in the garden. My original love for that shrub had grown not only into a passion for plants but into gaining horticultural knowledge and meeting a fellow nerd whose love for plants was as strong as mine. Like me, she yearned to experience the sensory joys of plants, to play with them, and recognized their worth in forwarding the cause of restoring our connection to nature, all while gaining the physical and mental health benefits. The butterfly bush dome represented my journey of green leisure come full circle.

A MODERN SOCIETY THAT DOESN'T SUPPORT LEISURE

So how can you, who by now might have discovered your need for leisure with nature, continue to leaf your troubles behind on a regular basis? Well, to my mind, the first step is to acknowledge its importance. Make time for green leisure, even for fifteen minutes. In America, we work, we raise kids, run errands, attend meetings and events, maybe exercise, accomplish, accomplish, accomplish, but we don't take enough *time off*. The government doesn't encourage it and we don't do it. The US government doesn't mandate paid time off for vacation or holidays. Nor paid sick leave. Many corporations offer it, but it's not *required*. I could open a business, hire you as an employee, and then expect you to work every day that I want, even if you're sick. If you don't, I could fire you. Isn't that sad?

Even when employers offer extra paid vacation days off, chances are you don't take them. A US Travel Association study found workers did not take 768 million days in 2018 that they could have. An incredible 236 million days were completely lost, meaning Americans couldn't roll over the time into the next year. Finally, 55 percent of Americans reported not using their given number of days off.[1] A 2019 *Turnkey* survey found more than 73 percent of Americans felt guilty for taking time off.[2] We didn't feel this way years ago. In fact, a *Harvard Business Review* article found "Americans used to take almost three weeks of vacation a year (20.3 days) in 2000, but they took only 16.2 days of vacation in 2015."[3]

I don't know the reason for this trend, but I suspect it has to do with corporations pressuring employees to work harder, faster, and longer. Yet salaries have increased very little during these last thirty years. The Pew Research Center says unless you're a high earner, your weekly wages, adjusting for inflation, have barely increased since the 1980s.[4] Some researchers blame the rising cost of health care, the decline of unions, lagging education, and other factors, but the bottom line is the middle and lower classes are working harder but not earning more.

ESTABLISHING THE HEALTHY HABIT OF GREEN LEISURE

This is a good argument for taking time off. If you do have paid time off, even more so. But how do we get into the habit of changing our ways? Well, guidance comes from one of my favorite books, *Atomic Habits* by James Clear (see appendix for more recommended reading). It's a simple, straightforward, convincing book about how to build good habits and break bad ones. Though I can't speak to your bad habits, I can help you create the positive one of taking time out for no-goals leisure with nature. Clear offers a four-pronged formula for creating a habit. He says you must make your new habit obvious, attractive, easy, and satisfying. So let's apply that to starting a habit of taking time for plant-oriented leisure time.

Think back to chapter 3 and your exploration of your favorite nature activities. Let's say you discovered you want to walk in the woods as your green leisure time, but you don't have woods outside your door. The woods are thirty minutes away. In that case, you'll have to commit to setting aside travel time. In total, you'll need one and a half to two hours: a half hour each way for travel time, then about a half hour to an hour for walking. This demands that you book about two hours of "Me Time" on your calendar, *regularly*, to do it. That's fine. It's certainly not impossible but it's not that easy.

Let's say you have to arrange a babysitter for your kids, schedule or book transportation (drive a car, take a ride share, bus, train, etc.), and buy the coats and boots you'll need for rough terrain. Again, no biggie if that's what you're into. But if not, you might want to ask yourself if this outing is a better means of green leisure than, say, a walk in a nearby park. The point is to make the activity obvious, attractive, easy, and satisfying. If a walk in the woods thirty minutes away still meets your criteria, go for it! If not, be easy on yourself and start out small.

One other scenario: let's say you have a townhome with a backyard. Right now, it's a patch of boring lawn with small strips of dirt surrounding it on three sides of a fence. But you'd like to create an outdoor green refuge with three mixed borders of trees, shrubs, and perennials, replace the lawn with a hardscape and patio, and add a nice dining table, chairs, and a lounge chair near a fountain. Even outdoor party lights. If you do that, you'll have created an outstanding green experience. It will be fantastic and definitely increase your chances of keeping a green leisure habit. It will be obvious (you can see it from your window), attractive (the plants and sitting areas will beckon you), and certainly satisfying (you'll be surrounded by a lovely sanctuary outside your door). But is it, after the time and cost involved, *easy*?

Well, it will be once it's finished, right? But in the short term, it's not. And if you don't have a lot of experience with gardening, you may put it off until it never happens. Or get involved, become frustrated, and want to abandon all things green forever. Instead, I suggest you do what I've always recommended to my clients: simplify your aims. Prioritize. What features of the courtyard bother you the most? What do you *want* to do in your courtyard the most? Since the priority is to get some plants and their healing properties into your life, I'd suggest focusing on growing plants in those empty borders along the fence and getting a lounge chair. Leave the hardscaping, dining table, and fountain for phase two of your plant refuge plan. Modifying large ambitions into smaller, attainable goals works well. This way, you'll be able to easily and immediately begin restoring your attention and lowering your stress through plants.

Another key I've found in creating a good habit is to identify a trigger that helps you do that activity, automatically without thinking. Journalist Charles Duhigg identified how our brains work with triggers and habits. We get a cue or reminder to do something, then we crave and act on it in a routine, and we receive a reward.[5] It's important we get a cue that triggers a positive response in order to form a good habit. So ask yourself what can be your trigger to start your regular green leisure habit?

For instance, if a walk in the woods is your green leisure (GL) activity, then you'll need a cue to trigger the activity. James Clear says triggers can be based on time, location, a preceding event, other people, or an emotional state. For instance, if you know that you want to walk in the woods, you could use noticing the trees (location) outside your window every Saturday morning (time) as you eat breakfast (preceding event) before you and your spouse, who is putting on his hiking boots (people), head out so that you can leave behind the workweek's stress and feel content (emotion). In this case, I worked in all of the triggers but you need only one to launch your GL activity. It could be noticing your GL mission statement on the fridge or getting an automated reminder through your phone. In my case, every day when I open my bedroom curtains and see the fir trees outside the window, I do my "Five-Minute, Five-Breath Fractal Meditation" activity. Opening the curtains to the outside view is my cue.

In the plant refuge scenario, your trigger might be smelling your coffee in the morning. Or noticing a comfy sweater on a hook, the sweater you always wear when you water your plants. Through a window, you might see your empty chair and beautiful plant pets waiting outside for you. You may hear the breeze blow in leaves and think, *Time for my tree walk.* Whatever the trigger, create an alluring one so it spawns your craving to relax amid greenery. Over time and with repetition, that habit loop will deepen, and you'll feel more attached and devoted to the ritual. During your green leisure lull, try your best to soak in the peaceful feeling you experience. The memory will motivate you to do it again and make it a part of everyday life.

WHAT IS THE ULTIMATE GREEN LEISURE ACTIVITY?

What if, after all the journaling and reading and exploring, you still crave the ultimate green leisure activity? The most bang for your buck, so to speak. What if you want one activity that encompasses all of the destressing strategies? What is the *ultimate* green leisure activity?

I'll tell you straightaway: volunteering at a botanic garden. First, you'll certainly *learn* about plants. Though I've been in the industry for a long time, I'm not familiar with all of the new or faraway cultivars that public gardens grow. You'll *experience* the sights, sounds, smells, and feel of the garden, engaging your senses and enabling you to breathe deeply in the fresh air. You'll *idly play* and have fun, helping the staff gardeners create new and interesting features. You'll of course *support* a worthy cause in maintaining plants for the public and *unite* with some wonderful people. I can attest that gardeners are usually very kind. Also, you'll *recognize* how wonderful it is to spend time in such a pretty setting for such a worthy cause. Lastly, you'll *exercise* by moving your body and feel tired but satisfied by the day's end. Those are some great reasons to be leisurely in a botanic garden!

Whatever you do, make your GL time obvious, easy, attractive, and satisfying. If you're trapped inside a little white screen for hours at a time, make it a point to close your laptop and get outside. As forest bathing researcher Qing Li notes, "Our eyes weren't designed to look at screens. . . . Nature is what we have been accustomed to looking at."[6] Set a timer for fifteen minutes and sit beneath a tree. Eat lunch in a park. Rent those kayaks you've been talking about. Maybe a butterfly bush won't change your life but sharing your life with a philodendron might. Lazing in a hammock wouldn't hurt. Every little bit helps. The science tells us so. And as James Clear says, all of our "atomic" or micro-habits add up to not only one larger routine, but also a new, better identity.

A new identity. Wow! You have the enormous power to transform yourself. Are you one of those people who will "leaf" your troubles? And by "leaf," I mean connect with nature to get happy? I think you might be. So now I ask what will you choose to kick off this transformative journey?

THE WORLD IS A NATURE DISTRIBUTOR

I'm reminded of an art installation I saw in Paris in 2017. At the Jardin Botanique de Paris in the Jardin des Serres d'Auteuil, our family visited the lovely conservatories. Tucked away in the back of one greenhouse was a vending machine. At first, I thought it was your typical soda or candy machine but as I approached, I noticed there were chunks of plant material nestled in between the spiral rings. Some real, some artificial. A hydrangea head, a magnolia flower, seed packets, poppies, and more. Though the plants each held a symbolic representation, the idea of this vending machine, called "Le distributeur de nature," or the nature distributor, is very literal to me.

The natural world is like your own personal vending machine of choices. Flowers, trees, seeds. Forests, prairies, deserts, swamps. Fake plantery, houseplant collections, backyard gardens. It's all out there. Ready for you to be as carefree as you were as a kid. Ready to welcome you into its healing magic. To indulge in that aimless state of mind where time and goals don't exist. Where your body is at ease and your attention simply exists. Restore and revitalize your wholesome spirit. Feel like you've got this life thing once again. Remember, plants don't have expectations or harsh demands. They don't gossip; they don't judge. They simply live their sweet lives and create soothing greenery to help you honor what Mary Oliver called in her poem "The Summer Day," "your one wild and precious life."

Are you ready to push the buttons on the nature distributor machine, choose the letter-number combo that turns the spiral and drops your natural treat? What will it be? Maybe to start, you'll frame a vacation photo of palm trees, grow a cutting for a friend, plant a huckleberry, picnic under an oak, walk among mesquites, or canoe amidst the cypress. It doesn't really matter. What matters is you're putting your mental health first. Helping your being be well. Learn, experience, idly play, support, unite, recognize, and exercise to live a life fully worth living. So what will you choose? The good news is the nature distributor is free. It charges no money. No quarters required. It's ripe with choices and freely gives. And when you do commit, when you honor your life, you'll not only destress and heal your soul, you'll leaf your troubles behind and a pure, boundless joy will bloom.

Acknowledgments

This book began as a fun, pass-the-time project. My friend Gretel, a longtime nonfiction editor, needed a practice client for a coaching certification program, and I, feeling lost about what to do during the pandemic, needed an excuse to write "that book about plants and mental health" I'd had in my mind for years. Through her vast experience and steady guidance, I clarified my vision and shaped this book. It was an unexpected yet precious way to get through a lot of sadness in my life during 2020. Friendships are valuable, so much so that sometimes with a friend's support, you do your best work. So first off, I can't express enough gratitude for Gretel Hakanson (www.gretelhakanson.com). I'm in awe of your patience, your ability to keep a stable perspective, your professional and personal wisdom, and your gushing support (which I know only comes when real). Thank you, my dear friend.

Thanks to my wonderful husband Ethan, who acts as if my talent is obvious and not to be questioned. Also, I want to acknowledge my kids who always are ready to make their own dinner or clean up when I need help. Thank you to Kara Fellows, who rendered these illustrations with such a cool, modern, playful eye. (You draw exactly as I would if I could!) Thanks to my friends Hemu and Kimberly, who gave me feedback and cheered me on. Thanks to my agent, the sharp, upbeat Jill Marsal, who makes a busy work life look easy. To my editor, Jake Bonar, for his enthusiastic, adept support, and to everyone at Prometheus Books who helped bring this book to life. Thanks to all the fellow gardeners and nature lovers who shared healing stories, and lastly, thank you, lovely soul, for reading!

Appendix
Branching Outward

Here are some resources if you'd like to dive further into leafing your troubles behind. I've included favorite online sites, some notable botanical gardens, reputable plant resources, and a suggested reading list.

FAVORITE PLANT IDENTIFICATION AND INFORMATION APPS

I like apps that don't force me to jump through hoops or sign up for limited free trials before allowing me to use the service. The apps below work fairly well for identifying plants and providing information about them. They all work better with close-up photos. One note: if you want care instructions and reminders, choose apps like Planta or PictureThis. They're super useful, but they charge fees. In the meantime, I recommend the following four.

1. Seek by iNaturalist: accurate plant identification, allows you to scan rather than photograph, also identifies wildlife, respects privacy, great for kids, created by the partnership of the California Academy of Sciences and National Geographic Society. No ads.

2. PlantNet: accurate plant identification with other photo suggestions, a citizen science project to identify plants from around the world, a huge database you can add to, fun groups to join, and run by the Agropolis Foundation in France. No ads.
3. PlantIdentify: clean and simple to use, accurate plant identification, easily keeps track of what you've photographed, good for casual explorers. Will prompt you to upgrade to a subscription.
4. LeafSnap: simple-to-use, accurate, fast plant identification, plays short ads.

MASTER GARDENER AND EXTENSION PROGRAMS

To find master gardener and university extension programs in your local area, visit the Extension Master Gardener website: https://mastergardener.extension.org/contact-us/find-a-program/. It links to programs in all fifty states.

TWENTY NOTABLE BOTANICAL GARDENS TO VISIT IN THE UNITED STATES

1. The Arnold Arboretum, Boston, Massachusetts: www.arboretum.harvard.edu
2. New York Botanical Garden, New York, New York: www.nybg.org
3. The Biltmore Estate, Ashville, North Carolina, www.biltmore.com/visit/biltmore-estate
4. Atlanta Botanical Garden, Atlanta, Georgia: www.atlantabg.org
5. Naples Botanical Garden, Naples, Florida: www.naplesgarden.org
6. New Orleans Botanical Garden, New Orleans, Louisiana: www.neworleanscitypark.com/botanical-garden
7. The Dallas Arboretum and Botanical Garden, Dallas, Texas: www.dallasarboretum.org
8. Missouri Botanical Garden, St. Louis, Missouri: www.missouribotanicalgarden.org

9. Pittsburgh Botanic Garden, Pittsburgh, Pennsylvania: www .pittsburghbotanicgarden.org
10. Chicago Botanic Garden, Chicago, Illinois: www.chicagobo tanic.org
11. Minnesota Landscape Arboretum, Minneapolis, Minnesota: www.arb.umn.edu
12. ABQ BioPark Botanic Garden, Albuquerque, New Mexico: www.cabq.gov/artsculture/biopark/garden
13. Myriad Botanical Gardens, Oklahoma City, Oklahoma: www .oklahomacitybotanicalgardens.com
14. Denver Botanic Gardens, Denver, Colorado: www.botanicgar dens.org
15. Red Butte Garden, Salt Lake City, Utah: www.redbuttegarden .org
16. Arizona-Sonoran Desert Museum, Tucson, Arizona: www .desertmuseum.org
17. The Huntington Botanical Gardens, Los Angeles, California: www.huntington.org/gardens
18. San Francisco Botanical Garden, San Francisco, California: www.sfbg.org
19. Washington Park Gardens, Portland, Oregon: www.explore washingtonpark.org
20. Bellevue Botanical Garden, Seattle, Washington: www.belle vuebotanical.org

OUTDOOR ACTIVITY ONLINE RESOURCES

Here are some online resources for ideas about what to do outside.

Websites

1. Recreation.gov (www.recreation.gov): This is a huge, wonderful website packed with information about various kinds of outdoor adventures in multiple locations around the United States.
2. National Park Service: www.nps.gov

3. *Outside* magazine online: www.outsideonline.com
4. American Hiking Society: www.americanhiking.org
5. *Outdoor Families* magazine: www.outdoorfamiliesonline.com
6. Appalachian Mountain Club: www.outdoors.org
7. Pacific Crest Trail Association: www.pcta.org
8. Continental Divide Trail Coalition: www.continentaldivide trail.org/
9. Active Outdoors: www.activeoutdoors.info
10. The Outdoor Activity: www.theoutdooractivity.com
11. The REI Co-Op Blog: www.rei.com/blog
12. PMags: www.pmags.com
13. Outdoor Canada: www.outdoorcanada.ca
14. *The Great Outdoors* magazine. www.tgomagazine.co.uk

YouTube Channels

- Go Traveler: www.youtube.com/gotraveler
- National Park Service: www.youtube.com/nationalparkservice
- Adventure Archives: www.youtube.com/c/AdventureArchives
- Homemade Wanderlust: www.youtube.com/c/HomemadeWan derlust
- Guide You Outdoors: www.youtube.com/guideyououtdoors

GEOCACHING RESOURCES

- Geocaching: www.geocaching.com/play
- National Geographic Society Geocaching: www.nationalgeo graphic.org/encyclopedia/geocaching/
- How to Get Started Geocaching, REI: www.rei.com/learn/expert -advice/gps-geocaching.html

MY FAVORITE HOUSEPLANT WEBSITES AND BLOGS

Many houseplant websites look dreamy but are rather shallow in terms of information. Or they cease publication after a few years.

Sometimes, they're actually online stores. That's fine, but here are five, low-ad sites with reliable advice by longtime experts.

1. House Plants Expert (www.houseplantsexpert.com): a deep site with reliable advice about houseplants and their care
2. Houseplant Guru (https://thehouseplantguru.com): down-to-earth, unique topics by a longtime garden writer
3. World of Succulents (www.worldofsucculents.com): a broad range of good info with a no-nonsense interface, but you'll find what you need
4. Healthy Houseplants (www.healthyhouseplants.com): not a sexy website but contains lots of excellent information and videos by a respected gardening journalist
5. Guide to Houseplants (www.guide-to-houseplants.com): solid advice with a plant encyclopedia and useful articles, although there's no search feature and some ads

My Favorite YouTube Channel

Epic Gardening (www.epicgardening.com): a wonderfully huge amount of useful info provided in friendly, to-the-point videos

My Favorite Podcast

"On the Ledge" with Jane Perrone. Jane is one of the United Kingdom's leading gardening experts and talks about useful houseplant topics. (Disclosure: I've been on Jane's podcast. I talked about how to keep your plants safe from cats and vice versa.)

My Favorite Gardening Websites and Blogs

1. Missouri Botanical Garden Plant Finder (www.missouribotanicalgarden.org/plantfinder/plantfindersearch.aspx): a comprehensive, searchable database for plant info; home gardener friendly

2. Oregon State University Landscape Database (www.landscape plants.oregonstate.edu): a comprehensive, searchable database for botanical info, helps with identification
3. A Way to Garden (www.awaytogarden.com): a knowledgeable New York expert's advice
4. Gardening Know How (www.gardeningknowhow.com): reliable information from established gardeners
5. You Grow Girl (www.yougrowgirl.com): focuses on affordability and DIY projects
6. Creative Vegetable Gardener (www.creativevegetablegardener.com): simple, useful advice from a prolific expert
7. The Spruce (www.thespruce.com): dreamy; stays on top of trends; easy to use
8. Gardenista (www.gardenista.com): offers stylish design advice
9. Treehugger (www.treehugger.com): trusted info on all things related to sustainability
10. Dave's Garden (www.davesgarden.com): a great database of citizen plant info

MY FAVORITE FUN WEBSITE

Garden Rant (www.gardenrant.com): ranty, often humorous articles on all kinds of industry topics, news, and trends; outstanding how-to articles (Disclosure: I've written for them.)

ZONES FOR TWENTY MAJOR CITIES IN THE UNITED STATES

These zones are an approximation, as some cities lay in two zones or a city falls in one and its suburbs in another, but this list will give you an idea.

1. New York, New York: 7a
2. Los Angeles, California: 10b
3. Chicago, Illinois: 6a

4. Dallas, Texas: 8a
5. Phoenix, Arizona: 9b
6. Philadelphia, Pennsylvania: 7b
7. Salt Lake City, Utah: 7b
8. Atlanta, Georgia: 8a
9. New Orleans, Louisiana: 9b
10. Jacksonville, Florida: 9a
11. San Francisco, California: 10b
12. Cleveland, Ohio: 6b
13. Charlotte, North Carolina: 8a
14. Indianapolis, Indiana: 6a
15. Seattle, Washington: 8b
16. Denver, Colorado: 5b
17. Washington, DC: 7b
18. Boston, Massachusetts: 7a
19. Detroit, Michigan: 6b
20. Nashville, Tennessee: 7a

To identify the zone where you live, visit the USDA website: https://planthardiness.ars.usda.gov

SOURCES FOR GOOD FAUX PLANTS

Michael's: www.michaels.com
Pottery Barn: www.potterybarn.com
Ikea: www.ikea.com
Target: www.target.com
TJ Maxx: www.tjmaxx.com
Home Goods: www.homegoods.com
Crate and Barrel: www.crateandbarrel.com
Wayfair: www.wayfair.com

FAVORITE BOOKS FOR YOUR EXPLORATION

Bailey, Fran. *The Healing Power of Plants: The Hero Houseplants That Will Love You Back.* New York: Sterling, 2019.

Bloom, Jessi. *Creating Sanctuary: Sacred Garden Spaces, Plant-Based Medicine, Daily Practices to Achieve Happiness and Well-Being*. Portland: Timber Press, 2018.

Brown, Stuart, with Christopher Vaughn. *Play: How It Shapes the Brain, Opens the Imagination, and Invigorates the Soul*. New York: Avery, 2009.

Clear, James. *Atomic Habits: An Easy and Proven Way to Build Good Habits and Break Bad Ones*. New York: Avery, 2018.

Coulthard, Sally. *Biophilia: You + Nature + Home*. London: Hachette, 2020.

Duhigg, Charles. *The Power of Habit: Why We Do What We Do in Life and Business*. New York: Random House, 2012.

Emmons, Robert A. *Thanks! How the New Science of Gratitude Can Make You Happier*. New York: Houghton Mifflin, 2007.

Gay, Ross. *Catalog of Unabashed Gratitude*. Pittsburgh: University of Pittsburgh Press, 2015.

Kondo, Marie. *The Life-Changing Magic of Tidying Up: The Japanese Art of Decluttering and Organizing*. Berkeley: Ten Speed Press, 2014.

Levitin, Daniel. *The Organized Mind: Thinking Straight in the Age of Information Overload*. New York: Dutton, 2014.

Li, Qing. *Forest Bathing: How Trees Can Help You Find Health and Happiness*. New York: Viking, 2018.

Lieberman, Matthew. *Social: Why Our Brains Are Wired to Connect*. New York: Crown, 2013.

Louv, Richard. *Last Child in the Woods. Saving Our Children from Nature-Deficit Disorder*. Chapel Hill, NC: Algonquin, 2005.

———. *The Nature Principle: Reconnecting with Life in a Virtual Age*. Chapel Hill, NC: Algonquin, 2011.

Lyubomirsky, Sonja. *The How of Happiness: A New Approach to Getting the Life You Want*. New York: Penguin, 2008.

Mortali, Micah. *Rewilding: Meditations, Practices, and Skills for Awakening in Nature*. Boulder, CO: Sounds True, 2019.

Newport, Cal. *Digital Minimalism: Choosing a Focused Life in a Noisy World*. New York: Portfolio, 2019.

Rubin, Gretchen. *The Happiness Project: Or Why I Spent a Year Trying to Sing in the Morning, Clean My Closets, Fight Right, Read Aristotle, and Generally Have More Fun*. New York: Harper, 2009.

———. *Better Than Before: What I Learned about Making and Breaking Habits—to Sleep More, Quit Sugar, Procrastinate Less, and Generally Build a Happier Life*. New York: Broadway Books, 2015.

Schaeffer, Charles E., and Athena A. Drewes. *The Therapeutic Powers of Play: 20 Core Agents of Change*. New York: Wiley, 2013.

Schildkret, Day. *Morning Altars: A 7-Step Practice to Nourish Your Spirit through Nature, Art, and Ritual*. New York: Countryman, 2018.

Selhub, Eva M., and Alan C. Logan. *Your Brain on Nature: The Science of Nature's Influence on Your Health, Happiness, and Vitality*. Mississauga, Ontario: John Wiley & Sons, 2012.

Seligman, Martin. E. P. *Learned Optimism: How to Change Your Mind and Your Life*. New York: Vintage, 1990.

Stuart-Smith, Sue. *The Well-Gardened Mind: The Restorative Power of Nature*. New York: Scribner, 2020.

Wall Kimmerer, Robin. *Braiding Sweetgrass: Indigenous Wisdom, Scientific Knowledge, and the Teachings of Plants*. Minneapolis, MN: Milkweeds Editions, 2013.

Wiking, Meik. *The Little Book of Hygge: Danish Secrets to Happy Living*. New York: William Morrow, 2017.

———. *The Little Book of Lykke: Secrets of the World's Happiest People*. New York: William Morrow, 2017.

Williams, Florence. *The Nature Fix: Why Nature Makes Us Happier, Healthier, and More Creative*. New York: W. W. Norton, 2017. (Love this book!)

Wilson, E. O. *Biophilia: The Human Bond with Other Species*. Cambridge: Harvard University Press, 1984.

Wohlleben, Peter. *The Secret Life of Trees: What They Feel, How They Communicate*. Vancouver: Greystone, 2016.

A GREEN LEISURE COCKTAIL

Finally, I thought I'd offer the green-colored drink I invented for relaxing in my garden. If you create a green leisure lounge and would like to enjoy it with a cocktail, try this recipe.

1 oz. tequila
½ oz. Midori
½ oz. lime juice
½ oz. lemon juice
1 oz. simple syrup
2 oz. (or top off with) soda water
1 ripe strawberry (optional)

In a lowball glass with ice, pour tequila, Midori, lime and lemon juices, syrup, and soda water. For a sweeter drink, substitute lemonade for lemon juice. Mix. Either drop the strawberry in the glass whole or mash in separate bowl, pouring berry and juice in. Enjoy!

Note: This drink can be made even more fun with the addition of mint leaf ice cubes. See my website, www.karenhugg.com, for how to make leaf ice cubes.

Notes

Chapter 1. A Modern Dilemma of Our Own Making

1. "The Stress Epidemic: Employees Are Looking for a Way Out," Wrike, September 2018, 6, www.wrike.com/blog/stress-epidemic-report -announcement/.

2. "42 Worrying Workplace Stress Statistics," The American Institute of Stress, September 25, 2019, www.stress.org/42-worrying-workplace -stress-statistics.

3. "Stress in America: Coping with Change," American Psychological Association, February 15, 2017, www.apa.org/news/press/releases /stress/2016/coping-with-change.pdf.

4. Leah Weiss, *How We Work: Live Your Purpose, Reclaim Your Sanity, and Embrace the Daily Grind* (New York: Harper Wave, 2018), 92.

5. Meik Wiking, *The Little Book of Lykke: Secrets of the World's Happiest People* (New York: HarperCollins, 2017), 24–30.

6. John Helliwell, R. Layard, and J. Sachs, "World Happiness Report 2019," Sustainable Development Solutions Network, 2019, 24–25, https://s3.amazonaws.com/happiness-report/2019/WHR19.pdf.

7. Neil E. Klepeis, William C. Nelson, Wayne R. Ott, John P. Robinson, Andy M. Tsang, Paul Switzer, Joseph V. Behar, Stephen C. Hern, and William H. Engelmann, "The National Human Activity Pattern Survey (NHAPS): A Resource for Assessing Exposure to Environmental Pollutants," *Journal of Exposure Science and Environmental Epidemiology* 11 (2001): 231–52.

8. Richard Louv, *Last Child in the Woods* (New York: Workman, 2008), 10.

9. E. O. Wilson, *Biophilia* (Cambridge: Harvard University, 1984), 1–2.

10. Marc Berman, J. Jonides, and S. Kaplan, "The Cognitive Benefits of Interacting with Nature," *Psychological Science* 19, no. 12 (2008): 1207–12.

11. Rita Berto, "The Role of Nature in Coping with Psycho-Physiological Stress: A Literature Review on Restorativeness," *Behavioral Sciences* 4, no. 4 (2014): 394–409.

Chapter 2. Slowing the Stress and Getting into Green Leisure

1. "The Nielsen Total Audience Report," www.nielsen.com, July 31, 2018.

2. Meik Wiking, "The Dark Side of Happiness," TEDx Copenhagen, Copenhagen, Denmark, video lecture, May 10, 2016, https://tedxcopen hagen.dk/talks/dark-side-happiness.

3. Cal Newport, *Digital Minimalism: Choosing a Focused Life in a Noisy World* (New York: Portfolio, 2019), 28.

4. Stephanie Watson and Kristeen Cherny, "The Effects of Sleep Deprivation on Your Body," *Healthline*, May 15, 2020; Jon Hamilton, "Scientists Discover a Link between Lack of Deep Sleep and Alzheimer's Disease," *All Things Considered*, transcript of radio report, November 16, 2020.

Chapter 3. Growing Your Green Personality

1. "APM Survey: How Often Do Americans Spend Free Time in Nature?" APM Research Lab, July 15, 2019, https://static1.squarespace .com/static/5c9542c8840b163998cf4804/t/5d88ddcf8e172d4fcc9f 9be6/1569250768435/apm-survey-july-15-2019-get-outside.pdf.

2. "Half of the U.S. population does not participate in outdoor recreation at all," Outdoor Foundation Participation Report 2019, Outdoor Foundation and "Increase in Outdoor Activities due to COVID-19," Outdoor Foundation Participation Report 2021, Outdoor Foundation. https:// outdoorindustry.org/article/increase-outdoor-activities-due-covid-19/.

Chapter 4. Learning and Imagining in Green

1. Bastien Blain and Rob Rutledge, "Happiness: Why Learning, Not Rewards, May Be the Key," *The Conversation*, February 1, 2021, https://theconversation.com/happiness-why-learning-not-rewards-may-be-the-key-new-research-153806.

2. "How Practice Changes the Brain," Australian Academy of Science, 2018, www.science.org.au/curious/people-medicine/how-practice-changes-brain.

3. Phillip Moeller, "Why Learning Leads to Happiness," *Chicago Tribune*, April 11, 2012.

4. Jeroen Nawijn, Miquelle A. Marchand, Ruut Veenhoven, and Ad J. Vingerhoets, "Vacationers Happier, but Most Not Happier after a Holiday," *Applied Research in Quality of Life* 5 (2010): 35–47.

5. Taylor Byers, "The Power of the Mind through Visualization," *Swimming World Magazine*, February 7, 2019, www.swimmingworldmagazine.com/news/the-power-of-the-mind-through-visualization/.

6. Jonah Lehrer, "The Virtues of Daydreaming," *The New Yorker*, June 5, 2012.

7. Kalina Christoff, Zachary C. Irving, Kieran C. R. Fox, R. Nathan Spreng, and Jessica R. Andrews-Hanna, "Mind-Wandering as Spontaneous Thought: A Dynamic Framework," *Nature Reviews Neuroscience* 17 (2016): 718–31.

8. Agata Blaszczak-Boxe, "Daydreaming Again? 5 Facts about the Wandering Mind," *Live Science*, September 15, 2016, www.livescience.com/56096-surprising-facts-about-daydreaming.html.

Chapter 5. Experiencing Plants through the Senses

1. Roger Ulrich, "View through a Window May Influence Recovery from Surgery," *Science* 224, no. 4647 (April 1984): 420–21.

2. Branka Spehar and Richard Taylor, "Fractals in Art and Nature: Why Do We Like Them?" Proceedings of SPIE–The International Society for Optical Engineering 8651 (2013).

3. Yoshifumi Miyazaki, "Nature Therapy," TEDx Tokyo, Tokyo, Japan, video lecture, June 30, 2012, www.tedxtokyo.com/tedxtokyo_talk/nature-therapy/.

4. Matilda Annerstedt, Peter Jonsson, Mattias Wallergard, Gerd Johansson, Bjorn Karlson, Patrik Grahn, Ase Marie Hansen, and Peter Wahrborg, "Inducing Physiological Stress Recovery with Sounds of Nature in a Virtual Reality Forest—Results from a Pilot Study," *Physiology & Behavior* 118 (2013): 240–50.

5. H. Woelk and S. Schläfke, "A Multi-Center, Double-Blind, Randomised Study of the Lavender Oil Preparation Silexan in Comparison to Lorazepam for Generalized Anxiety Disorder," *Phytomedicine* 17, no. 2 (2010): 94–99.

6. Qing Li, "Effect of Phytoncide from Trees on Human Natural Killer Cell Function," *International Journal of Immunopathology and Pharmacology* 22, no. 4 (2009): 951–59.

7. Qing Li, Ari Nakadai, Hiroki Matsushima, Yoshifumi Miyazaki, Alan Krensky, Tomoyuki Kawada, and Kanehisa Morimoto, "Phytoncides (Wood Essential Oils) Induce Human Natural Killer Cell Activity," *Immunopharmacology and Immunotoxicology* 28, no. 2 (2006): 319–33.

8. Diana Beresford-Kroeger, "Touch the Trees," *Call of the Forest* (blog), January 23, 2015, http://calloftheforest.ca/from-diana-touch-the-trees/.

9. Mary O'Brien, "SRL172 (Killed Mycobacterium Vaccae) in Addition to Standard Chemotherapy Improves Quality of Life without Affecting Survival, in Patients with Advanced Non-Small-Cell Lung Cancer: Phase III Results," *Annals of Oncology* 15, no. 6 (June 2004): 906–14.

10. C. A. Lowry, J. H. Hollis, A. de Vries, B. Pan, L. R. Brunet, J. R. F. Hunt, J. F. R. Paton, E. Van Kampen, D. M. Knight, A. K. Evans, G. A. W. Rook, and S. L. Lightman, "Identification of an Immune-Responsive Mesolimbocortical Serotonergic System: Potential Role in Regulation of Emotional Behavior," *Neuroscience* 146, nos. 2–5 (May 11, 2007): 756–72.

11. Rachel T. Buxton, Amber L. Pearson, Claudia Allou, Kurt Fristrup, and George Wittemyer, "A Synthesis of Health Benefits of Natural Sounds and Their Distribution in National Parks," *Proceedings of the National Academy of Sciences* 118, no. 14 (April 6, 2021).

12. Kazuko Koga and Yutaka Iwasaki, "Psychological and Physiological Effect in Humans of Touching Plant Foliage—Using the Semantic Differential Method and Cerebral Activity as Indicators," *Journal of Physiological Anthropology* 32, no. 1 (April 15, 2013): 7.

13. Gaétan Chevalier, Stephen T. Sinatra, James L. Oschman, Karol Sokal, and Pawel Sokal, "Earthing: Health Implications of Reconnecting

the Human Body to the Earth's Surface Electrons," *Journal of Environmental and Public Health* (January 12, 2012).

14. Djin Gie Liem and Catherine Georgina Russell, "The Influence of Taste Liking on the Consumption of Nutrient Rich and Nutrient Poor Foods," *Frontiers in Nutrition* (November 15, 2019).

Chapter 6. Idly Playing in the Plant World

1. Charles Schaefer, "Laughter, Play, and Love," *Fairleigh Dickinson University Magazine* (winter/spring 2006).

2. Robert Provine, "Cracking the Laughing Code," Chicago Humanities Festival, video lecture, February 2, 2010, www.chicagohumanities.org/media/robert-provine-cracking-laughing-code/.

3. Stuart Brown, "Play Is More Than Just Fun," TED, video lecture, May 2008, www.ted.com/talks/stuart_brown_play_is_more_than_just_fun.

4. "Chase Freedom Unlimited Card Survey Reveals a 'Fun Gap' in America," Business Wire, April 8, 2016, www.businesswire.com/news/home/20160408005471/en/.

5. "2020 Essential Facts about the Computer and Video Game Industry," Entertainment Software Association, report, July 2020, www.theesa.com/wp-content/uploads/2021/03/Final-Edited-2020-ESA_Essential_facts.pdf.

6. "Outdoor Foundation Study: Half of the US population Did Not Participate in Outdoor Recreation in 2019," 2020 Outdoor Participation Report, Outdoor Foundation, December 31, 2020, https://outdoorindustry.org/resource/2020-outdoor-participation-report/.

7. Bryan Robinson, "Is Time Famine Starving You? How to Satisfy Your Hunger for More," *Forbes*, September 5, 2019.

8. Amanda Dixon, "68% of Americans Have Skipped Recreational Activities in the Past Year Because of Cost," Bankrate, report, August 4, 2019, www.bankrate.com/surveys/recreational-spending-survey-august-2019/.

9. Seong-Hoon Cho et al., "Effects of Travel Cost and Participation in Recreational Activities on National Forest Visits," *Forest Policy and Economics* 40 (March 2014): 21–30.

10. Bryan Robinson, "Time Famine: How to Satisfy Your Hunger for More," *Psychology Today*, December 16, 2017.

11. Day Schildkret, video interview, *Good Morning LaLa Land*, October 30, 2018, https://youtu.be/vTJ1CGo5Shw.

12. Day Schildkret, *Morning Altars: A 7-Step Practice to Nourish Your Spirit through Nature, Art, and Ritual* (New York: Norton, 2018).

Chapter 7. Supporting a Little Green Life

1. Stephen G. Post, "Altruism, Happiness, and Health: It's Good to Be Good," *International Journal of Behavioral Medicine* 12, no. 2 (2005): 66–77.

2. Francesa Borgonovi, "Doing Well by Doing Good. The Relationship between Formal Volunteering and Self-Reported Health and Happiness," *Social Science and Medicine* 66, no. 11 (June 2008): 2321–34.

3. Ross Gay, "Unabashed Gratitude and Structures of Care, with Poet Gardener Ross Gay," *Cultivating Place*, podcast interview, November 28, 2019, www.cultivatingplace.com/post/2019/11/28/unabashed-gratitude -structures-of-care-with-poet-gardener-ross-gay.

4. Vanessa Rancaño, "Be Kind, Unwind: How Helping Others Can Help Keep Stress in Check," *NPR*, December 17, 2015.

5. Stephanie Brown, Dylan M. Smith, Richard Schulz, Mohammed U. Kabeto, Peter A. Ubel, Michael Poulin, Jaehee Yi, Catherine Kim, and Kenneth M. Langa, "Caregiving Behavior Is Associated with Decreased Mortality Risk," *Psychological Science* 20, no. 4 (2009): 488–94.

6. Mackenzie Nichols, "4 Gardening Trends You'll Want to Dig into in 2021," *Better Homes and Gardens*, December 22, 2020.

7. Kate Spirgen, "As IGCs Adapt and Grow with the Changes CO-VID-19 Has Made to the Retail World, Sales Are Booming and Business Is Better Than Ever," *Garden Center Magazine*, September 8, 2020.

8. Daisy Bowie-Sell, "UK buys 322 million more plants in 2020 than in 2019," *Gardens Illustrated*, July 9, 2020.

9. Sarah Marsh, "Indoor Plant Sales Boom, Reflecting Urbanisation and Design Trends," *The Guardian*, August 11, 2019.

10. Giulia Carabelli, email correspondence to author, June 9, 2021.

11. Sonja Lyubomirsky, Laura King, and Ed Diener, "The Benefits of Frequent Positive Affect: Does Happiness Lead to Success?" *Psychological Bulletin* 131, no. 6 (2005): 803–55.

12. S. Katherine Nelson, Kostadin Kushlev, Tammy English, Elizabeth W. Dunn, and Sonja Lyubomirsky, "In Defense of Parenthood: Children Are Associated with More Joy Than Misery," *Psychological Science* 24, no. 3 (2013).

13. Liesa Goins, "8 Therapist-Approved De-Stress Tactics," *PsyNet*, August 13, 2020.

14. Goins, "8 Therapist-Approved De-Stress Tactics."

Chapter 8. Uniting with Like Nature Minds

1. Ron Finley, "Ron Finley: Urban Gangsta Gardener in South Central LA," *Game Changers*, video interview, December 16, 2015, https://youtu.be/7t-NbF77ceM.

2. "Loneliness and the Workplace," Cigna, January 23, 2020, www.multivu.com/players/English/8670451-cigna-2020-loneliness-index/.

3. Elizabeth Hopper, "How Your Social Life Might Help You Live Longer," *Greater Good Magazine*, July 28, 2020, https://greatergood.berkeley.edu/article/item/how_your_social_life_might_help_you_life_longer.

4. Julianne Holt-Lunstad, "The Potential Public Health Relevance of Social Isolation and Loneliness: Prevalence, Epidemiology, and Risk Factors," *Public Policy & Aging Report* 27, no. 4 (2018): 127–30.

5. Ben Quinn, "Loneliness Linked to 30% Increase in Heart Disease and Stroke Risk," *The Guardian*, April 19, 2016.

6. Matthew Lieberman, "The Social Brain and Its Superpowers," TEDx St. Louis, St. Louis, Missouri, video lecture, October 7, 2013, https://tedxstlouis.com/speakers/matthew-d-lieberman-ph-d-professor-of-psychology-psychiatry-and-biobehavioral-sciences-university-of-california-los-angeles/.

7. Lieberman, "The Social Brain and Its Superpowers."

8. Julianne Holt-Lunstad, Timothy B. Smith, and J. Bradley Layton, "Social Relationships and Mortality Risk: A Meta-Analytic Review," *PLOS Medicine* 7, no. 7 (2010).

9. Anne Scelzo, Salvatore Di Somma, Paola Antonini, Lori P. Montross, Nicholas Schork, David Brenner, and Dilip V. Jeste, "Mixed-Methods Quantitative-Qualitative Study of 29 Nonagenarians and Centenarians in Rural Southern Italy: Focus on Positive Psychological Traits," *International Psychogeriatrics* 30, no. 1 (2017).

10. Dan Buettner, "The Island Where People Forget to Die," *New York Times*, October 24, 2012.

11. Stephen G. Post, "Altruism, Happiness, and Health: It's Good to Be Good," *International Journal of Behavioral Medicine* 12, no. 2 (2005): 66–77.

12. Michelle Berger, "Oxytocin, Vasopressin Flatten Social Hierarchy and Synchronize Behaviors," *Penn Today*, May 29, 2018, https://penntoday.upenn.edu/news/oxytocin-vasopressin-flatten-social-hierarchy-synchronize-behavior.

13. Miho Nagasawa, Shouhei Mitsui, Shiori En, Nobuyo Ohtani, Mitsuaki Ohta, Yasuo Sakuma, Tatsushi Onaka, Kazutaka Mogi, and Takefumi Kikusui, "Oxytocin-Gaze Positive Loop and the Coevolution of Human-Dog Bonds," *Science* 348, no. 6232 (2015): 333–36.

14. Susan Pollin and Carolin Retzlaff-Fürst, "The School Garden: A Social and Emotional Place," *Frontiers in Psychology*, April 22, 2021.

15. "Growing Social Connections through Gardening," *Mirage News*, August 27, 2019, www.miragenews.com/growing-social-connections-through-gardening/.

16. Janet Dyment, "Gaining Ground: The Power and Potential of School Ground Greening in the Toronto District School Board," Evergreen, 2005, www.evergreen.ca/downloads/pdfs/Gaining-Ground.pdf.

17. Jessie Sun, Kelci Harris, and Simine Vazire, "Is Well-Being Associated with the Quantity and Quality of Social Interactions?" *Journal of Personality and Social Psychology* 119, no. 6 (2019): 1478–96.

Chapter 9. Recognizing What We've Grown

1. Robert Emmons, "Why Gratitude Is Good," *Greater Good Magazine*, November 16, 2010, https://greatergood.berkeley.edu/article/item/why_gratitude_is_good.

2. Emmons, "Why Gratitude Is Good."

3. Lung Hung Chen and Chia-Huei Wu, "Gratitude Enhances Change in Athletes' Self-Esteem: The Moderating Role of Trust in Coach," *Journal of Applied Sport Psychology* 26, no. 3 (2014): 349–62.

4. Todd Kashdan, Gitendra Uswatte, and Terri Julian, "Gratitude and Hedonic and Eudaimonic Well-Being in Vietnam War Veterans," *Behavioral Research and Therapy* 44, no. 2 (2006): 177–99.

5. Nicola Petrocchi and Alessandro Couyoumdjian, "The Impact of Gratitude on Depression and Anxiety: The Mediating Role of Criticizing, Attacking, and Reassuring the Self," *Self and Identity* 15 (2013).

6. Alex Wood, John Maltby, Raphael Gillett, P. Alex Linley, and Stephen Joseph, "The Role of Gratitude in the Development of Social Support, Stress, and Depression: Two Longitudinal Studies," *Journal of Research in Personality* 42, no. 4 (2008): 854–71.

7. Lisa Williams and Monica Bartlett, "Warm Thanks: Gratitude Expression Facilitates Social Affiliation in New Relationships via Perceived Warmth," *Emotion* 15, no. 1 (2015): 1–5.

8. Sara Algoe, "Find, Remind, and Bind: The Functions of Gratitude in Everyday Relationships," *Social and Personality Psychology Compass* 6, no. 6 (2012).

9. Michael McCullough, Marcia B. Kimeldorf, and Adam D. Cohen, "An Adaptation for Altruism?" *Current Directions in Psychological Science* 17, no. 4 (2008): 281–85.

10. C. Nathan DeWall, Nathaniel Lambert, Richard Pond Jr., Todd Kashdan, and Frank Fincham, "A Grateful Heart Is a Nonviolent Heart: Cross-Sectional, Experience Sampling, Longitudinal, and Experimental Evidence," *Social Psychological and Personality Science* 3, no. 2 (2012): 232–40.

11. Robert Emmons, "Challenges to Gratitude," Greater Good Science Center, video lecture, November 17, 2010, https://greatergood.berkeley.edu/video/item/challenges_to_gratitude.

12. Sonja Lyubomirsky, *The How of Happiness: A New Approach to Getting the Life You Want* (New York: Penguin, 2008), 92–95.

13. Michael Bergeisen, "The Neuroscience of Happiness," *Greater Good Magazine*, September 22, 2010, https://greatergood.berkeley.edu/article/item/the_neuroscience_of_happiness.

14. Robert Emmons, *Thanks! How the New Science of Gratitude Can Make You Happier* (New York: Houghton Mifflin, 2007).

Chapter 10. Exercising Outside without Trying

1. "Benefits of Physical Activity," Centers for Disease Control, August 2021, www.cdc.gov/physicalactivity/basics/pa-health/index.htm.

2. Eva Selhub and Alan Logan, *Your Brain on Nature* (Mississauga, Ontario: John Wiley and Sons Canada, 2012), 115.

3. Jo Barton, "How We Started the Green Exercise Revolution," University of Essex, 2021, www.essex.ac.uk/research/showcase/how-we-started-the-green-exercise-revolution.

4. Watinee Kunpeuk, William Spence, Sirinya Phulkerd, Rapeepong Suphanchaimat, and Siriwan Pitayarangsarit, "The Impact of Gardening on Nutrition and Physical Health Outcomes: A Systematic Review and Meta-Analysis," *Health Promotion International* 35, no. 2 (April 1, 2020): 397–408.

5. A. E. Van Den Berg and M. H. G. Custers, "Gardening Promotes Neuroendocrine and Affective Restoration from Stress," *Journal of Health Psychology* 16, no. 1 (2010): 3–11.

6. Jamie Feldmar, "Gardening Could Be the Hobby That Helps You Live to 100," BBC, December 10, 2018, www.bbc.com/worklife/ar ticle/20181210-gardening-could-be-the-hobby-that-helps-you-live-to-100.

7. Qing Li, *Forest Bathing: How Trees Can Help You Find Health and Happiness* (New York: Viking, 2018), 77–84.

8. Yoshinori Ohtsuka, Noriyuki Yabunaka, and Shigeru Takayama, "Shinrin-Yoku (Forest-Air Bathing and Walking) Effectively Decreases Blood Glucose Levels in Diabetic Patients," *International Journal of Biometeorology* 41, no. 3 (February 1998): 125–27.

9. "Ecotherapy: The Green Agenda for Mental Health," Mind Week Report, May 2007, www.niagaraknowledgeexchange.com/wp-content/up loads/sites/2/2014/05/ECOTHERAPY.pdf.

10. Maria Bodin and Terry Hartig, "Does the Outdoor Environment Matter for Psychological Restoration Gained through Running?" *Psychology of Sport and Exercise* 4, no. 2 (2003): 141–53.

11. James Pennebaker and J. Lightner, "Competition of Internal and External Information in an Exercise Setting," *Journal of Personality and Social Psychology* 39, no. 1 (1980): 165–74.

12. "10 Health Benefits of Mountain Biking," travelbughealth.com, June 1, 2016, www.travelbughealth.com/bugs-blog/10-health-benefits-of -mountain-biking.

13. Steven McKenzie, "Sea Kayaking Helps My Recovery from Depression," BBC News, May 10, 2021.

14. Carly Wood, M. Flynn, R. Law, J. Naufahu, and N. Smyth, "The Effect of the Visual Exercise Environment on the Response to Psychological Stress: A Pilot Study," *Anxiety Stress Coping* 33, no. 6 (November 2020): 716–29.

15. Jo Barton, "How We Started the Green Exercise Revolution," University of Essex website, 2021, www.essex.ac.uk/research/showcase /how-we-started-the-green-exercise-revolution.

Chapter 11. The Healing Power of Houseplants

1. Linda Chalker-Scott, "The Myth of Stoic Trees," *Horticultural Myths*, 2021, https://s3.wp.wsu.edu/uploads/sites/403/2015/03/thigmo morphogenesis.pdf.

2. Peter Tompkins and Christopher Bird, *The Secret Life of Plants* (New York: Harper 1973), 145–62.

3. Seong-Hyun Park and Richard Mattson, "Ornamental Indoor Plants in Hospital Rooms Enhanced Health Outcomes of Patients Recovering from Surgery," *Journal of Alternative and Complementary Medicine* 15, no. 9 (September 2009): 975–80.

4. Virginia Lohr, "What Are the Benefits of Plants Indoors and Why Do We Respond Positively to Them?" *Acta Horticulturae* 881, no. 2 (2010): 675–82.

5. Chun-Yen Chang and Ping-Kun Chen, "Human Response to Window Views and Indoor Plants in the Workplace," *HortScience* 40 (2005): 1354–59.

6. Andrea Dravigne et al. "The Effect of Live Plants and Window Views of Green Spaces on Employee Perceptions of Job Satisfaction," *HortScience* 43, no. 1 (2008): 183–87.

7. Virginia Lohr, Caroline Pearson-Mims, and Georgia Goodwin, "Interior Plants May Improve Worker Productivity and Reduce Stress in a Windowless Environment," *Journal of Environmental Horticulture* 14, no. 2 (1996): 97–100.

8. Tove Fjeld, "The Effect of Interior Planting on Health and Discomfort among Workers and School Children," *HortTechnology* 10, no. 1 (2002): 46–52.

9. Ke-Tsung Han, "Influence of Limitedly Visible Leafy Indoor Plants on the Psychology, Behavior, and Health of Students at a Junior High School in Taiwan," *Environment and Behavior* 41, no. 5 (2009): 658–92.

10. Jennifer Doxey, T. Waliczek, and Jayne Zajicek, "The Impact of Interior Plants in University Classrooms on Student Course Performance and on Student Perceptions of the Course and Instructor," *HortScience* 44, no. 2 (2009): 384–91.

11. Michelle Baran, "Pick the House Plants for Your Room at This Hotel Pop-Up," *Afar*, September 16, 2019, www.afar.com/magazine/are-house-plants-the-new-must-have-hotel-room-amenity.

12. Magdalena van den Berg, Jolanda Maas, Rianne Muller, Anoek Braun, Wendy Kaandorp, René van Lien, Mireille N. M. van Poppel, Willem van Mechelen, and Agnes E. van den Berg, "Autonomic Nervous System Responses to Viewing Green and Built Settings: Differentiating between Sympathetic and Parasympathetic Activity," *International Journal of Environmental Research and Public Health* 12, no. 12 (December 2015): 15860–74.

Chapter 12. Creating an Indoor, Green Leisure Lounge

1. Esther Inglis-Arkell, "How Many Plants Would You Need to Generate Oxygen for Yourself in an Airlock?" *Gizmodo*, October 26, 2012, https://gizmodo.com/how-many-plants-would-you-need-to-generate-oxygen-for-y-5955071.

2. Kendra Cherry, "The Color Psychology of Green," *Very Well Mind*, May 28, 2021, www.verywellmind.com/color-psychology-green-2795817.

Chapter 14. Maintaining Nature's Magic

1. "Paid Time Off Trends in the U.S.," U.S. Travel Association, 2019, www.ustravel.org/sites/default/files/media_root/document/Paid%20Time%20Off%20Trends%20Fact%20Sheet.pdf.

2. "Leaving Work Behind—How U.S. Travelers Disconnect on Vacation," *Turnkey* (blog), 2019, https://blog.turnkeyvr.com/leaving-work-behind-on-vacation/.

3. Shawn Achor and Michelle Gielan, "The Data-Driven Case for Vacation," *Harvard Business Review*, July 13, 2016.

4. Drew DeSilver, "For Most U.S. Workers, Real Wages Have Barely Budged in Decades," Pew Research Center, August 7, 2018, www.pewresearch.org/fact-tank/2018/08/07/for-most-us-workers-real-wages-have-barely-budged-for-decades/.

5. Charles Duhigg, *The Power of Habit: Why We Do What We Do in Life and Business* (New York: Random House, 2012), 19.

6. Qing Li, *Forest Bathing: How Trees Can Help You Find Health and Happiness* (New York: Viking, 2018), 172–73.

About the Author
and Illustrator

Karen Hugg is a writer with a passion for plants. As a certified ornamental horticulturalist and Master Pruner, she created relaxing gardens for almost twenty years via her garden design and maintenance company. She's also the author of *Harvesting the Sky, The Forgetting Flower, The Dark Petals of Provence*, and *Song of the Tree Hollow*, all literary mysteries and thrillers inspired by the green world. Karen holds an MA in English from the University of Illinois and an MFA in fiction writing from Goddard College. She's been interviewed on several podcasts and has appeared on the TV show *New Day Northwest*. You can find her shorter writings on both gardening and books in *Garden Center Magazine, Garden Rant, The Big Thrill, Crime Reads, Thrive Global*, and other publications. Karen lives in the Seattle area with her husband, three kids, and dog Olive.

To get more ideas for growing a happier life and green leisure activities, visit Karen's website, www.karenhugg.com, and sign up for her newsletter. Follow her Instagram page to connect with other like-minded folks about nature outings, houseplant info, gardening tips, relaxation techniques, and other ways to "leaf" your troubles behind, www.instagram.com/karenhugg. Don't forget the hashtag #greenleisure.

If you enjoyed *Leaf Your Troubles Behind*, please write a few sentences on Amazon or Goodreads to help others find it. Thank you!

Kara Fellows lives in Boulder, Colorado, and has been a professional illustrator for thirty years. She holds an MFA in graphic design and can be found teaching illustration and printmaking workshops online and in person. She gets giddy about travel, vintage book hunting, trail running, and gardening. Her proudest achievement is her daughter, Daisy. For more, go to www.karafellows.com.